T0208204

NEW BOOK /||\ REAL MESSAGES OF `-GOD I, II; & III-!!!~' /||\

NEW BOOK /|\ REAL MESSAGES OF `-GOD I, II; & III-!!!~' /|\

Dwayne W. Anderson

NEW BOOK /||\ REAL MESSAGES OF `-GOD I, II; & III-!!!~' /||\

iUniverse books may be ordered through booksellers or by contacting:

iUniverse
1663 Liberty Drive
Bloomington, IN 47403
www.iuniverse.com
1-800-Authors (1-800-288-4677)

ISBN: 978-1-5320-9228-2 (sc)
ISBN: 978-1-5320-9230-5 (hc)
ISBN: 978-1-5320-9229-9 (e)

Library of Congress Control Number: 2020900739

Print information available on the last page.

iUniverse rev. date: 01/07/2020

BULLET POINTS FOR: `"-_/‖\ REAL MESSAGES of `-GOD I, II; & III-!!!~ /‖\'

- *THE LIFE AND DEATH OF CELEBRITIES –*
- *THE LIFE AND DEATHS OF PRESIDENTS & FIRST LADIES –*
- *THE LIFE AND DEATHS OF THE FOUNDING FATHERS of the UNITED STATES of AMERICA –*
- *THE LIFE AND DEATH OF COMMON PEOPLE –*
- *THE LIFE AND DEATH OF FAMILY –*
- *THE TIME CLOCK SEQUENCES of WORLD SHATTERING EVENTS –*
- *COMPARISON of the BIBLE'S PRESENTATIONS of PROPHECY to* **(Reciprocal-Sequencing-Numerology)/ (Reciprocal-Sequenced-Inversed-Realities)** *-*
- *READING; and, UNDERSTANDING a `-NEW`-SCIENCE in the FOCUS of Reciprocal-Sequencing-Numerology-RSN-'*
- *READING; and, UNDERSTANDING a `-NEW`-SCIENCE in the FOCUS of Reciprocal-Sequenced-Inversed-Realities-RSIR-'*
- *REVELATIONS by & from THE PROPHET DWAYNE W. ANDERSON through `-GOD -*
- *DISCOVERER & FOUNDER of RECIPROCAL (TRIGONOMETRY) INVERSE REALITIES – EQUATIONS of `-REALITY in LIFE & DEATH with BOTH AMERICAN & WORLD LEADERS - AUTHOR: DWAYNE W. ANDERSON –*

I've `-CREATED a NEW TYPE of PHILOSOPHY (Reciprocal-Sequencing-Numerology)/ (Reciprocal-Sequenced-Inversed-Realities) that `-PROVES without `-QUESTION the `-PRESENCE of GOD'S EXISTENCE in our DAILY `-LIVES & `-AFFAIRS!!!!!~'

'-**FOUNDING** '-**FATHERS** of the '-**UNITED** '-**STATES** of '-**AMERICA!!!**~'

'-**FOUNDING** '-**FATHER = ALEXANDER HAMILTON** '-**DAY** of '-**DEATH = JULY 12th** = (7/12) = (7 x 12) = '-**84**!~' DIED in ('-1**8**0**4**)!~' BORN in (**1757**) = (57 + 17) = ('-**74**) = "**JULY 4th**"!!!~' **RECIPROCAL** = '-**LIVED to be** ('-**47**) **YEARS of** '-**AGE!!!**~' '-**BORN** '-**DATE = JANUARY 11th, 1757** = (1 + 11 +17 + 57) = '-**86** = RECIPROCAL = '-**68**!~' '-**DEATH** '-**DATE** = JULY 12th, 1**8**0**4** = (7 + 12 + 18 + 4) = '-**41** = **BENJAMIN FRANKLIN'S** '-**BIRTHDAY # **'-**NUMBER!!!**~'

'-**FOUNDING** '-**FATHER = BENJAMIN FRANKLIN** '-**DAY** of '-**DEATH = APRIL 17th** = (4/17) = (4 x 17) = '-**68**!~' DIED at the '-**AGE** of ('-**84**) = RECIPROCAL = ('-**48**)!~' '-**BORN** '-**DATE** = **JANUARY 17th, 1706** = (1 + 17 + 17 + 6) = '-**41** = **ALEXANDER HAMILTON'S DEATH/DAY #** '-**NUMBER!!!**~' '-**DEATH** '-**DATE** = **APRIL 17th, 1790** = (4 + 17 + 17 + 90) = '-**128!!!**~' (41 + 41) = ('-**82**) = RECIPROCAL = ('-**28**)!!!~'

JULY 4th PRESIDENTS to DIE = (7 x 4) = '-**28** / (28 x 3) = '-**84!!!**~'

#1-PRESIDENT = GEORGE WASHINGTON '-DAY of '-DEATH = DECEMBER 14th = (12/14) = (12 x 14) = '-**168**!'

#2-PRESIDENT = JOHN ADAMS '-DAY of '-DEATH = JULY 4th = (7/4) = (7 x 4) = '-**28**!'

#3-PRESIDENT = THOMAS JEFFERSON '-DAY of '-DEATH = JULY 4th = (7/4) = (7 x 4) = '-**28**

#4-PRESIDENT = JAMES MADISON '-DAY of '-DEATH = JUNE 28th = (6 x 28) = '-**168**!'

#5-PRESIDENT = JAMES MONROE `-DAY of `-DEATH = JULY 4ᵗʰ = (7/4) = (7 x 4) = `-**28!!!~'**

#6-PRESIDENT = JOHN QUINCY ADAMS `-**DAY of `-DEATH** = **FEBRUARY 23ʳᵈ** = (2/23) = (2 x 23) = (`-**46**) / `-**23** = **RECIPROCAL** = `-**32!!!~'**

`-BORN JULY 11ᵗʰ, 1**767** /|\ `-DIED FEBRUARY **23**ʳᵈ, 1**848** = (`-**91**)

`-**1767** = (17 + 67) = `-**84** = **RECIPROCAL** = `-**48** = **DIED** in the **YEAR** of (`-**48**)!!!~'

#7-PRESIDENT = ANDREW JACKSON `-**DAY of `-DEATH** = **JUNE(6) 8** = (**6/8**) = (6 x 8) = `-**48** = RECIPROCAL = `-**84**!~' `-**AND;** `-**HE** `-**DIED on (6/8)**!!!~'

`-BORN MARCH 15ᵗʰ, 17**67** /|\ `-DIED **JUNE 8**ᵗʰ, 1845 = (`-**77**)

`-**ADD UP** `-**DEATH/DAY #** `-**NUMBERS for #6 & #7** = (**91** (ADAMS) + **77** (JACKSON)) = `-**168** /|\ FROM `-**BIRTH** to `-**BIRTH IT** `-**EQUALS** (`-**168**) for PRESIDENTS #6 & #7, `-**Too!!!~'** (`-**247**) DAYS = (24 x 7) = (`-**168**)!!!~'

#8-PRESIDENT = MARTIN VAN BUREN `-DAY of `-DEATH = JULY 24ᵗʰ = (7/24) = (7 x 24) = `-**168**!~'

#9-PRESIDENT = WILLIAM HENRY HARRISON `-DAY of `-DEATH = APRIL 4ᵗʰ = (4/4) = (4 x 4) = `-**16**!~' `-**DIED** at the `-**AGE** of (`-**68**)!~'

`-BORN FEBRUARY 9ᵗʰ, 17**73** /|\ `-DIED APRIL **4**ᵗʰ, 18**41**

(2 + 9 + 17 + **73**) = `-**101** /|\ (4 + 4 + 18 + 41) = `-**67**

$(101 + 67) =$ `-**168**!~'

#12-PRESIDENT = ZACHARY TAYLOR `-BORN NOVEMBER 24ᵗʰ, 17**84** /|\ `-DIED JULY 9ᵗʰ, **1850**!!!~'

`-17**84** = (84 (-) 17) = `-**67**!!!~'

`-**1850** = (18 + 50) = `-**68**!!!~'

#13-PRESIDENT = MILLARD FILLMORE `-**DIED** at the `-**AGE** of (`-**74**) = (**JULY 4ᵗʰ**) **in** (`-18**74**)!!!~'

#14-PRESIDENT = FRANKLIN PIERCE `-BORN NOVEMBER **23**ʳᵈ, 18**04** /|\ `-DIED OCTOBER 8ᵗʰ, 18**69**!!!~'

`-**23** = **RECIPROCAL** = `-**32**

#32-PRESIDENT = FRANKLIN D. ROOSEVELT `-DAY of `-DEATH = APRIL 12ᵗʰ = (**4/12**) = (4 x 12) = `-**48** = RECIPROCAL = `-**84**!!!~'

#33-PRESIDENT = HARRY S. TRUMAN `-BORN MAY 8ᵗʰ, 18**84** /|\ `-DIED DECEMBER 26ᵗʰ, 1972!!!~' **DECEMBER 26ᵗʰ** = (12 x 26) = `-**312** = (32 x 1) = `-**32**!!!~'

#34-PRESIDENT = DWIGHT D. EISENHOWER `-DAY of `-DEATH = MARCH **28**ᵗʰ = (3/**28**) = (3 x **28**) = `-**84** = RECIPROCAL = `-**48**!!!~'

(`-**84**) + (`-**48**) = (`-**132**)!!!~'

#45ᵗʰ UNITED STATES **PRESIDENT DONALD TRUMP** `-**BIRTH** `-**DATE** = **JUNE 14**ᵗʰ, 19**46**!!!~' **JUNE 14**ᵗʰ = (6 x 14) = (`-**84**)!!!~' (`-**46**) = (`-**23**) x (`-**2**)!!!~'

`-IT `-CONTINUES!!!~' `-SEE `-THE `-PATTERNS!!!~' `-IT'S `-IN `-THE `-BOOKS!!!~'

`"- The REAL PROPHET of DOOM (Kismet) - INTRODUCTION - `-PENDULUM `-FLOW - III -"`

With ALL POSSIBILITIES BEING POSSIBLE there `-EXISTS BOTH GOOD & BAD AND EVERY FLAVOR OF IT IN A `-GODLY EXISTENCE!~' THE BIBLE SAYS THAT WE WERE ALL MADE IN `-GOD'S `-IMAGE!~' WE ARE `-BABY `-GODS WITHOUT `-GOD'S ULTIMATE DEGREE OF POWERS!~' `-MESSAGES FROM `-GOD PART #1!!!!~'

`-GOD can `-TRANSPORT a `-PROPHET (`-40) YEARS' into the `-FUTURE; over and over, `-AGAIN; `-MAPPING `-OUT HIS `-LIFE; AND, `-PROJECTIONS!~' NOTHING EVER CHANGING; ALWAYS IN EXACT DETAILS!~' GOD'S `-MEMORY IS `-PRECISE!~' `-HE WOULD HAVE `-NO `-PROBLEM with the `-RESURRECTION!~'

`-EVERY `-HUMAN `-TALKS with `-GOD through their `-SUBCONSCIOUS & `-AUTONOMIC `-NERVOUS `-SYSTEMS!~' THEY are `-SUGGESTIONS of `-THOUGHT `-PATTERNS!~' `-GOD ` EXPERIENCES through `-US; HIS `-CREATION, for the `-POSSIBILITIES of `-BEING a `-GOD!~' `-MESSAGES FROM `-GOD PART #1!~'

FOR `-WHATEVER `-EPOCH of `-TIME; AND, FOR ALL of the GREATEST INVENTIONS that were `-EVER `-MADE; `-GOD `-PLANTED that `-THOUGHT in the `-INDIVIDUALS' `-MIND to `-CULTIVATE, `-ARTICULATE; AND, CULMINATE into `-EXISTENCE!~' FOR US TO `-SAVOR; until, `-HE was `-READY for ANOTHER!~

GOD can TAKE YOU into the `-FUTURE for 40 YEARS MONITORING `-ALL of YOUR WAKING THOUGHTS in all of YOUR `-WAKING `-HOURS for `-EVERY `-SECOND of `-THOSE `-40 YEARS of `-DAYS for EACH `-EXACT `-DAY; all `-WITHIN a `-VISION `-WINDOW of `-ONLY an `-8 HOURS/ of a `-NIGHT'S `-SLEEP!

GOD can `-ALLOW `-YOU to go through `-40 years of `-MEMORIES; and, to `-ALLOW YOU to`-SELECTIVELY `-FORGET `-ALL of those `-MEMORIES; `-UNTIL, THEY have `-ACTUALLY `-OCCURRED!~' HE `-NOW GIVES `-YOU the `-SENSATION of `-DÉJÀ VU' after a `-VISION `-MEMORY has been `-FULFILLED!!!~'

The `-PROPHET being `-49 YEARS of `-AGE (at the `-PRESENT) means `-GOD `-SPOKE to `-ME (the `-PROPHET) at the `-AGE of `-9!~' IT was `-TOUGH going through `-PUBERTY with an `-ADOLESCENCE of the `-MIND to an `-ADULT `-MENTAL `-DISPOSITION; but, `-IT was `-DONE & then `-FORGOTTEN!~

THEORETICAL PHYSICIST STEPHEN HAWKING'S BIRTH = JANUARY 8, 1942 / DEATH = MARCH 14, 2018!~' WAS `-BORN in (`-42) & `-DIED on (3/14) = (3 x 14) = `-42!~' (RECIPROCALS)!~' WAS `-BORN on (1/8) & `-DIED in (`-1/8)!~' STEPHEN HAWKING `-DIED at the `-AGE of (`-76) = (7 x 6) = (`-42)!~' (1942) = (42 (-) 19) = (`-23)

MARK = (`-42) x (`-2) = (`-84) / (`-84) x (`-2) = (`-168)!~' (42, 84, 168) are `-IDENTIFIABLE `-NUMBERS for the `-MARK of the

`-DEATHS for the "FOUNDING `-FATHERS of the `-UNITED `-STATES of `-AMERICA!~' This is THE "MARK of the `-BEAST" with `-GOD'S `-HAND!~' (7 x 6) = (`-42)!~'

MARK of MALCOLM X / BIRTH = MAY 19, 1925 = (5 + 19 + 19 + 25) = (68) / (5 + 19) = 24 = RECIPROCAL = 42!~' DEATH = FEBRUARY 21, 1965!~' (FEBRUARY (2) x 21) = 42!~' (1965) = (19 + 65) = 84!~' JACQUELINE KENNEDY DIED on HIS BIRTHDAY!~' MARTIN LUTHER KING, JR. DIED within HIS BIRTHDAY #!

MARK of JACQUELINE KENNEDY / BIRTH = JULY 28, 1929 / DEATH = MAY 19, 1994!~' (JULY(7) + 28) = 35!~' (1994) = (19 + 94) = 113!~' (35 + 113) = 148!~' (1929) = (19 + 29) = 48!~' JULY 28 = (7 x 28) = 196 = (96 x 1) = 96 / 2 = 48 = RECIPROCAL = 84!~' DIED at the AGE of MARTIN LUTHER'S BIRTHDAY # `-NUMBER (`-64)!!!~'

MARK of MARTIN LUTHER KING, JR. / BIRTH = JANUARY 15, 1929 = (1 + 15 + 19 + 29) = `-64 = DEATH/AGE OF JACQUELINE!~' (1929) = (19 + 29) = 48! DEATH = APRIL 4, 1968! APRIL 4 = (4 x 4) = 16! (68 + 16) = 84! DIED in (68)! JANUARY 15 = (1 + 15) = 16! BIRTHDAY (1/15) = DEATH/DAY (4/4) = ADD (1 + 15 + 4 + 4) = (`-24) = RECIPROCAL = (`-42)!!!~'

MARK = MARTIN LUTHER KING, JR. / BIRTH = (1/15/1929) & DEATH = (4/4/1968)!!!~' MALCOLM X / BIRTH = (5/19/1925) & DEATH = (2/21/1965)!!!~' FROM BIRTHDAY to BIRTHDAY there are (`-124) DAYS & FROM DEATH/DAY to DEATH/DAY there are (`-42) DAYS!!!~' (`-24) = RECIPROCAL = (`-42)!!!~'

MARK = JACQUELINE KENNEDY ONASSIS `-DIED on MALCOLM X'S BIRTHDAY (5/19); AND, WAS BORN IN THE SAME YEAR AS MARTIN LUTHER KING, JR. (29)!~'

MARTIN LUTHER KING, JR'S BIRTHDAY # ('-64) EQUALED HER AGE OF '-DEATH (64)!~' THE YEAR SHE '-DIED ('-1994) was the AGE of '-DEATH of LADY BIRD JOHNSON (94)!~' (9 x 4) = ('-36) = RECIPROCAL = ('-63)!!!~' JACQUELINE KENNEDY ONASSIS' BIRTHDAY is ('-194) DAYS AWAY from THE '-BIRTHDAY of MARTIN LUTHER KING, JR.!!!~'

MARK = MARTIN LUTHER KING, JR. '-DIED at the '-AGE of ('-39)!!!~' MALCOLM X '-DIED at the '-AGE of ('-39)!!!~' (39 + 39) = ('-78) = (7 x 8) = ('-56) = RECIPROCAL = ('-65)!!!~' MARTIN was '-BORN in ('-1929) = (19 + 29) = (48)!!!~' ('-48) = RECIPROCAL = ('-84)!!!~' MALCOLM was '-ASSASSINATED in ('-1965) = (19 + 65) = ('-84)!!!~'

MARK = MALCOLM X'S '-BIRTHDAY # '-NUMBER = ('-68)!!!~' MARTIN LUTHER KING, JR. was ASSASSINATED in ('-68)!!!~' JACQUELINE KENNEDY ONASSIS was ('-34) FOR WHEN HER HUSBAND #35/PRESIDENT JOHN F. KENNEDY was ASSASSINATED!!!~' (34 x 2) = ('-68)!!!~'

MARK = #35/PRESIDENT JOHN F. KENNEDY'S BIRTHDAY = (5/29) = (5 + 29) = ('-34) = "AGE of '-WIFE JACQUELINE KENNEDY for WHEN '-HE was '-ASSASSINATED"!!!~' #35/PRESIDENT JOHN F. KENNEDY was '-BORN in ('-1917) = (19 + 17) = ('-36) = RECIPROCAL = ('-63) = "HE was '-ASSASSINATED in ('-1963)!!!~' HIS '-CHILDREN JOHN F. KENNEDY JR. & CAROLINE KENNEDY were '-BORN ('-363) '-DAYS '-APART!!!~'

MARK = #35/PRESIDENT JOHN F. KENNEDY BIRTHDAY (5/29) & DEATH/DAY (11/22) = (5 + 29 + 11 + 22) = ('-67) = RECIPROCAL = ('-76)!!!~' HIS '-DAUGHTER CAROLINE KENNEDY was '-BORN = (11/27/1957)!!!~' (19 + 57) = ('-76)!!!~' CAROLINE KENNEDY was '-BORN ('-183) DAYS AWAY from

`-HER `-FATHER'S `-BIRTHDAY!!!~' CAROLINE KENNEDY'S BIRTHDAY = (11/27) = (11 + 27) = (`-38) = "AGE of `-HER `-BROTHER JOHN F. KENNEDY JRS. `-DEATH"!!!~' #35/ PRESIDENT JOHN F. KENNEDY was (`-180) DAYS AWAY from `-HIS `-SON JOHN F. KENNEDY, JR'S. = (6 x 3) = (18) = (18 + 0) = (`-180)!!!~'

MARK = JACQUELINE KENNEDY ONASSIS was `-BORN on JULY 28, 1929 & `-DIED on MAY 19, 1994!!!~' (7 + 28 + 19 + 29) = (`-83) = RECIPROCAL = (`-38) = "HER SON JOHN F. KENNEDY, JR. `-DIED at the `-AGE of (`-38)"!!!~' (5 + 19 + 19 + 94) = (`-137) = (37 + 1) = (`-38) = `-DEATH `-AGE of JOHN F. KENNEDY, JR.!!!~'

MARK = JACQUELINE KENNEDY ONASSIS was (`-122) DAYS AWAY (22 + 1) = (`-23) FROM BIRTHDAY to BIRTHDAY with `-HER `-DAUGHTER CAROLINE!!!~' JACQUELINE KENNEDY ONASSIS was (`-120) DAYS AWAY FROM BIRTHDAY to BIRTHDAY with `-HER `-SON JOHN F. KENNEDY JR.!!!~' (122 + 120) = (`-142)!!!~' JACQUELINE KENNEDY ONASSIS was (`-305) DAYS AWAY (35 + 0) = (`-35) FROM BIRTHDAY to BIRTHDAY with `-HER `-HUSBAND the #35th/PRESIDENT JOHN F. KENNEDY!!!~'

MARK = JACQUELINE KENNEDY ONASSIS was `-BORN on JULY 28 & `-DIED on MAY 19th!!!~' (7 x 28) = (`-196) = (96 (-) 1) = (`-95)!!!~' (5 x 19) = (`-95)!!!~' (`-95) = RECIPROCAL = (`-59)!!!~' (7 + 28 + 5 + 19) = (`-59)!!!~' (95 (-) 59) = (`-36) = RECIPROCAL = (`-63) = "YEAR that `-HER `-HUSBAND #35/PRESIDENT JOHN F. KENNEDY was `-ASSASSINATED"!!!~' JACQUELINE'S `-BIRTHDAY = (7 + 28) = (`-35)!!!~'

MARK = JACQUELINE KENNEDY ONASSIS was `-BORN on JULY 28 & `-DIED on MAY 19th = (519) = (59 x 1) = (`-59)!!!~'

(7 x 28) = (`-196) = (96 x 1) = (`-**96**) = RECIPROCAL = (`-**69**)!!!~' HER `-SON JOHN F. KENNEDY, JR. was `-BORN in (`-1**96**0) & `-DIED in (`-1**999**)!!!~' (1999 + 1960) = (`-**39/59**)!!!~' (`-**39**) = **3(9's)**!!!~' HE was `-MARRIED from (`-19**96**) TO (`-1**999**) to CAROLYN BESSETTE-KENNEDY WHO was `-BORN in (`-**66**) & `-DIED in (`-**99**)!!!~'

MARK = #35/PRESIDENT JOHN F. KENNEDY BIRTHDAY = (5/29) = (`-34) = "AGE of `-DEATH of the `-SISTER of CAROLYN BESSETTE-KENNEDY (LAUREN BESSETTE)"!!!~' #35/ PRESIDENT JOHN F. KENNEDY DEATH/DAY = (11/22) = (`-33) = "AGE of `-DEATH of CAROLYN BESSETTE-KENNEDY on the `-FLIGHT that `-KILLED `-ALL (`-3) of `-THEM; including, JOHN F. KENNEDY, JR.!!!~' LAUREN BESSETTE was `-BORN in (`-1964) = (19 + 64) = (`-83) = RECIPROCAL = (`-38) = "AGE of `-DEATH of JOHN F. KENNEDY, JR. at the `-TIME of the `-PLANE `-CRASH"!!!~'

MARK = JOHN F. KENNEDY, JR. `-BIRTHDAY = (11/25) = (11 + 25) = (`-36) = RECIPROCAL = (`-63) = "YEAR of `-FATHER'S (JOHN F. KENNEDY'S) `-ASSASSINATION"!!!~' JOHN F. KENNEDY, JR. `-DEATH/DAY = (7/16) = (7 + 16) = (`-23)!!!~' (BIRTHDAY # (36) + (23) DEATH/DAY #) = (`-59) = RECIPROCAL = (`-95) = "HIS `-MOTHER JACQUELINE KENNEDY ONASSIS"!!!~' (11 + 25 + 7 + 16) = (`-59) = RECIPROCAL = (`-95)!!!~' (95 (-) 59) = (`-36) = RECIPROCAL = (`-63)!!!~'

BASEBALL'S TYLER SKAGGS BIRTHDAY = JULY 13, 1991!~' DEATH/DAY = JULY 1, 2019!~' `-91 = RECIPROCAL = `-19 / 1991 = (91 (-) 19) = `-72 = RECIPROCAL = `-27 = `-AGE of

`-DEATH!~' `-BIRTHDAY # = (7 + 13 + 19 + 91) = `-130 = (13 + 0)
= `-13 = `-DIED (`-13) DAYS BEFORE HIS NEXT BIRTHDAY

THE `-WORLD has become so `-SIMPLE-MINDED as to `-HOW
`-MUCH `-GOD `-CAN `-DO!!!!!~' `-STOP, `-LOOK, `-LEARN;
AND, `-LISTEN!!!!!~' DWAYNE W. ANDERSON!!!!!~' THE
`-PROPHET!!!~'

INDEPENDENCE DAY (JULY 4th)!!!~'

INDEPENDENCE DAY (JULY 4th)!!!~' (3) of **FIRST (5)**
PRESIDENTS `-**DIED** on **JULY 4th!~'** JOHN ADAMS (**90**)
(**1826**), THOMAS JEFFERSON (**83**)(**1826**), JAMES MONROE
(**73**)(**1831**)!~' **FIRST 2 PRESIDENTS** to `-**DIE ADD**-**UP** to the

3rd PRESIDENT'S `-AGE of `-DEATH!-' (90 + 83) = `-173 = (73 x 1) = (`-73)!-'

(1826) = (18 + 26) = `-44!-' (PRESIDENT/VICE-PRESIDENT)-(PRESIDENT/VICE-PRESIDENT)-(PRESIDENT/VICE-PRESIDENT)!!!-' $1^{st}$ PRESIDENT GEORGE WASHINGTON was `-BORN in 17$\underline{32}$!-' (1732 + 44) = `-1776 = 1st INDEPENDENCE DAY (JULY 4th)!-' (32 = RECIPROCAL = 23) = 1776 + 23 = 1799 = PRESIDENT

`-GEORGE `-WASHINGTON DIES at the `-AGE of (`-67)!-' (76 = RECIPROCAL-INVERSE-REALITY = 67)!!!!!-' JAMES MONROE (JULY 4th, 1831) = (18 + 31) = `-49 = GEORGE WASHINGTON (FEBRUARY 22, 1732/Birth) = (17 + 32_) = `-49!!!!!-' (FEBRUARY 22 = (2 x 22) = (`-44)!!!!!-' (100 (-) 44) = `-56!!!!!-

`-56 = "The DELEGATES that `-SIGNED the `-DECLARATION of `-INDEPENDENCE!-' `-ALL `-INTERTWINED `-within `-the `-CENTURIES `-of `-TIME!!!!!-' BENJAMIN FRANKLIN (JANUARY 17, 1706-Birth)(APRIL 17, 1790-Death)!-' `-BORN on a (`-$17^{th}$) & `-DIED on a (`-$17^{th}$)!-' `-DIED at the `-AGE of (`-84)!-'

`-84 = (8 x 4) = `-32!-' (1706) = (0 + 76 x 1) = `-76!-' (17 + 6) = `-23!-' BENJAMIN FRANKLIN `-STARTED "POOR RICHARD'S ALMANACK" in (`-1732)!-' FOUNDING `-FATHER of the `-UNITED STATES of `-AMERICA!-' ANDREW JACKSON `-BORN on (MARCH 15, 1767)!-' REVERSE = (67 (-) 17 (-) 15 (-) 3) = `-32!-'

`-BENJAMIN FRANKLIN `-LIVED to be (`-84)!-' (84 / 2) = `-42 "HALF of `-HIS `-LIFE" = (7 x 6) = "BORN in (`-1706) = `-AS `-HE `-HELPED `-DRAFT the `-DECLARATION of

`-INDEPENDENCE in (`-17<u>76</u>)!!!~' (<u>17</u> x <u>4</u> = <u>FRANKLIN</u>) = `-<u>68</u>!~' PRESIDENT ANDREW JACKSON `-<u>DIED</u> on <u>JUNE</u>(6) <u>8</u>th = (`-<u>68</u>)!~'

`-PRESIDENT ANDREW JACKSON was `-<u>BORN</u> in (`-1<u>767</u>)!~' (<u>67</u> + 17) = `-<u>84</u> = THE `-YEARS BENJAMIN FRANKLIN `-<u>LIVED</u>!~' PRESIDENT GEORGE WASHINGTON'S DEATH/DAY # = (12 + 14 + 17 + 99) = `-<u>142</u> = (42 x 1) = `-<u>42</u> = (<u>6</u> x <u>7</u>)!~' 1st PRESIDENT GEORGE WASHINGTON `-<u>DIED</u> at the `-<u>AGE</u> of (`-<u>67</u>)!~'

`-<u>DEATH</u> `-<u>YEARS</u> of the 1st <u>THREE</u> of the <u>FIRST FIVE</u> `-<u>PRESIDENTS</u> to `-<u>DIE</u> on JULY 4th INDEPENDENCE DAY = (<u>1826</u> & <u>1831</u>) = (18 + 26 + 18 + 31) = `-<u>93</u>!~' The `-<u>YEARS</u> from the `-*FOUNDING* `-*FATHER* BENJAMIN FRANKLIN'S `-<u>BIRTH</u> to the `-1st PRESIDENT GEORGE WASHINGTON'S `-<u>DEATH</u> = (`-<u>93</u>)!!!-

AGAIN, BENJAMIN FRANKLIN `-<u>LIVED</u> to be (`-<u>84</u>) with `-HIS `-DEATH/DAY BEING (<u>4/17</u>)!~' (4 x 17) = `-<u>68</u> = PRESIDENT ANDREW JACKSON'S DAY of `-DEATH = JUNE(6) <u>8</u>th!~' WHAT is (<u>6</u> X <u>8</u>) but `-<u>48</u> = <u>RECIPROCAL</u> = `-<u>84</u>!~' PRESIDENT GEORGE WASHINGTON'S DEATH/DAY = (<u>12/14</u>) = (12 x 14) = (`-<u>168</u>)!~

PRESIDENT GEORGE WASHINGTON was `-<u>BORN</u> in (`-<u>32</u>); and, `-<u>DIED</u> (`-<u>23</u>) YEARS LATER AFTER (`-76) at the `-<u>AGE</u> of (`-<u>67</u>)!~' (<u>reciprocals</u>) `-<u>123</u> years later; PRESIDENT WOODROW WILSON `-<u>DIED</u> on (<u>2/3</u>) at the `-<u>AGE</u> of (`-<u>67</u>)!~' (<u>2/3/19<u>24</u></u>) = (2 + 3 + 19 + 24) = `-<u>48</u> = <u>RECIPROCAL</u> = `-<u>84</u>!~'

PRESIDENT GEORGE WASHINGTON'S BIRTHDAY = (<u>2/22</u>) = (2 + 22) = (`-<u>24</u>) = <u>RECIPROCAL</u> = (`-<u>42</u>) = (<u>6</u> X <u>7</u>) with PRESIDENT GEORGE WASHINGTON <u>DYING</u> on

`-HIS `-BIRTHDAY # `-NUMBER at the `-<u>AGE</u> of (`-<u>67</u>)!-'
U.S. PRESIDENTS that have `-<u>DIED</u> in `-<u>SUCCESSION</u> /the
`-AVERAGE `-AGE = (`-<u>67</u>)/(<u>76</u>)-'

PRESIDENT GEORGE WASHINGTON'S BIRTHDAY # = (2
+ 22 + 17 + 32) = `-<u>73</u>!-' FOUNDING FATHER BENJAMIN
FRANKLIN `-<u>DIED</u> in (`-<u>1790</u>) = (90 - 17) = `-<u>73</u>!- (<u>1776</u>) 1ST
INDEPENDENCE DAY = (17 + 76) = `-<u>93</u>!-' AGAIN, from the
`-BIRTH of `-FRANKLIN to the `-DEATH of `-WASHINGTON
= (<u>93</u>-years)!-'

PRESIDENT GEORGE WASHINGTON'S BIRTH = (<u>2</u>/<u>22</u>)
= (<u>2 + 22</u>) = `-<u>24</u>!- FROM `-<u>123</u> YEARS that (<u>lie-in-between</u>)
TO an `-ACTUAL `-<u>124</u> YEARS to PRESIDENT WOODROW
WILSON'S DEATH = (<u>124</u>) = (1 x 24) = `-<u>24</u> = <i>RECIPROCAL</i>
= `-<u>42</u> = (<u>6</u> X <u>7</u>) = <u>WILSON</u> <i>DIES</i> AT THE `-<u>AGE</u> of `-<u>67</u> <i>just
like</i> <u>WASHINGTON</u>!-

PRESIDENT GEORGE WASHINGTON was `-<u>BORN</u> in (`-
<u>32</u>); and, `-<u>DIED</u> (`-<u>23</u>) YEARS LATER AFTER (`-<u>76</u>) at the
`-<u>AGE</u> of (`-<u>67</u>)!-' (<u>reciprocals</u>) `-<u>123</u> years that (lie-in-between)
PRESIDENT WOODROW WILSON `-<u>DIED</u> on (<u>2</u>/<u>3</u>) at the
`-<u>AGE</u> of (`-<u>67</u>)!-' The (<u>23</u>rd) PRESIDENT <u>DYING</u> at the `-<u>AGE</u>
of (`-<u>67</u>)!-'

<u>#23</u>/PRESIDENT BENJAMIN <u>HARRISON</u> `-<u>DIED</u> at the
`-<u>AGE</u> of (`-<u>67</u>)!-' Note the `-LAST `-NAME!-' #9/PRESIDENT
WILLIAM HENRY <u>HARRISON</u> `-WHO `-DIED at the `-<u>AGE</u>
of (`-<u>68</u>)/<u>DIED</u> on this `-<u>DATE</u>: APRIL 4, 1841 = (4 + 4 +18 +
41) = (`-<u>67</u>)!-' <u>HAPPY</u> `-<u>INDEPENDENCE</u> `-<u>DAY</u> (`-17<u>76</u>)!!!-'
`-<u>PATTERNS</u> (23 + 9) = `-<u>32</u>!!!-'

The REAL PROPHET of DOOM (Kismet) - INTRODUCTION - `-PENDULUM `-FLOW - III -"`

`-HEY; HAS ANYONE HEARD OF THE MUSICAL GROUP "CHICAGO": (67,68), "DOES ANYONE KNOW WHAT TIME IT IS", "I'M A MAN, YES I AM, AND I CAN'T HELP BUT LOVE YOU SO", "SATURDAY, IN THE PARK, I THINK IT WAS THE 4th OF JULY…WILL YOU HELP ME CHANGE THE WORLD…CAN YOU DIG `-IT…YES I CAN"…!

THE FIRST LANDING ON THE MOON = APOLLO 11 = 240,000 MILES (386,242.6 km) / (76) HOURS to ENTER the MOON'S `-ORBIT!~' LAUNCH DATE = JULY 16 = (7/16) = (76 x 1) = `-76 = INDEPENDENCE `-DAY!~' (6:32 AM) GMT-7!~' (7/20/1969) = (69 (-) 19 (-) 20 (-) 7) = `-23!~' 23 = RECIPROCAL = 32!-

"THAT'S ONE SMALL STEP FOR MAN"!~' "ONE GIANT LEAP FOR ALL MANKIND"!~' "WE CAME IN PEACE FOR ALL MANKIND"!~' RETURN LAUNCH = JULY 21, 1969 (17:54 UTC) (54 (-) 17) = 37!~' (3 x 7) = 21 = JULY!~' EVA DURATION: 2 HOURS, 31 MINUTES, 40 SECONDS 2/3rds = 2 HOURS, 32 MINUTES = (`-232)!~

MARK = MARY TODD LINCOLN had `-DIED on (7/16)!~' (7 + 16) = 23!~' SHE was `-MARRIED to ABRAHAM LINCOLN for (23) YEARS!~' SHE DIED on (7/16/1882)!~' (7 + 16 + 18 + 82) = `-123!~' (1882) = (82 (-) 18) = `-64 = RECIPROCAL = `-46!~' EQUALS HER `-AGE at the TIME of the `-DEATH of `-ABE!~'

MARK of the '-BEAST of FIRST LADY MARY TODD LINCOLN was BORN on DECEMBER 13, 1818!~ (DECEMBER (12) x 13) = '-156 = (56 x 1) = '-56 = '-AGE of '-DEATH of PRESIDENT ABRAHAM LINCOLN!~' (1818) = (18 + 18) = '-36 = RECIPROCAL = '-63 = '-AGE of '-DEATH of FIRST LADY MARY TODD LINCOLN!~

MARK of ABRAHAM LINCOLN BORN on (2/12/1809) DIED on (4/15/1865)!~' (415 (-) 212) = 203!~' (4/15) = (4 x 15) = 60!~ (2/12) = (2 x 12) = 24!~' (60 + 24) = (84)!~' MARY DIED on (7/16/1882)!~' (82 (-) 18 (-) 16 (-) 7) = 41 = (2 + 12 + 18 + 09) = ABE'S BIRTHDAY # = MARY'S DEATH/DAY #!

MARK of the '-BEAST of PRESIDENT ABRAHAM LINCOLN OFFICE of the PRESIDENCY = MARCH 4, 1861 to APRIL 14, 1865!~' (3 + 4 + 18 + 61) = 86 = RECIPROCAL = 68!~' (1861) = (61 (-) 18) = '-43 = RECIPROCAL = 3/4!~' APRIL(4) 14 = (4 x 14) = 56 = AGE of '-DEATH of PRESIDENT ABRAHAM LINCOLN!~

MARK of the '-BEAST for JOHN F. KENNEDY BORN MAY 29, 1917!~' (1917) = (19 + 17) = 36 = RECIPROCAL = 63 = WAS KILLED in 1963!~' DEATH NOVEMBER 22, 1963!~' (5/29) = (5 + 29) = 34 = AGE of JACKIE at his ASSASSINATION (11/22) = (11 x 22) = 242!~' (29 (-) 5 = 24 = RECIPROCAL = 42!~'

JOHN F. KENNEDY BIRTH = 5/29 / DEATH = 11/22!~' (5 + 29 + 11 + 22) = '-67 = RECIPROCAL = '-76 = INDEPENDENCE DAY!~' (5 + 29 + 19 + 17) = 70 / (11 + 22 + 19 + 63) = 115!~' (115 (-) 70 = 45!~' JACKIE = (7 + 28 + 19 + 29) = 83 / (5 + 19 + 19 + 94) = 137!~' (137 (-) 83) = 54!~ RECIPROCALS ('-45 = RECIPROCAL = '-54)!!!~'

MARY TODD LINCOLN '-MARRIED ABE in (42)/1842!~' JOHN PAUL STEVENS '-STARTED SERVICE on the

SUPREME COURT in (`-42)/1942!~' JOHN PAUL STEVENS BIRTH = APRIL 20, 1920!~' APRIL 20 = (4/20) = (42 + 0) = 42!~' BORN in (1920) & DIED in (2019)!~' FLIP THEM AROUND = RECIPROCALS = RECIPS!~

MARY TODD LINCOLN `-DIED at the `-AGE of (`-63)!~' JOHN PAUL STEVENS BIRTHDAY # `-NUMBER = APRIL 20, 1920 = (4 + 20 + 19 + 20) = (`-63)!~' JOHN PAUL STEVENS `-DIED at the `-AGE of (`-99) = RECIPROCAL = (`-66)!~' (99 + 66) = 165' = (65 x 1) = 65 = YEAR MARY'S HUSBAND was KILLED!~'

FIRST LADY ELEANOR ROOSEVELT BIRTHDAY # `-NUMBER = OCTOBER 11, 1884 = (10 + 11 + 18 + 84) = `-123 = DEATH/DAY # `-NUMBER of FIRST LADY MARY TODD LINCOLN!~' DEATH = NOVEMBER 7, 1962 = (11 + 7 + 19 + 62) = 99 = AGE of `-DEATH of JOHN PAUL STEVENS!~' MARRIED to the 32nd PRESIDENT!~'

NEIL ARMSTRONG BIRTH = AUGUST 5, 1930 / DEATH = AUGUST 25, 2012!~' (8 x 5) = 40!~' (8 x 25) = 200!~' (200 + 40) = 240 = MILES AWAY FROM EARTH to the `-MOON!~' (8 + 25 + 20 + 12) = 65 = YEAR ABE was KILLED!~' DIED at 82 = 2(8's) = 88 = (11 x 8) = APOLLO 11 & GEMINI 8 MISSIONS!!!~'

ORBITER PILOT MICHAEL COLLINS is CURRENTLY (`-88)!~ BORN OCTOBER 31, 1930!~' (OCTOBER (10) (-) 31) = 21 = (11 + 10) = APOLLO 11 & GEMINI 10 MISSIONS!~' STATED HE was 230,000 MILES AWAY from EARTH!~' 1930 = (30 (-) 19) = APOLLO 11 (ARMSTRONG & COLLINS)!~' 2012 = (20 + 12) = `-32!~

WALTER CRONKITE was on TV for (`-32) HOURS `-STRAIGHT!~' BIRTH = NOVEMBER 4, 1916 / DEATH = JULY 17, 2009!~' (11 x 4) = 44 = 2(4's)!~' (7 + 17) = `-24!~' (1916 &

2009) = (19 + 16 + 20 + 09) = 64 = (8 x 8) = 2(8's) = ('-88)!~' (88 x 2) = '-176 = (76 x 1) = '-76 = INDEPENDENCE DAY!~'

APOLLO 11 LUNAR MODULE PILOT BUZZ ALDRIN'S BIRTH = JANUARY 20, 1930!~' 1930 = (30 (-) 19) = 11 = APOLLO 11 for BUZZ ALDRIN JUST AS WELL!~' BUZZ ALDRIN'S BIRTHDAY WAS (188) DAYS after APOLLO 11's FLIGHT LAUNCH on (7/16)!~' SPACE MISSIONS = APOLLO 11 & GEMINI 12 = (11 + 12) = '-23!

WALTER CRONKITE was on TV for ('-32) HOURS '-STRAIGHT!~' BIRTH = NOVEMBER 4, 1916 / DEATH = JULY 17, 2009!~' (2009 (-) 1916) = ('-93)!~' WALTER CRONKITE '-DIED within '-HIS (93rd) YEAR of '-EXISTENCE!~' ALL ASTRONAUTS were '-BORN in ('-93)!~' COVERING the APOLLO 11 SPACE MISSION!

APOLLO 11 LUNAR LANDING with NEIL ARMSTRONG & BUZZ ALDRIN TAKING 122 PHOTOGRAPHS WHILE on the MOON!~' (122) = (22 + 1) = ('-23')!~' REMEMBER THE FELT TIPPED PEN for the BROKEN CIRCUIT BREAKER AFTER THE STABILITY CONTROL BREAKER (PANEL 16/ROW 2) FOR ESCAPING = (16 x 2) = ('-32)!~'

APOLLO 11 EARTH RE-ENTRY UNDER HEAT SHIELD TRAVELING at (24,(67)7) MPH into ATMOSPHERE!~' (24 x 7) = 168!~' ON THE MOON'S SURFACE FOR LESS THAN 24 HOURS (23) UPON SAFELY LANDING & GATHERING WENT ON A ('-24) COUNTRY WORLD TOUR!~' ALL OF '-THIS AFTER CATCHING A ROCKET AT 9:32 AM!~'

APOLLO 11 PART OF WHAT WAS LEFT ON THE MOON FROM THE MISSION WERE MESSAGES FROM ('-73) WORLD LEADERS!~' ALSO; A '-PATCH from the APOLLO

1 MISSION THAT KILLED 3 U.S. ASTRONAUTS IN 19(67) DURING A TRAINING EXERCISE!~' ALSO, MEDALLIONS for FALLEN RUSSIAN COSMONAUTS in (67) & (68)!~'

(67') NEW ENGLAND PATRIOTS FOOTBALL GUARD MITCH PETRUS `-DIES at `-AGE `-32!~' BIRTH MAY 11, 1987 / DEATH JULY 18, 2019!~' (5 + 11 + 19 + 87) = 122 = (22 + 1) = `-23 = RECIPROCAL = `-32!~' (7 + 18 + 20 + 19) = 64 / 2 = 32!~' MAY(5) (.) (JULY(7) + 18) = 5.25 = 40 YARD DASH TIME!~'

(67') NEW ENGLAND PATRIOTS MITCH PETRUS `-DIES at `-AGE (`-32)!~' BIRTH MAY 11, 1987 / DEATH JULY 18, 2019!~' (5 x 11) = `-55 = (23 + 32)!~' (7 x 18) = `-126 / 2 = `-63 = `-HE was 6' 3" in `-HEIGHT!~' (1987) = (87 (-) 19) = `-68!~' `-HE DIED (`-68) DAYS AFTER HIS LAST BIRTHDAY!~'

MARK/BEAST for BOXING'S PERNELL WHITAKER BIRTH JANUARY 2nd, 1964 / DEATH JULY 14th, 2019!~' JANUARY 2 = 12 = RECIPROCAL = 21!~ JULY 14 = (7 + 14) = 21!~' (21 + 21) = 42!~' 1964 = (64 (-) 19) = 45!~' 2019 = (20 + 19) = 39!~' (45 + 39) = 84!~' DIED 193 DAYS AFTER HIS LAST BIRTHDAY!

MARK of the BEAST for BOXING'S PERNELL WHITAKER BIRTH JANUARY 2nd, 1964 / DEATH JULY 14th, 2019!~' (1964) / (2019) = (19 + 64 + 20 + 19) = 122 = (22 + 1) = 23 = RECIPROCAL = 32!~' DIED AT THE AGE OF 55 = (23 + 32)!~' (1 + 2 + 19 + 64) = 86 = RECIPROCAL = 68!~' THE MARK OF DEATH!~

MARK of the `-BEAST for BOXING'S GREAT PERNELL WHITAKER BIRTH JANUARY 2nd, 1964 / DEATH JULY 14th, 2019!~' (1 + 2 + 19 + 64) = 86!~' (7 + 14 + 20 + 19) = 60!~' (86 + 60) = 146 = (46 X 1) = `-46 = RECIPROCAL = `-64 = BOXING'S GREAT PERNELL WHITAKER WAS BORN IN (`-64) = (2 x 32)!~'

MARK of the `-BEAST for `-BOXING'S GREAT PERNELL WHITAKER BIRTH JANUARY 2nd, 1964 / DEATH JULY 14th, 2019!-' JULY 14th = JULY (1 X 4) = JULY 4th = INDEPENDENCE DAY!-' (7 X 14) = 98!-' JANUARY(1) x 2 = 2!-' (98 (-) 2) = 96 = 32 x 3!-' The `-MARK of the `-BEAST; `-INDEFINITELY!!!-'

ACCORDING to the `-BIBLE; WHY do `-HUMANS deserve to have EVERLASTING `-LIFE; or, `-LIFE ETERNAL!-' WHAT ELSE has THAT!-' YOU KILLED for that BACON, CHICKEN, PORK CHOPS, RIBS; and, EGGS!-' YOU'VE even `-KILLED for those ORANGES, APPLES; and, BANANAS; `-TOO!-' WHAT 'SAY "YOU"!!!-'

The BIBLE says that there will be an IMMORTALITY for CHRIST'S BROTHERS!-' HOW can INDIVIDUALS who have only LIVED a 100 YEARS or LESS have IMMORTALITY due to TRIBULATIONS when the ANGELS never became DEMONS and have been FAITHFUL unto `-GOD for BILLIONS of YEARS and not IMMORTAL!

The BIBLE says that the LIONS will EAT GRASS; and, that the CHILD will play upon the COBRA'S DEN!-' PEACE would be RESTORED to what was PRIOR to ADAM & EVE'S SIN!- THE DINOSAURS were there before ADAM & EVE!-' Was LIFE then that PEACEFUL for DINOSAURS for THOSE MILLIONS of YEARS!

Hmm, `-LION; a `-CYCLE of `-LIFE!-' THE `-BIBLE SAYS that SATAN is a ROARING LION SEEKING to DEVOUR SOMEONE!-' THAT'S `-FOOD for `-THOUGHT!-' "THE LION KING"!-' IF A REAL PROPHET were HERE right now;

here on EARTH; WOULD you BE ABLE to IDENTIFY HIM!~'
ONE that TALKS with `-GOD!~'

HOW MUCH CORRUPTION CAN CORRUPTION
STAND!~' HOW MUCH CORRUPTION CAN ONE STAND
FOR CORRUPTION!~' DEMOCRATIC PRESIDENTIAL
PRIMARY DEBATE (6/26) = (6 + 26) = `-32!~' DEMOCRATIC
PRESIDENTIAL PRIMARY DEBATE (7/30) = (30 (-) 7) = `-23!~'
32 = RECIPROCAL = 23!~' The MARK of the `-BEAST!

LONGTIME MANHATTAN DISTRICT ATTORNEY `-DIES
AT 99!~' ROBERT MORGENTHAU BIRTH JULY 31st, 1919 /
DEATH JULY 21st, 2019!~' 10 DAYS SHY of 100!~' JULY 31st = (7 x
31) = 217 = RECIPROCAL = 721 = DAY OF `-DEATH!~' (7 + 31) =
38 = (19 + 19) = 38!~' (38 + 38) = 76 = INDEPENDENCE DAY!!!~'

LONGTIME MANHATTAN DISTRICT ATTORNEY `-DIES
AT 99!~' ROBERT MORGENTHAU BIRTH JULY 31st, 1919 /
DEATH JULY 21st, 2019!~' (7 X 21) = 147 = RECIPROCAL = 714 =
JULY 14th = JULY (1 X 4) = JULY 4th = INDEPENDENCE DAY!~'
(7 + 31 + 19 + 19) = 76 = RECIPROCAL` = 67 = (7 + 21 + 20 + 19)!~'

MUSICIAN ART NEVILLE BORN DECEMBER 17, 1937 /
DEATH: JULY 22, 2019!~' (12 x 17) = 204 = (24 + 0) = 24 =
RECIPROCAL = 42!~' DECEMBER 17 = (12 + 17) = 29!~' JULY
22 = (7 + 22) = 29!~' (29 + 29) = 58 = (5 ı 8) = 13!~' DECEMBER
17, 1937 = (12 + 17 + 19 + 37') = 85 = (8 + 5) = `-13!~'

MUSIC/ARTIST ART NEVILLE BORN DECEMBER 17, 1937
/ DEATH: JULY 22, 2019!~' (7 + 22 + 20 + 19) = 68!~' (MARK of
the `-BEAST!~') DECEMBER 17, 1937 = (12/17/19/37) = (1 + 2 +
1 + 7 + 1 + 9 + 3 + 7) = 31 = RECIPROCAL = 13!~' (19'37') (20'19)
= (19 + 37 + 20) = 76' = INDEPENDENCE DAY!~'

ART NEVILLE BORN DECEMBER 17, 1937 / DEATH JULY 22, 2019!~' (7/22/20/19) = (7 + 2 + 2 + 2 + 0 + 1 + 9) = '~23 = RECIPROCAL = '~32!~' INDEPENDENCE DAY = 76 = (7 + 6) = '~13!~' DIED (217) DAYS AFTER HIS LAST BIRTHDAY = ROBERT MORGENTHAU!~' (365 (-) 217) = 148!~' (21 x 7) = '~147!~'

NASA MISSION CONTROL'S FOUNDING FATHER CHRISTOPHER COLUMBUS KRAFT JR. BIRTH FEBRUARY 28, 1924 / DEATH JULY 22, 2019!~' (2 + 28 + 19 + 24) = 73!~' (7 + 22 + 20 + 19) = 68!~' DIED 144 DAYS AFTER HIS LAST BIRTHDAY!~' (14 x 4) = 56!~' FEBRUARY 28 = (2 x 28) = 56!~' (365 (-) 144) = 221!~' 221 = (2 x 21) = 42!~' 221 = (2 + 21)= 23!~'

NASA MISSION CONTROL'S FOUNDING FATHER CHRISTOPHER COLUMBUS KRAFT JR. BIRTH FEBRUARY 28, 1924 / DEATH JULY 22, 2019!~' (2 + 2 + 8 + 1 + 9 + 2 + 4) = 28!~' BORN on a ('~28)!~' (1924) / (2019) = (19 + 24 + 20 + 19) = '~82 = RECIPROCAL = '~28!~' DIES AT THE AGE OF 95!~' (95 (-) 82) = '~13!~'

NASA MISSION CONTROL'S FOUNDING FATHER CHRISTOPHER COLUMBUS KRAFT JR. BIRTH FEBRUARY 28, 1924 / DEATH JULY 22, 2019!~' BIRTHDAY # '~NUMBER = 73!~' DEATH/DAY # '~NUMBER = '~68!~' (73 + 68) = 141!~' DEATH/ DAY 7/22 = (7 x 22) = 154!~' (154 (-) 141) = '~13!~' CAN '~YOU AGAIN SEE THE # '~NUMBERS of the FOUNDING FATHERS!~'

DEPARTMENT OF TREASURY BUDGET DEAL SUSPENDS DEBT CEILING to BORROW MONEY FOR 2 YEARS; AND, INCREASE SPENDING BY $320 BILLION DOLLARS!~'

INCREASE OVERALL GOVERNMENT SPENDING BY A $1.37 TRILLION DOLLARS NEXT YEAR 2019/2020!~' IN THE HOUSE, 132 REPUBLICANS VOTED AGAINST IT!~' SPECIAL INVESTIGATOR ROBERT MUELLER HAD DECLINED OR DEFLECTED QUESTIONS 123 TIMES!~'

DEPARTMENT OF TREASURY BUDGET DEAL SUSPENDS DEBT CEILING to BORROW MONEY FOR 2 YEARS; AND, INCREASE SPENDING BY $'(32)0 BILLION DOLLARS!~' IN THE HOUSE, 1(32)' REPUBLICANS VOTED AGAINST IT!~' MUELLER HAD DECLINED OR DEFLECTED QUESTIONS 1(23)' TIMES!~' `-23 = RECIPROCAL' = `-32!~'

THE BIBLE SAYS THAT `-GOD RESTED ON THE 7th DAY!~' FROM 'CREATION that may be; but, as to `-ACTUALLY `-WORKING with `-HIS `-CREATION; `-HE has; and, continues to `-DO so; `-EVERYDAY!~' `-GOD is a `-MATHEMATICIAN; and, `-HE 'LOVES `-USING `-RECIPROCALS in 'LIFE & DEATH!~' (23/32)

TO UNDERSTAND A LITTLE BIT MORE ABOUT 'GOD; HE ARTICULATES YOUR SLEEP, TOO!~' FROM SCOPE, STRUCTURE, SYNTAX, SYNTHESIS; and, ACUTE STYLE; HE does ALL of THIS just as WELL; as AWAKEN!~' IS IT a Distant Relative, Friend; OR, FOE; you KNOW!~' ALL of this; ENCAPSULATED, just for YOU!

TO UNDERSTAND A LITTLE BIT MORE ABOUT `-GOD; FOR WHEN YOU SLEEP `-HE ARTICULATES THIS JUST AS WELL!~' FROM `-SCOPE, `-STRUCTURE, `-SYNTAX; `-SYNTHESIS; and, `-ACUTE `-STYLE; `-HE does `-ALL of `-THIS just as `-WELL; as `-AWAKEN!~' IS `-IT a Distant Relative, Friend; OR, FOE!~' ALL of this `-YOU know; `-ENCAPSULATED, just for `-YOU!~'

SOMETHING THAT BAFFLES THE PROPHET is HOW 'GOD "SNAPS A LINE" THROUGHOUT ALL SPACE & TIME AND THROUGH EVERY BIT & PART OF HIS CREATIONS TO MOVE IN A 'FLUX OF MOTION IN AN ARTICULATED FASHION TO AN EVENTUALITY OF DESTINY!~' A 'FLUIDITY for EVERY 'MICROSECOND of EVERY 'MICROATOM!~'

ANNE FRANCIS "HONEY WEST" (65) & "FORBIDDEN PLANET" (56) (BIRTHDAY #: SEPTEMBER 16, 1930) (9 + 16 + 19 + 30) = 74!~' (DEATHDAY #: JANUARY 2, 2011) (1 + 2 + 20 + 11) = 34!~' (74 + 34) = ('-108)!~' 'SHE DIED ('-108) DAYS AFTER HER LAST BIRTHDAY in HER 81st YEAR at the AGE of (80)!~

FIRST LADY BARBARA PIERCE BUSH WAS BORN JUNE 8th, THE VERY SAME DAY THAT #7/PRESIDENT ANDREW JACKSON `-DIED (6/8)!~' FIRST LADY BARBARA BUSH DIED SAME DAY AS BENJAMIN FRANKLIN APRIL 17 = (4/17) = (4 x 17) = `-68!~' DIED 52 DAYS BEFORE HER BIRTHDAY = RECIPROCAL = 25 = YEAR BORN!~'

#7/PRESIDENT ANDREW JACKSON was BORN in (1767) = (67 + 17) = 84 = AGE of DEATH of BENJAMIN FRANKLIN!~ FOUNDING FATHER BENJAMIN FRANKLIN DIED 90 DAYS AFTER HIS BIRTHDAY in the YEAR of (90)!~' ANDREW JACKSON DIED 85 DAYS AFTER HIS BIRTHDAY = RECIPROCAL = 5' 8" = BARBARA'S HEIGHT!~'

FROM ALEXANDER HAMILTON, BENJAMIN FRANKLIN, to the FIRST (9)/ALL PRESIDENTS of USA; their DAY of DEATHS or BIRTHS ADD UP to/MULTIPLY to (84) and = (84 x 2) = 168!~ (3) PRESIDENTS to DIE on JULY(7) 4th (7 x 4) = 28 = (28 x 3) = `-84! DON'T SEE the HAND of GOD HERE; YOU'RE STUPID!~

BASEBALL'S TYLER SKAGGS BIRTH = JULY 13, 1991!~'
DEATH/DAY = JULY 1, 2019!~' `-91 = RECIPROCAL = `-19
/ 1991 = (91 (-) 19) = `-72 = RECIPROCAL = `-27 = `-AGE of
`-DEATH!~' `-BIRTHDAY = JULY 13 = (7 x 13) = 91!~' (91)19(91)
and DEATH in (`-19)!~' LEFT (7/1/20) = 28 = 13 DAYS AWAY!

Ethel Kennedy's daughter; COURTNEY KENNEDY HILL, was
BORN on SEPTEMBER 9th!~' (9 x 9) = (`-81)!~' HER DAUGHTER
SAOIRSE ROISIN HILL died ON (`-81) = AUGUST 1st!~'
(8/1/2019) = (8 + 1 + 20 + 19) = 48 = RECIPROCAL = 84!~' ETHEL
KENNEDY (4/11) = (4 x 11) = 44/2 = 22 = AGE of DEATH!~

JOHN F. KENNEDY JR. BIRTHDAY = NOVEMBER 25, 1960!~'
(11 + 25) = 36 = RECIPROCAL = 63 = YEAR HIS FATHER
was KILLED!~' (11 + 25 + 19 + 60) = `-115!~' HIS FATHER'S
DEATH/DAY = (11 + 22 + 19 + 63) = `-115!~' JR.S BIRTH # =
HIS FATHER'S DEATH #!~' (JFK 115 (+) JFK, JR 115) = (`-230)!~'

JOHN F. KENNEDY JR. DEATH = JULY 16, 1999!~' (7 + 16) =
`-23!~' DIED THE SAME DAY AS FIRST LADY MARY TODD
LINCOLN!~' FIRST LADY MARY TODD LINCOLN WAS
46 WHEN HER HUSBAND ABRAHAM LINCOLN WAS
ASSASSINATED!~' HIS FATHER WAS KILLED AT THE AGE
OF 46!~' 46 = (23 x 2) = (`-232) = RECIPROCALS!!!~'

JOHN F. KENNEDY JR. was MARRIED to CAROLYN
BESSETTE-KENNEDY from (1996-1999)!~' SHE WAS BORN
in (66) & DIED in (99) = RECIPROCALS!~' HER BIRTH =
JANUARY 7, 1966 = (1 + 7 + 19 + 66) = 93 = RECIPROCAL = 39
= THE AGE that HER HUSBAND was 132 DAYS AWAY FROM
BY BIRTHDAY!~' (23/\32)!~'

LAUREN BESSETTE FLIGHT TOOK OFF at 8:38 = `-83 =
RECIPROCAL = `-38!~' BIRTHDAY = NOVEMBER 5th, 1964 =

(11 + 5 + 19 + 64) = 99 = SHE DIED in (`-99)!~' 1964 = (19 + 64) = (83)!~' JFK, JR. DIED at the AGE of (38)!~' JULY 16th = (7 x 16) = 112 = SHE DIED 112 DAYS FROM HER BIRTHDAY!~'

CAROLYN BESSETTE-KENNEDY AGE of DEATH = '33!~' LAUREN BESSETTE AGE of DEATH = '34!~' (33 + 34) = 67 = RECIPROCAL = 76 = DIED on 7/16!~' 8:38 = (8 + 38) = '46 = RECIPROCAL = '64 = YEAR LAUREN BESSETTE was BORN!~' AGE of DEATH of JFK, JR.'S MOTHER JACQUELINE KENNEDY ONASSIS (64)!~'

BENJAMIN FRANKLIN DIED ON 68!~' PRESIDENT GEORGE WASHINGTON DIED ON 168!~' PRESIDENT JAMES MADISON DIED ON 168!~' PRESIDENT ANDREW JACKSON DIED ON 6/8 ADDED TO PRESIDENT QUINCY ADAMS = 168!~' PRESIDENT MARTIN VAN BUREN DIED ON 168!~' PRESIDENT WILLIAM HENRY HARRISON DIED AT 68!~'

ALEXANDER HAMILTON DIED ON 84 IN (`1804)!~' BENJAMIN FRANKLIN DIED AT AGE 84!~' PRESIDENTS JOHN ADAMS, THOMAS JEFFERSON & JAMES MONROE that DIED on JULY 4th ADDED up to 84!~' PRESIDENT JOHN QUINCY ADAMS DIED IN 1848!~' ZACHARY TAYLOR was BORN in 84!~' FRANKLIN PIERCE in (1804)!~'

#32/PRESIDENT FRANKLIN D. ROOSEVELT died on 48 = RECIPROCAL = 84!~' #33/PRESIDENT HARRY S. TRUMAN was BORN in 84!~' #34/PRESIDENT DWIGHT D. EISENHOWER DIED on 84!~' #44/PRESIDENT BARACK OBAMA was BORN AUGUST 4th (84)!~' #45/PRESIDENT DONALD TRUMP = JUNE 14th = (6 x 14) = (`-84)!~

#35/PRESIDENT JOHN F. KENNEDY DIED ON (242)!~'
#37/PRESIDENT RICHARD M. NIXON DIED ON (4/22)!~'
242/422!~ #39/PRESIDENT JIMMY CARTER & #41/
PRESIDENT GEORGE H. W. BUSH were BORN in (24)!~'
#40/PRESIDENT RONALD REAGAN DIED in 2004!~' #43/
PRESIDENT GEORGE W. BUSH was BORN on (42)!~'

#35-JOHN F. KENNEDY, #36-LYNDON B. JOHNSON; and, #37-RICHARD NIXON `-ALL had `-DIED on a (`-22<sup>nd</sup>); of the `-MONTH, `-in a `-ROW!!!~'

TIMED & INTERTWINED!!!~'

THE SOLUTION that I had IMAGINED has already been CREATED by MIT's MEDIA LAB-(was CONCEIVED in a 1984 PROPOSAL)!~' NEW WIRELESS CELLPHONE - YOU SPEAK WITHOUT UTTERING A WORD or MOVING YOUR LIPS (SIGNALS to the VOCAL CORDS MIGRATION)!~' MIT'S MEDIA LAB (230 STUDENTS/302 PATENTS)!~

FOR 40 DAYS AND FOR 40 NIGHTS of the NOAH ACCOUNT!~' IF THIS ACCOUNT IS REAL ALL ANIMALS COULD AND WOULD HAVE BEEN DIRECTED TO APPROACH NOAH AND THE ARK!~' 600th YEAR on the 17th DAY A HIBERNATION OCCURRED including VEGETATION!~' GOD directs HUMANS as WELL as CAN CLEARLY BE SEEN!

WHEN YOU LOOK to the BIBLE for ITS WRITERS & PROPHETS with every WORD SEMANTIC, LETTER; and, NUMBER; THEY can be AND are DICTATED DIRECTLY by GOD for EXACT PLACEMENT on PAPER unbeknownst TO THE WRITER like WRITING A SCRIPT!~' AND THAT'S EXACTLY WHAT GOD DOES, HE WRITES SCRIPTS!~'

#8/PRESIDENT MARTIN VAN BUREN DIED on 24ᵗʰ!~' #12/ PRESIDENT ZACHARY TAYLOR was BORN on 24ᵗʰ!~' #13/ PRESIDENT MILLARD FILLMORE DIED on (24)!~' #22/#24/ PRESIDENT GROVER CLEVELAND DIED on 24ᵗʰ!~' #27/ PRESIDENT WILLIAM HOWARD TAFT DIED ON 24!~' #28/ PRESIDENT WOODROW WILSON DIED IN 24

#22/#24/PRESIDENT GROVER CLEVELAND WAS `-BORN in `-18(**37**) with #36-PRESIDENT LYNDON B. JOHNSON BEING `-BORN in (`-**1908**); AND, `-HE `-DYING in `-19(**73**)!!!~' AND; `-WITH #22/#24-PRESIDENT GROVER CLEVELAND `-DYING in (`-**1908**)!!!~' **(RECIPROCAL-INVERSED-REALITY-RECIPROCAL-SEQUENCING)!**

MANY PRESIDENTS WERE BORN in 19(46)!~' #42/WILLIAM JEFFERSON CLINTON, #43/GEORGE W. BUSH; and, #45/ DONALD J. TRUMP!~' `-46 = (4 x 6) = 24 = RECIPROCAL = 42!~' #44/PRESIDENT BARACK H. OBAMA was BORN in 1961 = (61 (-) 19) = 42!~' PRESIDENTS OBAMA & CLINTON SHARE THE BIRTH # OF 92!~

#44/PRESIDENT BARACK H. OBAMA & #42/WILLIAM JEFFERSON CLINTON SHARE THE SAME BIRTHDAY # `-NUMBER of (`-92)!~' (92 X 2) = (184) = (`-84)!~' # OF THE FOUNDING FATHERS!~' (44 + 42) = `-86 = RECIPROCAL = `-68!~' # OF THE FOUNDING FATHERS!~' THESE NUMBERS are the MARKS of the BEAST!~'

#16/PRESIDENT ABRAHAM LINCOLN was `-BORN FEBRUARY 12ᵗʰ, 1809 = (2 + 12 + 18 + 09) = `-**41**!~' `-DIED APRIL 15ᵗʰ, 1865 = (4 + 15 + 18 + 65) = `-**102**!~' (102 (-) 41) = `-**61** = **JUNE 1ˢᵗ** = #15/PRESIDENT JAMES BUCHANAN'S `-**DAY of** `-**DEATH**!~' #15/PRESIDENT JAMES BUCHANAN

`-**DIED** in (`-**1868**)! One `-**PRESIDENT** `-BACK `-**CLOCKS** the # `-**NUMBER!!!~'** (`-**16**) = RECIPROCAL = (`-**61**)!!!~'

#1/PRESIDENT GEORGE WASHINGTON was BORN in 32!~'
#6/PRESIDENT JOHN QUINCY ADAMS DIED on a 23rd!~'
#14/PRESIDENT FRANKLIN PIERCE was BORN on a 23rd!~'
#15/PRESIDENT JAMES BUCHANAN was BORN on a 23rd!~'
#18/PRESIDENT ULYSSES S. GRANT DIED on a 23rd!~ #28/
WOODROW WILSON DIED on 2/3!

#29/PRESIDENT WARREN G. HARDING DIED the YEAR of
23!~' #36/PRESIDENT LYNDON B. JOHNSON DIED on 23
(JAN. 22) = (1 + 22) = 23!~' #35/PRESIDENT JOHN F. KENNEDY;
AND, #36/PRESIDENT LYNDON B. JOHNSON `-BOTH
HAVE the `-VERY `-SAME `-DEATH/DAY # `-NUMBER OF
(`-115)!~' (115 + 115) = 230!

#37/PRESIDENT RICHARD M. NIXON DIED in 1994; WHILE,
#36/LYNDON B. JOHNSON'S WIFE LADY BIRD JOHNSON
DIED at the AGE of (94)!~' NIXON was BORN in 1913 = (19 + 13)
= 32 = -a PROPHETIC NUMBER!~' #38/PRESIDENT GERALD
FORD `-DAY of `-DEATH = DECEMBER 26th = (12/26) = (12 x
26) = 312!~'

#40/PRESIDENT RONALD REAGAN'S BIRTHDAY is on
FEBRUARY 6th = (2/6); WHILE, #38/PRESIDENT GERALD
FORD `-DIED on APRIL 26th in 2006!!!~' BIRTHDAY = (2/6);
WHILE, #38/PRESIDENT GERALD FORD `-DIED on a 26 in
2006!~'_#38/GERALD FORD; AND, #40/RONALD REAGAN
BOTH DIED at the AGE of 93!~'

#40/PRESIDENT RONALD REAGAN & #38/PRESIDENT
GERALD FORD DIED AT THE SAME AGE OF '93!~' (93 x 2) =
186 = 86 = RECIPROCAL = 68!~' (93 (-) 26) = 67 = RECIPROCAL

= 76 = INDEPENDENCE DAY!~' NOTE MANY FIRST LADYS THESE NUMBERS APPLY TO: HILLARY CLINTON & MELANIA TRUMP BORN on a 26th!~'

#2/PRESIDENT JOHN ADAMS DIED JULY 4th!~' #3/ PRESIDENT THOMAS JEFFERSON DIED JULY 4th!~' #5/ PRESIDENT JAMES MONROE DIED JULY 4th!~' #30/ PRESIDENT CALVIN COOLIDGE WAS BORN ON JULY 4th!~ #38/PRESIDENT GERALD FORD was BORN on JULY 14!~' LOOK for the PRESIDENTS/FIRST LADYS & (76)!!!~'

WHEN A PROPHET ENTERS PROPHECY; HE ENTERS GOD'S MIND AND IMAGINATION!~' WHEN A PROPHET SEES HIMSELF WATCHING TELEVISION 40 YEARS INTO THE FUTURE; AND, ANALYZES TO COMPREHENSION THE STATUS OF THE CURRENT EVENTS AT HAND; ONE IS THANKFUL TO FORGET THE SITUATIONS!~' PERFECT MEMORY!~'

A PROPHET IS A TIME TRAVELER THROUGH THE IMAGINATION OF GOD!~' ONE CAN TRAVEL TO THE PAST AND ONE CAN TRAVEL INTO THE FUTURE!~' FOR WHAT I HAVE DONE; GOD HAS NEVER DONE BEFORE!~' IT'S A SPECIAL ARRANGEMENT!~' AN ARRANGEMENT FOR AN AGREEMENT; OF SOMETHING TERMED, `-ARMAGEDDON!!!~'

THE `-FATE of `-US; `-ALL!!!!!~'

AMERICAN ACTOR RUTGER HAUER (75) (BIRTH: JANUARY 23, 1944) (DEATH: JULY 19, 2019)

BIRTHDAY # `-NUMBER = (1 + 23 + 19 + 44) = 87

DEATH/DAY # `-NUMBER = (7 + 19 + 20 + 19) = 65

(87 (-) 65) = `-22

HE DIED (`-177) DAYS FROM HIS LAST BIRTHDAY!!!~'

(365 (-) 177) = (`-188)!!!~'

HE DIED AT THE `-AGE of (`-75) /|\ (7 x 5) = (`-35)!!!~'

(35 + 22) = `-57 = RECIPROCAL = `-75 = `-AGE of `-DEATH!!!~'

AMERICAN THEATRICAL PRODUCER HAROLD PRINCE (91) (BIRTH: JANUARY 30, 1928) (DEATH: JULY 31, 2019)

BIRTHDAY # `-NUMBER = (1 + 30 + 19 + 28) = 78

DEATH/DAY # `-NUMBER = (7 + 31 + 20 + 19) = 77

(78 + 77) = `-155 = (55 x 1) = `-55 = (23 + 32)!!!~'

HE DIED (`-182) DAYS FROM HIS LAST BIRTHDAY!!!~'

(365 (-) 182) = (`-183)!!!~'

HE DIED AT THE `-AGE of (`-91) /|\ (91 x 2) = (`-182)!!!~'

AMERICAN PROFESSIONAL WRESTLER HARLEY RACE (76) (BIRTH: APRIL 11, 1943) (DEATH: AUGUST 1, 2019)

BIRTHDAY # `-NUMBER = (4 + 11 + 19 + 43) = 77

DEATH/DAY # `-NUMBER = (8 + 1 + 20 + 19) = 48

(77 + 48) = `-125

125 (-) 13 = `-112

HE DIED (`-112) DAYS FROM HIS LAST BIRTHDAY!!!~'

(365 (-) 112) = (`-253)!!!~'

HE DIED AT THE `-AGE of (`-76) = (7 + 6) = (`-13)!!!~'

AMERICAN NOVELIST TONI MORRISON (88) (BIRTH: FEBRUARY 18, 1931) (DEATH: AUGUST 5, 2019)

FEBRUARY 18 = 2(1 x 8) = 2(8) = 2(8's) = 88 = AGE OF DEATH!!!~'

BIRTHDAY # `-NUMBER = (2 + 18 + 19 + 31) = 70

DEATH/DAY # `-NUMBER = (8 + 5 + 20 + 19) = 52

(70 (-) 52) = `-18 = "THE DAY SHE WAS BORN"!!!~'

SHE DIED (`-168) DAYS FROM HER LAST BIRTHDAY!!!~'

(365 (-) 168) = (`-197)!!!~'

SHE DIED AT THE `-AGE of (`-88)!!!~'

SUSHMA SWARAJ (FORMER MINISTER of EXTERNAL AFFAIRS for INDIA) (67) (BIRTH: FEBRUARY 14, 1952) (DEATH: AUGUST 6, 2019)

FEBRUARY 14 = (2 x 14) = 28 = 2(8) = 2(8's) = 88!!!~'

(214 (-) 86) = (`-128) = (1 x 28) = 28 = 2(8) = 2(8's) = 88!!!~'

(88 + 88) = (`-176) = (1 x 76) = (`-76) = RECIPROCAL = (`-67) = `-AGE of `-DEATH of SUSHMA SWARAJ!!!~'

BIRTHDAY # `-NUMBER = (2 + 14 + 19 + 52) = 87

DEATH/DAY # `-NUMBER = (8 + 6 + 20 + 19) = 53

(87 + 53) = `-140 = (14 + 0) = 14 = "THE DAY SHE WAS BORN"!!!~'

SHE DIED (`-173) DAYS FROM HER LAST BIRTHDAY!!!~'

(365 (-) 173) = (`-192)!!!~'

SHE DIED AT THE `-AGE of (`-67)!!!~'

INDIA's INDEPENDENCE from the UNITED KINGDOM in 1947 /|\ 47 = RECIPROCAL = 74 = JULY 4th = AMERICAN INDEPENDENCE!!!~'

AUGUST 15th = (8 + 15) = `-23

AUGUST 6th = (`-86) = RECIPROCAL = (`-68) = "THE `-MARK of the `-BEAST"!!!~'

AMERICAN FINANCIER JEFFREY EPSTEIN (66) (BIRTH: JANUARY 20, 1953) (DEATH: AUGUST 10, 2019)

(120 + 810) = 930 = (93 + 0) = (`-93) = RECIPROCAL = (`-39) = (20 + 19) = "YEAR `-HE had `-DIED"!!!!!~'

BIRTHDAY # `-NUMBER = (1 + 20 + 19 + 53) = 93

DEATH/DAY # `-NUMBER = (8 + 10 + 20 + 19) = 57

(93 (-) 57) = `-36 = 3(6) = 3(6's) = 666 = DIED at the AGE of (`-66)!!!~'

HE DIED (`-202) DAYS FROM HIS LAST BIRTHDAY!!!~'

(365 (-) 202) = (`-163) = (1 x 63) = (`-63) = RECIPROCAL = (`-36)!!!~'

HE DIED AT THE `-AGE of (`-66)!!!~' BODY was FOUND at 6:30AM!~'

JANUARY 20, 1953 = (1 + 2 + 0 + 1 + 9 + 5 + 3) = 21

AUGUST 10, 2019 = (8 + 1 + 0 + 2 + 0 + 1 + 9) = 21

(21 + 21) = (`-42) = "THE MARK of the `-BEAST"!!!!!~'

THE `-<u>FATE</u> of `-<u>PRESIDENTS</u>; and, their <u>LADIES</u>!!!~'

MARTHA WASHINGTON BIRTHDAY JUNE 13, 1731!~' (6 + 13 + 17 + 31) = 67 = AGE HER HUSBAND #1/PRESIDENT GEORGE WASHINGTON DIED!~' DEATH/DAY MAY 22, 1802 = (5 + 22 + 18 + 02) = 47 = RECIPROCAL = 74 = JULY 4th!~' (6 x 13) = 78!~' (5 x 22) = 110!~' (110 (-) 78) = 32 = YEAR HE WAS BORN!~'

FIRST LADY MARTHA WASHINGTON DIED MAY 22nd = 22 DAYS before HER NEXT BIRTHDAY!~' BIRTH/YEAR (1731) / DEATH/YEAR (1802)!~' (17 + 31 + 18 + 02) = 68!~' MARRIED to GEORGE WASHINGTON for 40 YEARS!~' MARRIED TO DANIEL PARKE CUSTIS FOR 7 YEARS!~' 40/7 = 47 = DEATH/ DAY # `-NUMBER '47!~'

#1/PRESIDENT GEORGE WASHINGTON DIED AT THE AGE OF 67!~' 76 YEARS LATER #17/PRESIDENT ANDREW JOHNSON DIED IN HIS 67th YEAR of EXISTENCE at the AGE of 66!~' PRESIDENT ANDREW JOHNSON'S WIFE FIRST LADY ELIZA MCCARDLE JOHNSON died IN 18(76)!~' ANDREW & ELIZA were MARRIED for 48 YEARS!

#1/PRESIDENT GEORGE WASHINGTON & #17/PRESIDENT ANDREW JOHNSON DEATH to DEATH = 230 DAYS!~' #17/PRESIDENT ANDREW JOHNSON & #16/PRESIDENT ABRAHAM LINCOLN BIRTH to BIRTH = 46 DAYS APART ~ (23x2)!~' #16/PRESIDENT ABRAHAM LINCOLN & #7/ PRESIDENT ANDREW JACKSON BIRTH to BIRTH = 32 DAYS!

GEORGE WASHINGTON BORN in 17(32); AND, DIED AGE of 67!~' ANDREW JACKSON BORN in 1(767); AND, (`-32) YEARS later PRESIDENT GEORGE WASHINGTON DIED!~'

PRESIDENT ANDREW JACKSON'S BIRTHYEAR 1767 & DEATHYEAR 1845!~' (17+67+18+45) = 147 = (47 x 1) = 47 = MARTHA WASHINGTON'S DEATH/DAY #!

#37/PRESIDENT RICHARD M. NIXON & LADY PAT NIXON DIED at the AGE of 81!~' BOTH DIED on a 22nd of the MONTH!~' FROM LADY PAT NIXON'S BIRTH 3/16 to DEATH of #37/ PRESIDENT RICHARD M. NIXON (4/22) THERE ARE 37 DAYS!~' (81 + 22) = '103 = THE DAYS AFTER HIS BIRTHDAY THAT RICHARD DIED!~'

#38/PRESIDENT GERALD FORD & LADY BETTY FORD DIED at the AGE of 93!~' FIRST LADY BETTY FORD was BORN on an 8th & DIED on an 8th!~' #38/PRESIDENT GERALD FORD'S DEATH/DAY 12/26 = (12 + 26) = 38!~' BETTY FORD was BORN in 1918 = (19 + 18) = 37 = RICHARD NIXON!~ PAT NIXON DIED in 93!~'

FIRST LADY PAT NIXON BIRTH (3/16) = (3 + 1 + 6) = 10!~' FIRST LADY PAT NIXON DEATH (6/22) = (6 + 2 + 2) = 10!~ #37/PRESIDENT RICHARD M. NIXON BIRTH (1/9) = (1 + 9) = 10!~' #37/PRESIDENT RICHARD M. NIXON DEATH (4/22) = (4 + 2 + 2) = 8!~' (10 + 10 + 10 + '8) = `-38 = GERALD FORD!~'

#37/PRESIDENT RICHARD NIXON BORN 186 DAYS before #38/PRESIDENT GERALD FORD!~' BOTH BORN in 1913 = (19 + 13) = 32!~' #38/PRESIDENT GERALD FORD DEATH/ DAY (12/26) = (26 (-) 12) = 14 = DAY of BIRTH!~' PAT NIXON DEATH (6/22) = (6 x 22) = 132!~ PAT NIXON BIRTH (3/16) = (3 x 16) = 48!~'

#38/PRESIDENT GERALD FORD & FIRST LADY BETTY FORD HAVE 194 DAYS FROM DEATH/DAY TO DEATH/ DAY that EXISTS BETWEEN with LADY BIRD JOHNSON

DYING at the AGE of 94!~' FIRST LADY BETTY FORD BIRTH/
YEAR 1918 & DEATH/YEAR 2011!~' (19 + 18 + 20 + 11) = 68!~'
(94 (-) 68 = 26 = DAY of DEATH!~

#36/PRESIDENT LYNDON B. JOHNSON DEATH (1/22)!~'
LADY BIRD JOHNSON BIRTH (12/22)!~' #36/PRESIDENT
LYNDON B. JOHNSON, #37/PRESIDENT RICHARD M.
NIXON; and, FIRST LADY PAT NIXON all DIED on the (`-22nd)
of the MONTH; while, LADY BIRD JOHNSON was BORN on
a (`-22$^{nd}$)!~ KENNEDY (`-22nd)!

FIRST LADY NANCY REAGAN DIED (122) DAYS BEFORE
HER NEXT BIRTHDAY!~' LADY NANCY REAGAN
BIRTH (7/6/1921) = (7+6+19+21) = '53!~' #40/PRESIDENT
RONALD REAGAN DEATH = (6/5/2004) = (6+5+20+4) = '35
= RECIPROCAL = '53!~' RONALD & NANCY REAGAN were
BORN on a 6th!~' NANCY DIED on a 6th!~'

FROM FIRST LADY NANCY REAGAN DEATH (3/6)
to the DEATH of #40/PRESIDENT RONALD REAGAN
(6/5) EQUALS 91 DAYS!~' 91 = RECIPROCAL = 19!~' #40/
PRESIDENT RONALD REAGAN DIED 119 DAYS AFTER HIS
BIRTHDAY!~' NANCY REAGAN DIED 74 DAYS AFTER THE
BIRTHDAY OF LADY BIRD JOHNSON BOTH DYING at 94!

FROM FIRST LADY NANCY REAGAN DEATH (3/6) to
the DEATH of #40/PRESIDENT RONALD REAGAN (6/5)
EQUALS 91 DAYS!~' #40/PRESIDENT RONALD REAGAN
BIRTHDAY (2/6) & DEATH/DAY (6/5)!~' (26 + 65) = 91!~' FIRST
LADY NANCY REAGAN DIED on a (6th); AND, was BURIED
(`-5) DAYS LATER!~' (94/2) = 47!

#40/PRESIDENT RONALD REAGAN BIRTH (2/6/1911)
= (2+6+19+11) = 38!~' FROM THE DEATH/DAY of #41/

PRESIDENT GEORGE H. W. BUSH to the DEATH/DAY of FIRST LADY BARBARA BUSH there are 138 DAYS!~' GEORGE H. W. BUSH BIRTHDAY (6/12) & BARBARA PIERCE BUSH BIRTHDAY (6/8)!~' (6+1+2+6+8) = `-23!

FIRST LADY BETTY FORD BIRTH/YEAR 1918 & DEATH/YEAR 2011!~' (19+18+20+11) = 68!~' #40/PRESIDENT RONALD REAGAN & FIRST LADY NANCY REAGAN were BORN on a 6th!~' FIRST LADY NANCY REAGAN DIED on a 6th!~' LADY BETTY FORD was BORN on an 8th & DIED on an 8th!~' (`-68) MARK of the BEAST!~'

#38/PRESIDENT GERALD FORD & FIRST LADY BETTY FORD BIRTHDAYS & DEATH/DAYS!~' FIRST LADY BETTY FORD (4/8)/(7/8) = (48 + 78) = 126 = HUSBAND'S #38/PRESIDENT GERALD FORD'S DEATH/DAY!~' FIRST LADY BETTY FORD DIED 91 DAYS AFTER HER LAST BIRTHDAY = #40/PRESIDENT RONALD & NANCY REAGAN!~'

#38/PRESIDENT GERALD FORD & FIRST LADY BETTY FORD BIRTHDAYS & DEATH/DAYS!~' #38/PRESIDENT GERALD FORD (7/14)(12/26)!~' (7+14+12+26) = 59!~' LADY BETTY FORD (4/8)(7/8) = (4+8+7+8) = 27!~' (59 (-) 27) = 32 = A PROPHETIC NUMBER!~' (59 + 27) = 86 = RECIPROCAL = 68 = THE MARK/BEAST!~'

Reciprocal-Sequencing-Numerology-RSN!!!!!~'

&

Reciprocal-Sequenced-Inversed-Realities-RSIR!!!!!~'

AUTHOR: DWAYNE W. ANDERSON = "The "PROPHET"!!!~'

FOUNDER & DISCOVERER of -this `-NEW `-PHILOSOPHY!!!~'

FIRST LADY BESS TRUMAN'S BIRTHDAY = 2/13/1885; DEATH = 10/18/1982!~' (1018 (-) 213) = (`-805) = RECIPROCAL = (`-508) = MAY 8th = BIRTHDAY of HUSBAND #33/PRESIDENT HARRY S. TRUMAN!~' HARRY DIED 12/26 = (12 x 26) = 312 = RECIPROCAL = 213 = WIFE FIRST LADY BESS TRUMAN'S BIRTHDAY!~'

FIRST LADY BESS TRUMAN'S BIRTHDAY = 2/13/1885 = (2 + 13 + 18 + 85) = 118!~' JUST ADD A (`-0) ZERO; and, YOU HAVE HER DAY of DEATH (`-1018)!~' DEATH = 10/18/1982!~ FIRST LADY BESS TRUMAN DIED 118 DAYS BEFORE HER NEXT BIRTHDAY!~' WAS MARRIED FOR 53 YEARS and ENDED HER DUTIES IN 53!

AMERICAN ACTOR PETER FONDA (79) (BIRTH: FEBRUARY 23, 1940) (DEATH: AUGUST 16, 2019)

BIRTHDAY # `-NUMBER = (2 + 23 + 19 + 40) = 84

DEATH/DAY # `-NUMBER = (8 + 16 + 20 + 19) = 63

(84 + 63) = (`-147)

HE DIED (`-174) DAYS FROM HIS LAST BIRTHDAY!!!~'

(365 (-) 174) = (`-191)

HE DIED AT THE `-AGE of (`-79) = (7 X 9) = (`-63)!!!~'

PETER FONDA BIRTH: FEBRUARY 23, 1940 / DEATH: AUGUST 16, 2019!~' BIRTHDAY # = (2+23+19+40) = 84!~' DEATH/DAY # = (8+16+20+19) = 63!~' (84 + 63) = `-147!~' Mr. FONDA DIED `-174 DAYS AFTER HIS LAST BIRTHDAY!~' HE DIED at the AGE of 79 = (7x9) = `-63 = DEATH/DAY #!~' 23/47=RECIP=74!~'

(2/23/1940) / (8/16/2019) = (2 + 2 + 3 + 1 + 9 + 4 + 0 + 8 + 1 + 6 + 2 + 0 + 1 + 9) = `-48 = RECIPROCAL = `-84 = BIRTHDAY # `-NUMBER!!!~'

AMERICAN FOOTBALL PLAYER CEDRIC MYRON BENSON (36) (BIRTH: DECEMBER 28, 1982) (DEATH: AUGUST 17, 2019)

WAS `-BORN in (`-82); AND, `-DIED on a (`-28ᵗʰ) = RECIPROCALS!!!~'

BIRTHDAY # `-NUMBER = (12 + 28 + 19 + 82) = 141

DEATH/DAY # `-NUMBER = (8 + 17 + 20 + 19) = 64

(141 (-) 64) = (`-77)

DECEMBER 28, 1982 = (82 (-) 19 (-) 28 (-) 12) = (`-23)!!!~'

HE DIED (`-232) DAYS AFTER HIS LAST BIRTHDAY!!!~

40

WAS (`-32) at the GREEN BAY PACKERS & WAS (`-32) at the CINCINNATI BENGALS!!!~' (`-2(32's))!!!~' (`-232) = (2 x 32) = (`-64) = `-DEATH/DAY #!!!~'

(365 (-) 232) = (`-133)

HE DIED AT THE `-AGE of (`-36)!!!~'

AMERICAN FOOTBALL PLAYER CEDRIC MYRON BENSON (BIRTH: 12/28/1982) (DEATH: 8/17/2019)!!!~' HE DIED (`-232) DAYS AFTER HIS LAST BIRTHDAY!!!~ WAS (`-32) at the GREEN BAY PACKERS & the CINCINNATI BENGALS!!!~' (2(`-32's))!~' (`-232) = (2x32) = (`-64) = `-DEATH/ DAY # = (8+17+20+19)!!!~'

AMERICAN FOOTBALL PLAYER CEDRIC MYRON BENSON (BIRTH:12/28/1982) (DEATH:8/17/2019)!~' HE DIED 232 DAYS AFTER HIS LAST BIRTHDAY!~ WAS 32 at the GREEN BAY PACKERS & the CINCINNATI BENGALS!~' (2(32's))!~' (232) = (2x32) = 64 = DEATH/DAY# = (8+17+20+19)!~' (8x17) = 136 = AGE of DEATH!~'

ACCORDING to the BIBLE `-MAN has been on this EARTH for some 6,000 years!~' The CORRECT TIME is 60,000 YEARS!~ The BIBLE TEACHES that there was one ADAM & EVE!~' THERE were ACTUALLY `-FIRST `-COUPLES in the `-BEGINNING per `-GEOGRAPHIC `-LOCATIONS according to the 'HUMAN GENOME!~

KATHLEEN BLANCO FORMER LOUISIANA GOVERNOR DURING HURRICANE KATRINA (76) (BIRTH: DECEMBER 15, 1942) (DEATH: AUGUST 18, 2019)!~'

BIRTHDAY # `-NUMBER = (12 + 15 + 19 + 42) = 88

DEATH/DAY # `-NUMBER = (8 + 18 + 20 + 19) = 65

(88 (-) 65) = (`-23)

(88 + 65) = (`-153)

(`-153/2) = (`-76.5) = AGE at TIME of `-DEATH for KATHLEEN BLANCO!!!~'

(12 + 15) = (`-27) / (8 + 18) = (`-26) / (27 + 26) = (`-53)

SHE DIED (`-119) DAYS BEFORE HER NEXT BIRTHDAY!!!~'

(365 (-) 119) = (`-246) = (46/2) = (`-23)!!!!!~'

(`-246) = (24 x 6) = `-144 = (14 x 4) = (`-56) = (7 x 8) = (`-78) = (8 + 16 + 19 + 35) = HUSBAND'S BIRTHDAY # `-NUMBER!!!!!~'

DEATH/DAY = (8 X 18) = (`-144)!!!~'

SHE DIED AT THE `-AGE of (`-76) = (7 X 6) = (`-42) = BORN in (`-42); `-again)!!!~' HOW MANY THIS `-YEAR at (76/42); and, LAST `-YEAR!!!~'

`-46 = RECIPROCAL = `-64

MARRIED in (`-1964) FOR (`-55) YEARS!!!~' (`-55) = (23 + 32)!!!~' (64/2) = (`-32) = RECIPROCAL = (`-23)!!!~'

`-53 = RECIPROCAL = `-35

HUSBAND RAYMOND BLANCO was BORN in (`-1935); AND, (`-84) at the TIME of `-HER `-DEATH!!!~'

RAYMOND BLANCO `-BORN on AUGUST 16th (8/16) = (86 X 1) = (`-86) = RECIPROCAL = (`-68)!!!~'

(8 X 16) = (`-128) = (28 X 1) = 28 = 2(8's) = (`-88) = KATHLEEN BLANCO'S `-BIRTHDAY # `-NUMBER!!!~'

`-48 = RECIPROCAL = `-84

KATHLEEN BLANCO `-DIED two DAYS (`-48) HOURS after HER HUSBAND'S `-BIRTHDAY of (`-84)!!!~'

BIRTH = (`-1942) = (42 x 2) = (`-84)!!!!!~'

KATHLEEN BLANCO DIED 119 DAYS BEFORE HER NEXT BIRTHDAY!~' (365(-)119) = (246) = (24x6) = 144 = (14x4) = (56) = (7x8) = (78) = (8+16+19+35) = HUSBAND'S BIRTHDAY #!~' SHE DIED two DAYS (48) HOURS after HER HUSBAND'S (84th) BIRTHDAY!~' 48=RECIPROCAL=84!~' BIRTH=(1942)=(42x2)=(84)!~

AMERICAN SPORTSCASTER JOHN FRANCIS WHITAKER (95) (BIRTH: MAY 18, 1924) (DEATH: AUGUST 18, 2019)

WAS `-BORN on an (`-18th); AND, `-DIED on an (`-18th)!!!~'

BIRTHDAY # `-NUMBER = (5 + 18 + 19 + 24) = 66

DEATH/DAY # `-NUMBER = (8 + 18 + 20 + 19) = 65

$(66 + 65) = (`-131) / `-13 = RECIPROCAL = `-31$

$(5 + 18) = (`-23) / (8 + 18) = (`-26) / (23 + 26) = (`-49) = RECIPROCAL = (`-94)!!!~'$

$(5 + 18 + 19) = (`-42)!!!~'$

HE DIED (`-92) DAYS FROM HIS LAST BIRTHDAY!!!~'

KATHLEEN BLANCO DIED (`-119) DAYS BEFORE HER NEXT BIRTHDAY = RECIPROCAL = 911 = (91 + 1) = (`-92)!!!~'

$(365 (-) 92) = (`-273)$

HE DIED AT THE `-AGE of (`-95)!!!~'

$(5 + 1 + 8 + 1 + 9 + 2 + 4 + 8 +1 + 8 + 2 + 0 + 1 + 9) = (`-59) = RECIPROCAL = (`-95) = `-AGE of `-DEATH for JOHN FRANCIS WHITAKER!!!~'$

AMERICAN SPORTSCASTER JOHN FRANCIS WHITAKER (BIRTHDAY: MAY 18, 1924) (DEATH/DAY: AUGUST 18, 2019)!~' HE DIED AT THE `-AGE of (`-95)!!!~' $(5 + 1 + 8 + 1 + 9 + 2 + 4 + 8 +1 + 8 + 2 + 0 + 1 + 9) = (`-59) = RECIPROCAL = (`-95) = `-AGE of `-DEATH for Mr. JOHN FRANCIS WHITAKER!~'$ WWII~

PATRICK SWAYZE LOST HIS LIFE AT THE AGE of (`-57) = RECIPROCAL = (`-75)!~' MR. PATRICK SWAYZE was MARRIED in (`-1975) to 'LISA NIEMI WHOSE BIRTHDAY = $(5/26/1956) = (5+2+6+1+9+5+6) = (`-34) = HOW MANY YEARS$

THEY WERE MARRIED!!!~' (`-1956) = (19 + 56) = (`-75)!~'
#IAmPatrickSwayze

BONNIE & CLYDE KNOWN FOR ROBBERY & VIOLENCE
WERE SHOT DEAD ON MAY 23rd, 1934!!!~' (5 + 23 + 19 + 34) =
(`-81)!!!~' (5 x 23) = (`-115)!!!~' (115 (-) 81) = (`-34) = "THERE were
some (`-134) ROUNDS that `-KILLED `-THEM"!!!~' (`-43)!!!~'

THE (`-34th) PRESIDENT of the UNITED STATES of AMERICA
DWIGHT D. EISENHOWER DIED (`-165) DAYS AFTER
HIS LAST BIRTHDAY!!!~' HE `-DIED in (1969)!!!~' HIS WIFE
FIRST LADY MAMIE EISENHOWER was BORN in (1896) and
`-DIED (`-13) DAYS before HER NEXT BIRTHDAY!!!~' THEY
WERE MARRIED in (1916) for (`-53) YEARS; `-AGAIN the
`-PATTERN of (`-53)!!!~' SEE the PATTERNS!!!~'

PRESIDENTIAL TERM `-STARTED in (`-1953)!!!~'

(`-69) = RECIPROCAL = (`-96) = BORN in (`-96); and, DIED
in (`-69)!!!~'

FIRST LADY MAMIE EISENHOWER was BORN in (`-1896)
= (96 (-) 18) = (`-78) = AGE of DEATH of HER HUSBAND #34/
PRESIDENT DWIGHT D. EISENHOWER!!!~'

(`-165) + (`-13) = (`-178)!!!~'

#34/PRESIDENT DWIGHT D. EISENHOWER LIVED to be
(`-78) YEARS of AGE!!!~' FIRST LADY MAMIE EISENHOWER
LIVED to be (`-82) YEARS of `-AGE!!!~'

#34/PRESIDENT DWIGHT D. EISENHOWER `-DIED in (`-1969)!!!~' (69 + 19) = (`-88) = 2(8's) = 28 = RECIPROCAL = (`-82) = `-AGE of `-DEATH of FIRST LADY MAMIE EISENHOWER!!!~'

OCTOBER 14ᵗʰ, 1890 = #34/PRESIDENT DWIGHT D. EISENHOWER'S BIRTHDAY = (10 + 14 + 18 + 90) = (`-**132**)!!!~' **HE `-DIED on MARCH 28ᵗʰ** = (3 x 28) = (`-**84**)!!!~'

MARCH 28ᵗʰ, 1969 = (3 + 28 + 19 + 69) = (`-**119**)!!!~'

(1014 (-) 328) = (`-686)!!!~' = MARK of the `-BEAST!!!~'

BORN (`-1890) / DEATH (`-1969) = (18 + 90 + 19 + 69) = (`-1**96**)!!!~'

#34/PRESIDENT DWIGHT D. EISENHOWER:

BIRTH: OCTOBER 14ᵗʰ, 18**90** /|\ DEATH: MARCH 28ᵗʰ, 19**69**

(**90/69**) = **THE `-AGES of `-DEATH of #31/PRESIDENT HERBERT CLARK HOOVER & WIFE FIRST LADY LOU HENRY HOOVER!!!~'**

(90 (-) 18 (-) 14 (-) 10) = (`-**48**) /|\ (69 (-) 19 (-) 28 (-) 3) = (`-**19**)

(48 + 19) = (`-**67**) = **"THE DEATH of `-PRESIDENTS"!!!~'**

FIRST LADY MAMIE EISENHOWER:

BIRTH: NOVEMBER 14ᵗʰ, 18**96** /|\ DEATH: NOVEMBER 1ˢᵗ, 19**79**

(96 (-) 18 (-) 14 (-) 11) = (`-**53**) /|\ (79 (-) 19 (-) 1 (-) 11) = (`-**48**)

(48/48) = **PRESIDENT'S BIRTH = FIRST LADY'S DEATH!!!~'**

(48 + 48) = (`-**96**)!!!~' **SEE THE `-PATTERNS!!!~'**

(53 (-) 19) = (`-**34**) = **For the** (`-**34**th) **PRESIDENT DWIGHT D. EISENHOWER!!!~'**

#31/PRESIDENT HERBERT CLARK HOOVER & WIFE FIRST LADY LOU HENRY HOOVER were **BORN** (`-**134**) **DAYS APART!!!~'**

FIRST LADY LOU HENRY HOOVER LIVED TO BE (`-**69**) **YEARS of `-AGE!!!~'**

#31/PRESIDENT HERBERT CLARK HOOVER LIVED TO BE (`-**90**) **YEARS of AGE!!!~'**

BOTH were `-**BORN** in (`-**74**) = **JULY 4**th, **INDEPENDENCE DAY!!!~'**

FIRST LADY LOU HENRY HOOVER'S DEATH/DAY = JANUARY 7th, 1944 = (1 + 7 + 19 + 44) = (`-**71**)!!!~'

#31/PRESIDENT HERBERT CLARK HOOVER `-DIED (`-**71**) DAYS after HIS LAST BIRTHDAY!!!~'

(71 + 71) = (`-**142**) = (42 X 1) = (`-**42**) = **"THE MARK OF THE `-BEAST"!!!~'**

JANUARY 7th = (`-**17**) = RECIPROCAL = (`-**71**)!!!~'

JANUARY 7th, 1944 = (44 (-) 19 (-) 7 (-) 1) = (`-**17**)!!!~'

#31/PRESIDENT HERBERT CLARK HOOVER:

BIRTH: AUGUST 10th, 18**74** /|\ DEATH: OCTOBER 20th, 19**64**

(74 (-) 18 (-) 10 (-) 8) = (`-**38**) /|\ (64 (-) 19 (-) 20 (-) 10) = (`-**15**)

(38 (-) 15) = (`-**23**) = -a PROPHETIC NUMBER!!!~'

(38 + 15) = (`-**53**) = "THE WAR of the WORLDS"!!!~'

FIRST LADY LOU HENRY HOOVER'S:

BIRTH: MARCH 29th, 18**74** /|\ DEATH: JANUARY 7th, 19**44**

(3 x 29) = (`-**87**) = RECIPROCAL = (`-**78**) = `-AGE of `-DEATH of #34/PRESIDENT DWIGHT D. EISENHOWER & #32/FIRST LADY ELEANOR ROOSEVELT!!!~'

#26/PRESIDENT THEODORE ROOSEVELT was BORN in (`-1858); AND, DIED in (`-1919)!!!~'

(`-1858) = (18 + 58) = (`-**76**) = INDEPENDENCE DAY!!!~'

(`-1919) = (19 + 19) = (`-**38**) = "The `-DEATH # `-NUMBERS"!!!~'

(`-**76/2**) = (`-**38**)!!!~'

PRESIDENTIAL TERM: SEPTEMBER 14, 1901 - MARCH 4, 1909!!!~'

(9 + 14) = (`-**23**)!!!~ /|\ (9 + 14 + 19 + 01) = (`-**43**) = RECIPROCAL = (`-**34**) = MARCH 4th /|\

(3 + 4 + 1 + 9 + 0 + 9) = (`-26) = FOR THE (`-26th) PRESIDENT!!!~'

BIRTH: OCTOBER 27th, 1858 /|\ DEATH: JANUARY 6th, 1919

(10 + 27 + 18 + 58) = (`-113)!!!~'

(1 + 6 + 19 + 19) = (`-45) = "YEAR of `-DEATH for #32/ PRESIDENT FRANKLIN DELANO ROOSEVELT"!!!~'

(113 (-) 45) = (`-68) = "THE `-MARK of the `-BEAST!!!~'

#32/PRESIDENT FRANKLIN DELANO ROOSEVELT was BORN in (`-1882); AND, DIED in (`-1945)!!!~'

(82 (-) 18) = (`-64)!!!~' /|\ (19 + 45) = (`-64)!!!~' BIRTH `-EQUALS = `-DEATH!!!~' (64 + 64) = (`-128)!!!~'

(64/2) = (`-32) = FOR THE `-32nd PRESIDENT of the UNITED STATES of AMERICA!!!~'

(45 (-) 19) = (`-26) = FOR THE `-26th PRESIDENT of the UNITED STATES of AMERICA THEODORE ROOSEVELT!!!~'

BIRTH: JANUARY 30th, 1882 /|\ DEATH: APRIL 12th, 1945

(1 + 30 + 18 + 82) = (`-131) = SWIPE 1 = (`-113) THEODORE ROOSEVELT!!!~'

(1 + 30 + 18 + 82) = (`-131) = (31 + 1) = (`-32) = FOR THE 32nd PRESIDENT!!!~'

(4 + 12 + 19 + 45) = (`-80)!!!~'

**FIRST LADY ELEANOR ROOSEVELT WIFE of #32/
PRESIDENT FRANKLIN DELANO ROOSEVELT; and,
NIECE of #26/PRESIDENT THEODORE ROOSEVELT!!!~'**

**FRANKLIN DIED (`-72) DAYS after HIS BIRTHDAY;
RECIPROCAL, WHILE; ELEANOR DIED (`-27) DAYS after
HER BIRTHDAY!!!~' THEODORE was BORN on a (`-27th);
AND, DIED within (`-72) DAYS AFTER HIS LAST BIRTHDAY
at the `-EXACT `-DAY of (`-71)!!!~'**

BIRTH: OCTOBER 11th, 1884 /|\ DEATH: NOVEMBER 7th,
1962

(1884) = (84 + 18) = (`-**102**)!!!~'

(1884) = (84 (-) 18) = (`-**66**)!!!~'

(1962) = (62 (-) 19) = (`-**43**) = RECIPROCAL = (`-**34**)!!!~'

(1962) = (62 + 19) = (`-**81**)

(102 + 43) = (`-**145**) = (45 x 1) = (`-**45**) = **The `-YEAR HER
HUSBAND `-DIED!!!~'**

(66 (-) 43) = (`-**23**) = RECIPROCAL = (`-**32**) = **`-HER `-HUSBAND
`-AGAIN!!!~'**

(81 + 102) = (`-**183**) = **"The `-DEATH # `-NUMBERS"!!!~'**

(81 + 66) = (`-**147**) = (47 x 1) = (`-**47**) = RECIPROCAL = (`-**74**) =
JULY 4th, INDEPENDENCE DAY!!!~'

(10 + 11 + 18 + 84) = (`-**123**) = (23 X 1) = (`-**23**) = RECIPROCAL =
(`-**32**) = **FOR the `-32nd PRESIDENT of the UNITED STATES
FRANKLIN DELANO ROOSEVELT!!!~'**

(11 + 7 + 19 + 62) = (`-**99**)!!!~'

(`-99) + (`-80) **FDR** = (`-**179**) = (79 (-) 1) = (`-**78**) = **AGE of `-DEATH of FIRST LADY ELEANOR ROOSEVELT!!!~'**

(`-99) + (`-80) FDR = (`-**179**) = (79 x 1) = (`-**79**) = (7 X 9) = (`-**63**) = **AGE of `-DEATH of #32/PRESIDENT FRANKLIN DELANO ROOSEVELT!!!~'**

FIRST LADY EDITH KERMIT CAROW ROOSEVELT DIED at the `-AGE of (`-**87**) = RECIPROCAL = (`-**78**) = FIRST LADY ELEANOR ROOSEVELT DIED AT THIS `-AGE!!!~'

#26/PRESIDENT THEODORE ROOSEVELT DIED AT THE `-AGE of (`-**60**); WHILE, #32/PRESIDENT FRANKLIN DELANO ROOSEVELT DIED AT THE `-AGE of (`-**63**)!!!~'

FIRST LADY GRACE COOLIDGE DIED at the `-AGE of (`-**78**); and, HER HUSBAND #30/PRESIDENT CALVIN COOLIDGE DIED at the `-AGE of (`-**60**!!!~'

(***RECIPROCALS***)!!!~'

AMERICAN BUSINESSMAN DAVID KOCH (79) (BIRTH: MAY 3, 1940) (DEATH: AUGUST 23, 2019)

ACTOR PETER FONDA was BORN on a (`-23<sup>rd</sup>); and, DIED at (`-79)!~' BUSINESSMAN DAVID KOCH DIED on a (`-23<sup>rd</sup>); and, at the AGE of (`-79)!!!~'

BIRTHDAY # `-NUMBER = (5 + 3 + 19 + 40) = 67

DEATH/DAY # `-NUMBER = (8 + 23 + 20 + 19) = 70

(67 + 70) = (`-137)

HE DIED (`-112) DAYS FROM HIS LAST BIRTHDAY!!!~'

(365 (-) 112) = (`-253)

HE DIED AT THE `-AGE of (`-79) = (7 X 9) = (`-63)!!!~'

PETER FONDA BIRTH: FEBRUARY 23, 1940 / DEATH: AUGUST 16, 2019!~' BIRTHDAY # = (2+23+19+40) = 84!~' DEATH/DAY # = (8+16+20+19) = 63!~' (84 + 63) = `-147!~' Mr. FONDA DIED `-174 DAYS AFTER HIS LAST BIRTHDAY!~' HE DIED at the AGE of 79 = (7x9) = `-63 = DEATH/DAY #!~' 23/47=RECIP=74!~'

(5/3/1940) / (8/23/2019) = (5 + 3 + 1 + 9 + 4 + 0 + 8 + 2 + 3 + 2 + 0 + 1 + 9) = `-47 = RECIPROCAL = `-74 = ACTOR PETER FONDA!!!~'

(8 x 23) = (`-184) = (84 x 1) = (`-84) = RECIPROCAL = (`-48) = IN JUNE (2019) WORTH (`-48) BILLION $ DOLLARS!!!~'

WAS `-MARRIED to JULIA MARGARET FLESHER for (`-23) YEARS!!!!!~' WAS `-MARRIED in (`-1996)!!!!!~'

HIS `-WIFE was `-BORN in (`-1963)!!!!!~'

WHAT IF!!!~'

What if ANGELS & DEMONS; and, SATAN & JESUS CHRIST never EXISTED!~' What if ALL of the PREVIOUS

PROPHETS mentioned in the BIBLES were NEVER REALLY ANY PROPHETS at ALL!~' What if ALL of the GOOD, GREAT, & MAGNIFICENT; and, BAD, WORSE, & HORRIBLE were ALL from ONE ENDEARING GOD!!!~

When ONE STUDIES the BODY with ITS ANATOMY & PHYSIOLOGY; and, the ENGINEERING SCIENCES; ONE is ONLY PERPLEXED; AND, CAPTURED; into the FOLD, 'of GOD'S GLORY!~' ONE KNOWS that `-GOD is THERE with UNDENIABLE CERTAINTY!~' ONE MUST NOW USE HIS/ HER POWER OF REASON; TO FIGURE, GOD OUT!

USING ONE'S GODLY POWER OF REASON, IS IT REASONABLE TO BELIEVE THAT GOD DAMNED ALL OF HIS GODLY CREATION INTO PERPETUAL DEATH AND NOT EVERLASTING LIFE; BECAUSE, HIS FIRST CREATION ATE A PIECE OF FRUIT THAT HE (GOD) HIMSELF HAD CREATED!!!~' HOW MUCH INTELLIGENCE DOES GOD HAVE!!!~'

INDIVIDUALS RAPE, MURDER, STEAL; AND, CAN BE FORGIVEN UNDER CHRIST'S RANSOM SACRIFICE FOR OUR SINS!~' AT THE END OF CHRIST'S MILLENNIAL REIGN SATAN IS RELEASED FOR A SHORT TIME AS A TEST TO A PERFECT MANKIND!~' HE CAN NOW BE DESTROYED FOREVER!~' IS THIS REASONABLE TO BELIEVE!!!~'

WITH ALL of the GOOD, GREAT, & MAGNIFICENT; and, BAD, WORSE, & HORRIBLE COMING from ONE ENDEARING GOD; HOW WAS `-I TO RESPOND TO HIM!~ THIS WENT CONTRARY TO ALL OF MY BELIEFS!~' HOW WAS THE PROPHET TO RESPOND FOR WHEN THE

PROPHET COULD BE EXTERMINATED AT ANY SECOND AT ANY TIME!~'

HUMANS & ANGELS were ALL CREATED through CHRIST!~' WHY WOULDN'T THE ANGELS BE CHRIST'S BROTHERS SINCE THEY'RE BOTH SPIRITS; AND, HAVE EXISTED TOGETHER FOR BILLIONS OF YEARS; VERSUS, HUMANS WHO HAVE ONLY BEEN ON EARTH FOR LESS THAN A HUNDRED YEARS BEING CALLED CHRIST'S BROTHERS!~'

IT'S NICE BEING THE FALSE PROPHET of the BIBLE; ALTHOUGH, BEING THE TRUE REVELATION AS TO THE EXISTENCE of `-GOD!~' WE ALL LOVE THOSE PERFECTLY TIMED EXPERIENCES OF LIFE WITH MUCH DEEP MEANING TO BE PONDERED UPON!~' AT A MOMENT'S NOTICE; `-PERFECTION, THROUGHOUT the `-UNIVERSE!~'

`SINS!!!~'

With ALL of the GOOD, GREAT, & MAGNIFICENT; and, BAD, WORSE, & HORRIBLE; ALL from ONE ENDEARING GOD, there is NO `-SIN!~ IS IT REASONABLE that GOD would ALLOW HIS OTHER CREATIONS to be KILLED in ORDER to PAY a DEBT that WE were CREATED WITH!~' JUDGED FOR HUMAN INSTINCT BY NATURE!

With ALL of the GOOD, GREAT, & MAGNIFICENT; and, BAD, WORSE, & HORRIBLE; ALL from ONE ENDEARING GOD, there is NO `-SIN!!!~' NOW; BEING a 50-YEAR-OLD-VIRGIN; IT'S A LITTLE LATE to be REMEMBERING THIS!~'

HOWEVER; ALL THINGS BEING 'POSSIBLE, IT IS STILL GOOD; TO PROTECT ONESELF!!!~'

With ALL of the GOOD, GREAT, & MAGNIFICENT; and, BAD, WORSE, & HORRIBLE; ALL from ONE ENDEARING GOD, there is NO `-SIN!~ NOW, ONE CAN BE RECKLESS; WITH WHAT CONSEQUENCES COME, BY BEING RECKLESS!~ OR; ONE CAN PUT LAWS INTO PLACE, THAT PROVIDE OPPORTUNITIES; FOR EVERYBODY INVOLVED!

With ALL of the GOOD, GREAT, & MAGNIFICENT; and, BAD, WORSE, & HORRIBLE; ALL from ONE ENDEARING GOD, there is NO `-SIN!!!~' MARRIAGE IS GOOD BY THE NATURE OF REASON!~' WOULD YOU LIKE FOR THERE TO BE TWENTY SEPARATE PARENTS FOR A CHILD IN BEING SINGLE!~' WHAT IMPACT ON THE FAMILY!

With ALL of the GOOD, GREAT, & MAGNIFICENT; and, BAD, WORSE, & HORRIBLE; ALL from ONE ENDEARING GOD, there is NO `-SIN!~' ONE CAN LOVE THE NUCLEAR BOMB; AND, HAVE AN EVENTUALITY LIKENED TO THAT OF THE DINOSAURS!~' GOD WILL ALLOW IT!~' OR; CREATE STRUCTURE FOR AN ENDURING FUTURE!~

With ALL of the GOOD, GREAT, & MAGNIFICENT; and, BAD, WORSE, & HORRIBLE; ALL from ONE ENDEARING GOD, there is NO `-SIN!~ IF ADAM & EVE were REAL; THEY WERE CREATED PERFECT with the ABILITY to be IMPERFECT because THEY HAD SINNED!~' ALL CREATION is IMPERFECT made PERFECTLY BY GOD!

DEATH!!!-'

THERE IS ONE SPIRIT BEING IN EXISTENCE TODAY; AND, THAT BEING IS GOD ALONE!- THERE IS NOTHING ELSE IN HEAVEN BUT HIM!-' WHEN YOU DIE, YOU DON'T GO TO HEAVEN; DESPITE, THE WISHES!-' THE QUESTION, IS; IF, YOU DON'T GO TO HEAVEN; WHERE DO YOU GO, FOR WHEN YOU DIE!-' 'TO THE GRAVE!-'

OUR DEATHS ARE ARTICULATED EXACTLY TO END AT A SPECIFIC TIME!-' FAMILY MEMBERS INCLUDING IN-LAWS ARE INTERWOVEN WITHIN TIME JUST AS WELL!-' FROM KIDS, TO GRANDPARENTS, TO GREAT-GRANDPARENTS ALL DONE BY THE HAND OF '-GOD!-' OUR RELATIONSHIPS OF ANY KIND ARE PICKED BY GOD; '-TOO!-'

I'M SORRY FOR THE DOUBTERS, ATHEIST, EVOLUTIONIST; and, AGNOSTICS; but, '-GOD REALLY REALLY DOES EXIST!-' IN MY PREVIOUS BOOKS I OUTLINED ON WHAT PHYSICAL REPRESENTATIONS THAT '-GOD MADE HIMSELF VISIBLY REPRESENT HIMSELF WITHIN!-' MY NAME IS NOBODY!-' THIS WAS THE VERY FIRST ONE!

WITH ADAM & EVE BEING CREATED PERFECT IN A PARADISE WOULD GOD HAVE SECLUDED THEIR RECOGNITION, MINDS AND BEHAVIORS TO NEVER SEE BAD FOR IF THEY HADN'T EATEN OF THE TREE OF THE KNOWLEDGE OF GOOD AND BAD!-' BAD NATURALLY EXISTS IN ALL OTHER CREATION!-' HOW WOULD GOD HAVE HIDDEN IT!

WOULD A WISE GOD HONESTLY ALLOW ANOTHER CREATION OF HIS TO EXIST (SATAN the DEVIL) AND WREAK HAVOC ON HIS OTHER CREATIONS FOR SOME 60,000 YEARS JUST BECAUSE ONE SPECIFIC CREATION (MAN) ATE A FORBIDDEN FRUIT HAVING THE KNOWLEDGE OF GOOD & BAD THAT ALREADY HAD EXISTED AROUND THEM!-

WERE ANGELS CREATED PERFECT!-' DO THEY NEED A RANSOM SACRIFICE FOR THE FORGIVENESS OF THEIR SINS SUCH AS THROUGH JESUS CHRIST for in REVELATIONS of the BIBLE; SATAN the DEVIL, took a 3RD OF THE ANGELS WITH HIM to MAKE THEM DEMONS!-' IF THEY WERE CREATED PERFECT WHY THE DEFECTION!

SINCE THE ANGELS CAN BECOME DEMONS AND SIN; WHAT KIND OF SACRIFICE WOULD THE ANGELS BE OFFERING UP TO GOD FOR THE FORGIVENESS OF THEIR MISSED IMPERFECTIONS!-' SINCE JESUS CHRIST HELPED IN THEIR CREATION; WOULD HE OFFER UP A SIMILAR SACRIFICE FOR THEM; BUT, IN THE HEAVENLY REALM!-

AS ADAM & EVE WERE ONCE PERFECT, THEN IMPERFECT; BUT, WITH JESUS CHRIST'S RANSOM SACRIFICE THEIR CHILDREN CAN BE FORGIVEN AND RECEIVE EVERLASTING LIFE!- CAN DEMONS CHANGE THEIR MINDS; AND, ASK FOR FORGIVENESS FROM GOD AND RECEIVE EVERLASTING LIFE JUST AS WELL WITH CHRIST'S RANSOM

SINCE ADAM & EVE ATE THE FORBIDDEN FRUIT OF KNOWLEDGE OF GOOD AND BAD; AND, RECEIVED DEATH within a DAY of a THOUSAND YEARS because of this

ACT; can THEY TOO be FORGIVEN of their ONE SIN; and, RECEIVE EVERLASTING LIFE just as well as for ALL of their DESCENDANTS through CHRIST!~'

FOR THOSE THAT HAVE THE BELIEF THAT ONCE THEY DIE THEY GO TO LIVE IN HEAVEN WILL THEY BE AMONGST THE ANGELS OR DEMONS!~' AND, ONCE IN HEAVEN; CAN THEY DEFECT LIKE THE DEMONS AND RUNAWAY WITH the DEVIL IN THEIR FUTURE AFTERLIFE PRESENCE; OR, WILL THEY BECOME ANGELS THEMSELVES!!!~'

HOW MANY THAT HAVE CHILDREN WOULD DISCIPLINE THEM SO SEVERELY FOR MAKING ONE MISTAKE!~' THAT ALL OF THEIR FUTURE CHILDREN SHOULD HAVE TO PAY THE PRICE FOR THEIR ONE MISTAKE!~' HOW MANY INVENTORS WOULD DESTROY THEIR CREATIONS BECAUSE YOU WANTED TO TEACH A LESSON OF YOUR IMPORTANCE

JESSICA COMBS "FASTEST WOMAN ON 4 WHEELS" (39) (BIRTH: JULY 27, 1980) (DEATH: AUGUST 27, 2019)

BIRTHDAY # `-NUMBER = (7 + 27 + 19 + 80) = 133

DEATH/DAY # `-NUMBER = (8 + 27 + 20 + 19) = 74

(133 + 74) = (`-207) = (27 + 0) = (`-27) = BORN on a (`-27th); AND, DIED on a (`-27th)!!!~'

SHE DIED (`-31) DAYS FROM HER LAST BIRTHDAY!!!~'

(365 (-) 31) = (`-334)

(`-334) = (33 x 4) = (`-132) = (32 X 1) = (`-32) = -a PROPHETIC NUMBER!!!~'

SHE DIED AT THE `-AGE of (`-39) = (3 X 9) = (`-27)!!!~'

JULY 27 = (7 x 27) = (`-189) /|\ AUGUST 27 = (8 x 27) = (`-216) /|\ (216 (-) 189) = (`-27)!!!~'

727 /|\ 827 = ALMOST `-RECIPROCALS of EACH OTHER!!!~'

JULY 27, 1980 = (7 + 2 + 7 + 1 + 9 + 8 + 0) = (`-34)!!!~'

AUGUST 27, 2019 = (8 + 2 + 7 + 2 + 0 + 1 + 9) = (`-29)!!!~'

(34 + 29) = (`-63)!!!~'

PETER FONDA BIRTH: FEBRUARY 23, 1940 / DEATH: AUGUST 16, 2019!~' BIRTHDAY # = (2+23+19+40) = 84!~' DEATH/DAY # = (8+16+20+19) = 63!~' (84 + 63) = `-147!~' Mr. FONDA DIED `-174 DAYS AFTER HIS LAST BIRTHDAY!~' HE DIED at the AGE of 79 = (7x9) = `-63 = DEATH/DAY #!~' 23/47=RECIP=74!~'

`-74 = RECIPROCAL = `-47

(74 (-) 47) = (`-27)!!!~'

JESSICA COMBS "FASTEST WOMAN ON WHEELS" BIRTH = (7+27+19+80) = 133!~' DEATH = (8+27+20+19) = 74!~' (133+74) = 207 = (27+0) = 27 = BORN on a (`-27th); AND, DIED on a (`-27th)!!!~' DIED at AGE 39 = (3x9) = 27!~' JULY 27 = (7x27) = 189 /\ AUGUST 27 = (8x27) = 216 /|\(216(-)189) = 27

ACCORDING TO THE BIBLE; WHEN ADAM & EVE SINNED, THEY AND THEIR CHILDREN HAD TO DIE!!-' WHEN THE ANGELS SINNED; AND, BECAME DEMONS; DID THEY, OR; THEIR CHILDREN HAVE TO DIE!!-' DID SATAN the DEVIL have to DIE BECAUSE HE HAD SINNED AND REBELLED AND FELL SHORT OF THE GLORY OF GOD!!-

WOULD A REAL GOD HAVE TO LET ONE SET OF HIS CREATIONS (ANGELS & DEMONS) TORMENT ANOTHER SET OF HIS CREATIONS (MANKIND) TO PROVE A LITTLE POINT ABOUT BREAKING HIS RULES!- TO ALLOW ONE SET OF HIS CREATIONS TO HAVE NO LIMITS; AND, TO HANDICAP THE OTHER TO ENDURE THE RAMIFICATIONS!-'

HOW WOULD THE ANGELS/DEMONS COMMUNICATE WITH MANKIND TO BLESS OR TORMENT THEM!- IS IT OUTRIGHT CONTROL; or, WOULD IT BE BY A SUGGESTION OF THOUGHT!- OPEN YOUR EYES; THIS IS JUST HOW GOD DOES IT!!!-' BY THE SUBTLE SUGGESTION OF A PASSING THOUGHT YOU ARE GUIDED IN YOUR DIRECTION!-'

AMERICAN ACTRESS VALERIE HARPER "RHODA" (80) (BIRTH: AUGUST 22, 1939) (DEATH: AUGUST 30, 2019)

BIRTHDAY # `-NUMBER = (8 + 22 + 19 + 39) = 88

DEATH/DAY # `-NUMBER = (8 + 30 + 20 + 19) = 77

(88 (-) 77) = (`-11) = "YIN/YANG" = "THE CYCLE of LIFE"!!!-'

(88 + 77) = (`-165) = (16 x 5) = (`-80) = "AGE of `-DEATH for MRS. VALERIE HARPER"!!!~'

SHE DIED (`-8) DAYS AFTER HER LAST BIRTHDAY at the AGE of (`-80)!!!~'

(8 X 8) = (`-64)!!!~'

(365 (-) 8) = (`-357) /|\ (35 X 7) = (`-245) /|\ (57 x 3) = (`-171) /|\ (245 (-) 171) = (`-74) = "AGE of on "DANCING with the STARS"" = "JULY 4th" = INDEPENDENCE DAY!!!~'

SHE DIED AT THE `-AGE of (`-80)!!!~' AUGUST 30th = (8/30) = (83 + 0) = (`-83) = "THE DEATH # `-NUMBERS"!!!~'

AUGUST 22 = (8 x 22) = (`-176) /|\ AUGUST 30 = (8 x 30) = (`-240) /|\ (240 (-) 176) = (`-64) = "WAS FIRST MARRIED to RICHARD SCHAAL in (`-1964)!!!~'

DIVORCED in (`-1978) from RICHARD SCHAAL (`-78) = RECIPROCAL = (`-87) = WAS REMARRIED in (`-1987) TO TONY CACCIOTTI!!!~'

WAS MARRIED to RICHARD SCHAAL for (`-14) YEARS!!!~' (32 + 14) = (`-46) = RECIPROCAL = (`-64)!!!~'

AUGUST 22, 1939 = (8 + 2 + 2 + 1 + 9 + 3 + 9) = (`-34)!!!~'

AUGUST 30, 2019 = (8 + 3 + 0 + 2 + 0 + 1 + 9) = (`-23)!!!~' (`-23) = RECIPROCAL = (`-32) = "WAS MARRIED to HER HUSBAND TONY CACCIOTTI for (`-32) YEARS!!!~'

(34 (-) 23) = (`-11) = "YIN/YANG" = "THE CYCLE of LIFE"!!!~'

VALERIE HARPER "RHODA" WAS `-BORN in (`-39); AND, `-DIED in (`-39) = (2019) = (20 + 19) = (`-39)!!!~' (39 + 39) = (`-78) = "REVIEW the # `-NUMBERS"!!!~'

VALERIE HARPER "RHODA" BIRTHDAY # `-NUMBER = (8 + 22 + 19 + 39) = 88!!!~' DEATH/DAY # `-NUMBER = (8 + 30 + 20 + 19) = 77!!!~' (88 + 77) = (`-165) = (16 x 5) = (`-80) = "AGE of `-DEATH for MRS. VALERIE HARPER"!!!~' SHE DIED (`-8) DAYS AFTER HER LAST BIRTHDAY at the AGE of (`-80)!!!~' (8/80) = (88 + 0) = (`-88) = `-HER `-BIRTHDAY # `-NUMBER)!!!~'

GOD has CREATED HIS OTHER CREATIONS WITH POISONS, STINGERS, TRANQUILIZERS, ETC., ETC., ETC... FOR THE `-KILL!!!~' ACCORDING TO JESUS WE ARE NOT TO BE VIOLENT AT ALL!!!!~' THE ISRAELITES WERE A WARRING NATION AT TIMES; AND, NOW; WE MUST STOP!!!!~' ALL OTHER CREATION WAS CREATED TO PREY; AND, TO `-KILL; BUT, `-WE; MUST `-STOP, WHY???~'

WHEN YOU THINK GOD IS WITH YOU; GOD IS WITH YOU!!!~' NOT ONLY WITH YOU; BUT, WITH EVERY SINGLE ENTITY OF HIS CREATION JUST AS WELL; SIMULTANEOUSLY!!!~' THIS INCLUDES ALL OF THE OTHER PLANETS AND STARS WITHIN ALL OF THE OTHER CONSTELLATIONS JUST AS WELL!!!~'

EVERY INSECT, EVERY AMOEBA, EVERY ATOM, EVERY PROTON, EVERY NEUTRON, EVERY ELECTRON!!!~' GOD IS THERE; AND, CONTROLLING `-AT THE VERY SAME TIME; SIMULTANEOUSLY, PERPETUALLY; and, FOREVER!!!~'

EVERY THOUGHT, EVERY INCLINATION, EVERY PASSING THOUGHT, `-EVERYTHING `-CAPTURED; and, MOVING; within the `-IMAGINATION of `-GOD'S; or, GOD'S `-MIND OF `-IMAGINATION at `-ALL `-TIMES; `-ALL LUMPED `-TOGETHER, MOVING `-TOGETHER; BEING BROUGHT `-TOGETHER, `-SEAMLESSLY!!!~' HOW DOES `-GOD-` DO `-IT!!!~' HOW DOES `-HE DO `-IT!!!~'

WE WERE CREATED WITH A SINGLE (ONE DIMENSIONAL) STREAM OF CONSCIOUS PROCESSING `-WITH OUR HUMAN BRAIN!!!~' ALTHOUGH; EXTREMELY INTELLIGENT, AT TIMES; IT (the BRAIN) PASSES OFF, as BEING very STUPID; AT MANY OTHER TIMES!!!~' FOR OTHER CREATIONS; WE JUST SAY, WELL; THEY JUST DIDN'T KNOW ANY BETTER!!!~'

AMERICAN COSTUME DESIGNER CHRIS MARCH (56) (BIRTH: FEBRUARY 25, 1963) (DEATH: SEPTEMBER 5, 2019)

BIRTHDAY # `-NUMBER = (2 + 25 + 19 + 63) = 109

DEATH/DAY # `-NUMBER = (9 + 5 + 20 + 19) = 53

(109 (-) 53) = (`-56) = `-AGE of `-DEATH of CHRIS MARCH

(109 + 53) = (`-162) = (62 + 1) = (`-63) = YEAR of `-BIRTH for CHRIS MARCH!!!~'

HE DIED (`-192) DAYS AFTER HIS LAST BIRTHDAY!!!~'

(365 (-) 192) = (`-173) = "PART of the `-MARK"!!!~'

HE DIED AT THE `-AGE of (`-56)!!!~'

SEPTEMBER 5th = (9/5) = ROBERT MUGABE'S AGE of DEATH!!!~'

(1963/2019) = (19 + 63 + 20 + 19) = (`-121) = (12/21) = ROBERT MUGABE!!!~'

FORMER PRIME MINISTER OF ZIMBABWE ROBERT MUGABE (95) (BIRTH: FEBRUARY 21, 1924) (DEATH: SEPTEMBER 6, 2019)

WAS MARRIED TO GRACE MUGABE (1996) FOR (`-23) YEARS; and, SALLY MUGABE (1961 - 1992) FOR (`-31) YEARS!!!~'

WAS MARRIED TO GRACE MUGABE in (`-96); and, `-DIED on (9/6)!!!~' (9 X 6) = (`-54)!!!~'

BIRTHDAY # `-NUMBER = (2 + 21 + 19 + 24) = 66

DEATH/DAY # `-NUMBER = (9 + 6 + 20 + 19) = 54

(66 + 54) = (`-120) = (12 + 0) = (`-12)

(66 (-) 54) = (`-12)

(12 + 12) = (`-24) = YEAR ROBERT MUGABE was `-BORN!!!~'

FEBRUARY 21 = (2 x 21) = `-42 = RECIPROCAL = `-24!!!~'

HE DIED (`-197) DAYS AFTER HIS LAST BIRTHDAY!!!~'

(`-95); (`-96); (`-97)!!!~'

(365 (-) 197) = (`-**168**) = **"The MARK of `-DEATH"!!!~'**

HE DIED AT THE `-AGE of (`-95) = (9 X 5) = `-45 = RECIPROCAL = `-54 = DEATH/DAY # `-NUMBER for ROBERT MUGABE!!!~'

FOR ALL OF THE OTHER PROPHETS BEFORE ME; I'M, THE ONLY ONE; THAT GOD HAS ACTUALLY TALKED TO!!!~' I ASKED; and, HE TOLD ME SO!!!~'

WHY DO PEOPLE THINK THAT GOD IS STUPID!!!~' THAT HE COULDN'T DO SOME OF THE GREAT FANTASTICAL THINGS LIKE IN THE MOVIES!!!~' LIKE ONLY WE COULD IMAGINE IT!!!~' HE CAN DO IT; AND, DOES; AND, THAT'S `-HIM!!!~' IN REAL LIFE; and, IN THE MOVIES!!!~'

PLEASE DON'T FORGET ABOUT THE NUMBERS (23/32) IN OUR DAILY AFFAIRS; and, IN LIFE IN GENERAL!!!~' IT'S ALWAYS ON THE NEWS!!!~' IT'S ALWAYS BEEN IN THE NEWS!!!~' (13/31); `-TOO!!!~'

AMERICAN COUNTRY MUSIC SINGER KYLIE RAE HARRIS (30) (BIRTH: MAY 15, 1989) (DEATH: SEPTEMBER 4, 2019)

BIRTHDAY # `-NUMBER = (5 + 15 + 19 + 89) = 128

DEATH/DAY # `-NUMBER = (9 + 4 + 20 + 19) = 52

(128 + 52) = (`-180)

(128 (-) 52) = (`-76)

SHE DIED (`-112) DAYS AFTER HER LAST BIRTHDAY!!!~'

(365 (-) 112) = (`-253)

SHE DIED AT THE `-AGE of (`-30)!!!~'

MAY 15, 1989 = (5 + 1 + 5 + 1 + 9 + 8 + 9) = (`-38)!!!~'

SEPTEMBER 4, 2019 = (9 + 4 + 2 + 0 + 1 + 9) = (`-25)!!!~'

(38 + 25) = (`-63) = RECIPROCAL = (`-36) = (9 X 4) = SEPTEMBER 4th!!!~'

MAY 15 = (5 X 15) = (`-75)!!!~'

SEPTEMBER 4 = (9 X 4) = (`-36)!!!~'

(75 (-) 36) = (`-39) = OIL TYCOON T. BOONE PICKENS!!!~'

AMERICAN COUNTRY MUSIC SINGER KYLIE RAE HARRIS & OIL TYCOON T. BOONE PICKENS `-both `-DIED (`-**112**) **DAYS** from their `-**DAY of** `-**BIRTH!!!~'**

OIL TYCOON T. BOONE PICKENS (91) (BIRTH: MAY 22, 1928) (DEATH: SEPTEMBER 11, 2019)

BIRTHDAY # `-NUMBER = (5 + 22 + 19 + 28) = 74

DEATH/DAY # `-NUMBER = (9 + 11 + 20 + 19) = 59

(74 + 59) = (`-133) = (33 (-) 1) = (`-32) = -a PROPHETIC NUMBER!!!~'

(74 + 59) = (`-133) = (13 X 3) = `-39 = AMERICAN COUNTRY MUSIC SINGER KYLIE RAE HARRIS!!!~'

HE DIED (`-112) DAYS AFTER HIS LAST BIRTHDAY!!!~'

(365 (-) 112) = (`-253)!!!~'

HE DIED AT THE `-AGE of (`-91)!!!~'

MAY 22, 1928 = (5 + 2 + 2 + 1 + 9 + 2 + 8) = (`-29)!!!~'

SEPTEMBER 11, 2019 = (9 + 1 + 1 + 2 + 0 + 1 + 9) = (`-23)!!!~'

(29 + 23) = (`-52) = RECIPROCAL = (`-25) = SEPTEMBER 4th, 2019 = AMERICAN COUNTRY MUSIC SINGER KYLIE RAE HARRIS!!!~'

MAY 22 = (5 X 22) = (`-110)!!!~'

SEPTEMBER 11 = (9 X 11) = (`-99)!!!~'

(110 + 99) = (`-209) = (29 + 0) = (`-29) = MAY 22, 1928!!!~'

AMERICAN COUNTRY MUSIC SINGER KYLIE RAE HARRIS & OIL TYCOON T. BOONE PICKENS `-both `-DIED (`-**112**) **DAYS** from their `-**DAY of** `-**BIRTH!!!~'**

CONCEPTS!!!~'

WHY HAVE HUMANS BEEN SO CONSUMED WITH WRITING ABOUT WHAT HAPPENS DURING; AND, AFTER DEATH!!!~' IT'S JUST TOO HARD TO ACCEPT THAT LIFE HAS A PRE-DESIGNED SET OF LIMITS INCLUDING TERM

LIMITS!!!~' WE WERE MADE TO LOVE; AND, CHERISH LIFE; AND, IT'S JUST TOO HARD TO LEAVE `-IT!!!~'

HOW ABOUT RELATIONSHIPS; AND, AS TO WHAT IS PROPER; AND, AS TO WHAT IS NOT!!!~' WHATEVER GOD HAS ALLOWED TO EXIST WITHIN HIS IMPERFECT EARTHLY CREATIONS; IS, WHAT IS ALLOWED; AND, WHAT IS NOT; BY HIS CREATIVE HANDS!!!~' ASK YOURSELF; WHAT IS REQUIRED FOR A CREATIVE LIFE TO CONTINUE TO EXIST!!!~' WITH YOUR `-POWER OF `-REASON, ACT ACCORDINGLY; OR, `-CEASE; TO 'EXIST!!!~'

WOULD `-YOU LIKE AN `-AFFAIR!!!~' WOULD `-YOU HAVE ANY SELF-CONTROL IN THE SITUATION!!!~' HOW DOES IT FEEL FOR YOU; WHEN SOMEONE IS IN A FAITHFUL RELATIONSHIP; AND, HOW DOES IT FEEL FOR YOU; WHEN SOMEBODY IS IN AN ADULTEROUS RELATIONSHIP!!!~' WITH YOUR POWER OF REASON; WHICH ONE, SEEMS MORE FEASIBLE; AS TO THE `-INTENDED `-TARGET, OF `-GOD'S ORIGINAL CREATIVE HANDS!!!~' HOW DO YOU FEEL???~'

FRIDAY the **13**th FULL MOON

THE FAST FACTS: SEPTEMBER **13**th, 2019 AT **9:32**PM

Also Called:

HARVEST MOON & MICROMOON

LAST OCCURRENCE OCTOBER **13**th, 2000

NEXT OCCURRENCE AUGUST 13th, 20**49**

(`-**30**) YEARS; UNTIL, THE NEXT ONE!!!~'

AMERICAN SINGER/SONGWRITER EDDIE MONEY (**70**) (BIRTH: MARCH 21, 19**49**) (DEATH: SEPTEMBER 13, 2019)

BIRTHDAY # `-NUMBER = (3 + 21 + 19 + 49) = 92

DEATH/DAY # `-NUMBER = (9 + 13 + 20 + 19) = 61

(92 (-) 61) = (`-**31**) = RECIPROCAL = (`-**13**)!!!~'

(92 + 61) = (`-153) = (53 + 1) = (`-**54**)!!!~'

HE DIED (`-1**76**) DAYS AFTER HIS LAST BIRTHDAY!!!~'

(365 (-) 176) = (`-1**89**)!!!~'

HE DIED AT THE `-AGE of (`-**70**)!!!~'

MARRIED HIS WIFE LAURIE MONEY IN (`-19**89**)!!!~' (89 (-) 19) = (`-**70**) = AGE of `-DEATH for AMERICAN SINGER/SONGWRITER EDDIE MONEY!!!~'

MARRIED FOR (`-**30**) YEARS!!!~'

(1949) = (19 + 49) = (`-**68**)!!!~'

(2019) = (20 + 19) = (**39**)!!!~'

(68 (-) 39) = (`-**29**)!!!~'

69

MARCH 21, 1949 = (3 + 2 + 1 + 1 + 9 + 4 + 9) = (`-**29**)!!!~' `-29 = RECIPROCAL = `-92

SEPTEMBER 13, 2019) = (9 + 1 + 3 + 2 + 0 + 1 + 9) = (`-25)!!!~'

(92 (-) 25) = (`-**67**) = RECIPROCAL = (`-**76**)!!!~'

MARCH 21 = (3 X 21) = (`-63)!!!~'

SEPTEMBER 13 = (9 X 13) = (`-117)!!!~'

(117 (-) 63) = (`-**54**)!!!~'

AMERICAN SINGER/SONGWRITER RIC OCASEK "THE CARS FRONTMAN" (75) (BIRTH: MARCH 23, 19**44**) (DEATH: SEPTEMBER 15, 2019)

BIRTHDAY # `-NUMBER = (3 + 23 + 19 + 44) = **89**

DEATH/DAY # `-NUMBER = (9 + 15 + 20 + 19) = **63**

(89 (-) 63) = (`-**26**)

(89 + 63) = (`-152) = (52 + 1) = (`-**53**)!!!~'

HE DIED (`-1**76**) DAYS AFTER HIS LAST BIRTHDAY!!!~'

(365 (-) 176) = (`-1**89**)!!!~'

HE DIED AT THE `-AGE of (`-75)!!!~' (7 X 5) = (`-**35**) = RECIPROCAL = (`-**53**)!!!~'

MARRIED HIS WIFE PAULINA PORIZKOVA IN (`-19**89**)!!!~'
EQUALS `-BIRTHDAY # `-NUMBER of AMERICAN SINGER/
SONGWRITER RIC OCASEK "THE CARS FRONTMAN"!!!~'

MARRIED FOR (`-**30**) YEARS to PAULINA FROM (1989 -
2019)!!!~' (EDDIE MONEY & WIFE)!!!~'

MARRIED to SUZANNE OCASEK for (`-17) FROM (1971 -
1988)!!!~' (`-71) = RECIPROCAL = (`-17)!!!~'

(30 (-) 17) = (`-13) /|\ (30 + 17) = (`-47)

MARCH 23, 1944 = (3 + 2 + 3 + 1 + 9 + 4 + 4) = (`-**26**)!!!~'

SEPTEMBER 15, 2019) = (9 + 1 + 5 + 2 + 0 + 1 + 9) = (`-27)!!!~'
(`-27) = RECIPROCAL = (`-72) = (8 X 9) = (`-89) = BIRTHDAY #
`-NUMBER & YEAR MARRIED WIFE (`-89)!!!~'

(26 + 27) = (`-**53**)!!!~'

MARCH 23 = (3 X 23) = (`-**69**)!!!~'

SEPTEMBER 15 = (9 X 15) = (`-**135**)!!!~' (35 X 1) = (`-**35**) =
RECIPROCAL = (`-**53**)!!!~'

(135 + 69) = (`-**204**)!!!~' (24 + 0) = (`-24) = (6 X 4) = **6' 4**" = HEIGHT
of RIC OCASEK "THE CARS FRONTMAN"!!!~'

(135 (-) 69) = (`-**66**) = (6 x 6) = (`-**36**) = RECIPROCAL = (`-**63**) =
DEATH/DAY # `-NUMBER!!!~'

71

AMERICAN SINGER/SONGWRITER EDDIE MONEY is an OVERLAY of AMERICAN SINGER/SONGWRITER RIC OCASEK "THE **CARS** FRONTMAN"!!!~'

AMERICAN NAS**CAR** LEGEND MIKE STEFANIK (61) (BIRTH: MAY 20, **1958** (DEATH: SEPTEMBER 15, **2019**)

BIRTHDAY # `-NUMBER = (5 + 20 + 19 + 58) = **102**

DEATH/DAY # `-NUMBER = (9 + 15 + 20 + 19) = **63**

(102 (-) 63) = (`-**39**)

(102 + 63) = (`-165) = (65 + 1) = (`-**66**)!!!~'

(66 (-) 39) = (`-**27**)!!!~'

HE DIED (`-1**18**) DAYS AFTER HIS LAST BIRTHDAY!!!~'

(365 (-) 118) = (`-247)!!!~' (24 x 7) = (`-**168**)!!!~'

HE DIED AT THE `-AGE of (`-61)!!!~' (61 x 2) = (`-**122**) = (22 + 1) = (`-**23**) = -a **PROPHETIC NUMBER!!!~'**

MAY 20, 1958 = (5 + 2 + 0 + 1 + 9 + 5 + 8) = (`-**30**)!!!~'

SEPTEMBER 15, 2019) = (9 + 1 + 5 + 2 + 0 + 1 + 9) = (`-**27**)!!!~'

(30 + 27) = (`-**57**)!!!~'

MAY 20 = (5 X 20) = (`-**100**)!!!~'

SEPTEMBER 15 = (9 X 15) = (`-135)!!!~' (35 X 1) = (`-**35**) = RECIPROCAL = (`-**53**)!!!~'

(135 + 100) = (`-**235**)!!!~'

(135 (-) 100) = (`-**35**)**!!!~'**

(235 + 35) = (`-**270**) = (27 + 0) = (`-**27**)!!!~'

`-1958 = (58 (-) 19) = (`-**39**)!!!~'

`-2019 = (20 + 19) = (`-**39**)!!!~'

(39 + 39) = (`-**78**) = **"The `-DEATH # `-NUMBER for (`-2019)"**!!!~'

`-BORN in (`-39) & `-DIED in (`-39)!!!~' (3 X 9) = (`-27) = DEATH/DAY # `-NUMBER of AMERICAN NASCAR LEGEND MIKE STEFANIK!!!~'

WHY DOES `-GOD NEED A GOVERNMENT WHEN HE IS `-GOD CONTROLLING EVERYTHING!!!~' JUST A `-THOUGHT!!!~'

LEGENDARY JOURNALIST COKIE ROBERTS (75) (BIRTH: DECEMBER **27**, 19**43** (DEATH: SEPTEMBER 17, **2**01**9**)
BIRTHDAY # `-NUMBER = (12 + 27 + 19 + 43) = **101**
DEATH/DAY # `-NUMBER = (9 + 17 + 20 + 19) = **65**
(101 (-) 65) = (`-**36**) = RECIPROCAL = (`-**63**)!!!~'
(101 + 65) = (`-1**66**) = (66 + 1) = (`-**67**) = RECIPROCAL = (`-**76**)!!!~'
(67 (-) 36) = (`-**31**) = RECIPROCAL = (`-**13**)!!!~'
(101 + 65) = (`-1**66**) = (66 x 1) = (`-**66**)!!!~'

MARRIED in (`-19**66**) TO STEVEN V. ROBERTS; and, MARRIED for (`-**53**) YEARS!!!~'
#36/PRESIDENT LYNDON B. JOHNSON `-ATTENDED THEIR WEDDING!!!~'

SHE DIED (`-**101**) DAYS BEFORE HER NEXT BIRTHDAY = LEGENDARY JOURNALIST COKIE ROBERTS BIRTHDAY # NUMBER (`-**101**)!!!~'
(365 (-) 101) = (`-**264**)!!!~'
SHE DIED AT THE `-AGE of (`-75)!!!~' (7 x 5) = (`-**35**)!!!~'

DECEMBER 27, 1943 = (1 + 2 + 2 + 7 + 1 + 9 + 4 + 3) = (`-**29**)!!!~'
SEPTEMBER 17, 2019) = (9 + 1 + 7 + 2 + 0 + 1 + 9) = (`-**29**)!!!~'
DEATH/DAY (`-**29**) = BIRTHDAY (`-**29**)!!!~' DIED in (`-**2**019)!!!~'
(29 + 29) = (`-**58**)!!!~'
HER `-FATHER POLITICIAN HALE BOGGS `-DIED at the `-AGE of (`-**58**) ON DECEMBER **29**th within 19**72** = (12 + 29 + 19 + 72) = (`-**132**) = (32 x 1) = (`-**32**) = -a **PROPHETIC NUMBER!!!~'**

DECEMBER 27 = (12 + 27) = (`-**39**)!!!~' POLITICIAN LINDY BOGGS BIRTHDAY (3/13) = (3 x 13) = (`-**39**)!!!~'
DECEMBER 27 = (12 X 27) = (`-324) = (24 X 3) = (`-**72**)!!!~'
SEPTEMBER 17 = (9 + 17) = (`-26)!!!~'
SEPTEMBER 17 = (9 X 17) = (`-153)!!!~' (53 X 1) = (`-**53**) = RECIPROCAL = (`-**35**)!!!~'
(39 (-) 26) = (`-**13**)!!!~'
(39 + 26) = (`-**65**) = DEATH/DAY # `-NUMBER of LEGENDARY JOURNALIST COKIE ROBERTS!!!~'
(324 + 153) = (`-**477**)!!!~'
(324 (-) 153) = (`-**171**) = (71 + 1) = (`-**72**) = RECIPROCAL = (`-**27**) = BIRTHDAY of LEGENDARY JOURNALIST COKIE ROBERTS**!!!~'**

`-1943 = (19 + 43) = (`-**62**)!!!~'

`-2019 = (20 + 19) = (`-**39**)!!!~' LINDY BOGGS (`-**97**) AGE OF
`-DEATH & HALE BOGGS (`-**58**) AGE OF `-DEATH = (97 (-)
58) = (`-**39**)!!!~'

(62 + 39) = (**101**)!!!~'

(62 (-) 39) = (`-**23**) = -a PROPHETIC NUMBER!!!~'

(101 (-) 23) = (`-**78**) = "The `-DEATH # `-NUMBER for
(`-2019)"!!!~'

**COKIE ROBERTS `-DAY of `-DEATH = SEPTEMBER 17
= (9/17) = (97 x 1) = (`-97) = `-AGE of `-DEATH of `-HER
`-MOTHER LINDY BOGGS!!!~'**

SHE `-DIED in `-HER (`-**76**[th]) YEAR of EXISTENCE!!!~'
AMERICAN JOURNALIST & HUSBAND STEVEN V.
ROBERTS was (`-**76**) YEARS of AGE FOR WHEN HIS `-WIFE
COKIE had `-DIED!!!~'
HUSBAND STEVEN V. ROBERTS WAS BORN FEBRUARY
11, 1943 = (2 + 11 + 19 + 43) = (`-**75**) = AGE of `-DEATH of `-HIS
`-WIFE LEGENDARY JOURNALIST COKIE ROBERTS!!!~'

HER MOTHER LINDY BOGGS `-DIED at the `-AGE of (`-
97) on a (`-**27**[th]) = JULY 27, 2013 = (7 + 27 + 20 + 13) = (`-**67**) =
RECIPROCAL = (`-**76**)!!!~' WAS BORN on a (`-**13**[th]) = MARCH
13, 1916!!!~' MARCH 13 = (`-**313**) = JOHN F. KENNEDY =
HUSBAND was on the WARREN COMMISSION = WARREN
COMMISSION was FOUNDED on NOVEMBER 29, 1963 =
(11 + 29 + 19 + 63) = (`-**122**) = (22 + 1) = (`-**23**) = -a PROPHETIC
NUMBER!!!~' (`-1916) = (19 + 16) = (`-**35**) = RECIPROCAL =
(`-**53**)!!!~' (`-**122**) – "THE PRESIDENTS & FIRST LADIES #
`-NUMBER"!!!~' LYNDON B. JOHNSON DIED ON (`-**122**) &
GAVE the ORDER for the WARREN COMMISSION!!!~'

POLITICIAN HALE BOGGS BIRTHDAY # `-NUMBER =
FEBRUARY 15, 1914 = (2 + 15 + 19 + 14) = (`-**50**)!!!~'

POLITICIAN LINDY BOGGS BIRTHDAY # `-NUMBER = MARCH 13, 1916 = (3 + 13 + 19 + 16) = (`-**51**)!!!-'

(51 + 50) = (`-**101**) = LEGENDARY JOURNALIST COKIE ROBERTS DIED (`-**101**) DAYS BEFORE HER NEXT BIRTHDAY & BIRTHDAY # NUMBER was (`-**101**)!!!-'

THE BIRTHDAY # `-NUMBERS of the `-PARENTS `-ADD `-UP to the `-BIRTHDAY # `-NUMBER of the `-DAUGHTER COKIE ROBERTS!!!-'

HALE BOGGS BIRTH/YEAR = (`-1914) = (`-**33**)!!!-'

LINDY BOGGS DEATH/YEAR = (`-2013) = (`-**33**)!!!-'

(33 + 33) = (`-**66**) = COKIE ROBERTS was MARRIED in (`-**66**)!!!-' (66 X 2) = (`-**132**) = (32 x 1) = (`-**32**) = -a **PROPHETIC NUMBER!!!-'**

HALE BOGGS DEATH/YEAR = (`-1972) = (72 (-) 19) = (`-**53**)!!!-'

LINDY BOGGS BIRTH/YEAR = (`-1916) = (`-**35**)!!!-'

(`-**35**) = **RECIPROCAL** = (`-**53**)!!!-'

HALE & LINDY BOGGS ARE `-RECIPROCALS-' of `-EACH `-OTHER (35/53)!!!-'

HALE BOGGS `-DIED (`-**48**) DAYS BEFORE HIS NEXT BIRTHDAY!!!-' (365 (-) 48) = (`-317) = (17 x 3) = (`-**51**) = LINDY BOGGS BIRTHDAY # `-NUMBER!!!-'

HALE BOGGS `-DIED (`-**48**) DAYS BEFORE HIS NEXT BIRTHDAY!!!-' (365 (-) 48) = (`-317) = (31 x 7) = (`-217) = (27 x 1) = (`-**27**) = LINDY BOGGS DEATH/DAY & COKIE ROBERTS

BIRTH/DAY & HALE BOGGS DEATH/YEAR RECIPROCAL (`-**72**)!!!~'

LINDY BOGGS `-DIED (`-1**36**) DAYS AFTER HER LAST BIRTHDAY!!!~' (36 x 1) = (`-**36**) = RECIPROCAL = (`-**63**)!!!~' (365 (-) 136) = (`-229) = (29 x 2) = (`-**58**) = **AGE of `-DEATH of HUSBAND HALE BOGGS!!!~'**

LINDY BOGGS `-DIED (`-1**36**) DAYS AFTER HER LAST BIRTHDAY!!!~' (36 x 1) = (`-**36**) = RECIPROCAL = (`-**63**)!!!~' (365 (-) 136) = (`-229) = (22 x 9) = (`-198) = (98 (-) 1) = (`-**97**) = **AGE of `-DEATH of LINDY BOGGS!!!~'**

(**48** + 136) = (`-1**84**) = (84 x 1) = (`-**84**) = RECIPROCAL = (`-**48**)!~'

LINDY BOGGS was MARRIED to HER HUSBAND HALE BOGGS in (1938)!!!~' (1972 (-) 1938) = (`-**34**) YEARS MARRIED = RECIPROCAL = (`-**43**) = YEAR HER DAUGHTER COKIE ROBERTS WAS `-BORN (`-19**43**)!!!~'

President Lyndon B. Johnson married Lady Bird Johnson in `-**1934**!!!!!~ Lady Bird Johnson died `-**34** years; after, the death of President Lyndon B. Johnson!!!!!~ Jacqueline Lee Kennedy was `-**34** years of age at the time of her husband's assassination; that of, President John F. Kennedy; and, the inauguration of President Lyndon B. Johnson!!!!!~ **April 30**th = 0**4**/**3**0 = `-**43** = **RECIPROCAL** = `-**34** !!!!!~

HALE BOGGS (1914/1972) /|\ LINDY BOGGS (1916/2013)!!!~'

(19 + 14 + 19 + 72) = (`-**124**)

(19 + 16 + 20 + 13) = (`-**68**) = (68 / 2) = (`-**34**)!!!~'

(124 (-) 68) = (`-**56**) = RECIPROCAL = (`-**65**) = **DEATH/ DAY # `-NUMBER of LEGENDARY JOURNALIST COKIE ROBERTS!!!~'**

LINDY BOGGS was `-<u>BORN</u> & `-<u>DIED</u> on `-<u>RECIPROCALS</u>-'  /|\  (`-**313**) /|\ (`-**727**)!!!~' (*Reciprocal-Sequenced-Numerology-RSN!~'*)!!!~'

`-<u>31</u> = RECIPROCAL = `-<u>13</u> /|\ `-<u>72</u> = RECIPROCAL = `-<u>27</u>!!!~'

GOD ORCHESTRATES `-ALL of OUR `-BIRTHS, `-DEATHS, `-BABIES, `-GRANDBABIES & `-MARRIAGES; EVEN TO `-INCLUDE IN-LAWS!!!~' COKIE ROBERTS & FAMILY ABOVE ARE A CLEAR REPRESENTATION OF THIS OF WHAT HAS ALREADY BEEN PRESENTED IN THE "REAL PROPHET of DOOM (KISMET) – INTRODUCTION – PENDULUM FLOW" `-SERIES of `-BOOKS; OF THESE EVENTUALITIES!!!~'

IT'S SAD TO SAY; BUT, AIRPLANE CRASHES LIKE HER FATHER'S, CANCERS, STORMS; and, MURDERS are `-ALL ORCHESTRATED JUST AS WELL; TO FIT WITHIN THE `-ASSIGNED `-STREAMLINED `-PIPELINE of `-EVENTS for the `-FIT `-PURPOSES of `-GOD'S `-WISHES!!!~' THAT'S THE REALITY of the `-MATTER; ALTHOUGH, CONFUSING; UNTIL, YOU ENVISION BEING AN INVENTOR/ CREATOR; AND, SEE THE NECESSITY OF SUCH STEPS OF PROGRESSION IN THE PART OF HAVING AN EXISTENCE; IN THAT ALL THINGS BEING POSSIBLE AND APPRECIATED, ALL of THIS WITH ALL OF ITS NUANCES!!!~'

THIS ALREADY SEEMS EXTREMELY COMPLEX FOR OUR ENTIRE FAMILIES TO BE SO INTERWOVEN AND INTERTWINED; BUT, GOD WILL ALSO ALLOW to INCLUDE OTHER FAMILIES; and, `-STRANGERS to OVERLAY their `-TIMELINES of `-EXISTENCE with `-OURS!!!~' THEIR MARRIAGES, THEIR BABIES, THEIR GRANDBABIES, THEIR BIRTHS; AND, THEIR DEATHS!!!~'

HAVE `-YOU `-NOTICED the MANY `-CELEBRITIES that have `-INTERTWINED among `-ANOTHER!!!~' CELEBRITIES were `-USED to be `-VERIFIED by the `-MASSES!!!~' NON-CELEBRITIES HAVE BEEN UTILIZED WHICH CAN BE `-VERIFIED by the `-MASSES through the `-INTERNET!!!~' ALL LINKED TOGETHER TO SHOW THAT IT'S NOT JUST ONE GROUP LIKE SUCH AS WITH THE CELEBRITIES; BUT, TO INCLUDE ALL OF `-CREATION `-ITSELF!!!~' EVERYONES `-INCLUDED!!!~'

NOT TO GIVE HONOR; OR, GLORY to WHERE `-IT'S RIGHTFULLY `-DESERVED; BUT, GOD is a PERFECT MATHEMATICIAN!!!~' HIS CONCEPTS ARE EXACT, PRECISE; AND, to the `-POINT!!!~' FOR `-ALL of the `-MATHEMATICS `-HE has `-ALLOWED US to `-DISCOVER; and, `-SCIENCES; IT IS `-TRULY a `-GRAND `-BLESSING INDEED for `-OUR `-UNDERSTANDING of `-HIS `-TRUE `-EXISTENCE!!!~' `-AND; THAT IS WHAT I HAVE DONE, with the `-DISCOVERY & `-CREATION of the **RECIPROCAL-SEQUENCING-NUMEROLOGY-RSN `-PIIILOSOPIIY!!!~'**

AMERICAN TELEVISION HOST & ACTRESS SUZANNNE WHANG (**56**) (BIRTH: SEPTEMBER 28, 1962) (DEATH: SEPTEMBER 17, 2019)

BIRTHDAY # `-NUMBER = (9 + 28 + 19 + 62) = **118**

DEATH/DAY # `-NUMBER = (9 + 17 + 20 + 19) = **65**

AGE OF DEATH (`-**56**) is the `-RECIPROCAL of HER DEATH/ DAY # `-NUMBER (`-**65**)!!!~'

(118 (-) 65) = (`-**53**) = RECIPROCAL = (`-**35**)!!!~'

(118 + 65) = (`-1**83**) = (83 + 1) = (`-**84**) = RECIPROCAL = (`-**48**)!!!~'

SHE DIED (`-**11**) DAYS BEFORE HER NEXT BIRTHDAY!!!~'

(365 (-) 11) = (`-354)!!!~' (54 x 3) = (`-162) = (62 + 1) = (`-**63**)!!!~'

(365 (-) 11) = (`-354)!!!~' (54 + 3) = (`-**57**) = RECIPROCAL = (`-**75**) = AGE of DEATH of COKIE ROBERTS!!!~'

COKIE ROBERTS DIED (`-101) DAYS FROM HER BIRTHDAY!!!~' TAKE OUT THE (`-0); AND, YOU HAVE (`-11) = SUZANNE WHANG!!!~'

SHE DIED AT THE `-AGE of (`-56)!!!~' (5 + 6) = (`-**11**) = DAYS SHE DIED BEFORE HER NEXT BIRTHDAY!!!~'

SEPTEMBER 28, 1962 = (9 + 2 + 8 + 1 + 9 + 6 + 2) = (`-**37**)!!!~'

SEPTEMBER 17, 2019) = (9 + 1 + 7 + 2 + 0 + 1 + 9) = (`-**29**)!!!~'

(37 + 29) = (`-**66**)!!!~' (6 X 6) = (`-**36**) = RECIPROCAL = (`-**63**)!!!~'

SEPTEMBER 28 = (9 + 28) = (`-**37**) = SEPTEMBER 28, 1962 (`-**37**)!!!~' (37 + 37) = (`-**74**) = (7 + 4) = (`-**11**) = DAYS OF DEATH BEFORE BIRTHDAY!!!~'

SEPTEMBER 28 = (9 X 28) = (`-**252**) = (25 X 2) = (`-**50**)!!!~'

SEPTEMBER 28 = (9 X 28) = (`-**252**) = (25 + 2) = (`-**27**) = RECIPROCAL = (`-**72**) = **COKIE ROBERTS & FAMILY!!!~'**

SEPTEMBER 17 = (9 + 17) = (`-**26**)!!!~'

SEPTEMBER 17 = (9 X 17) = (`-**153**)!!!~' (53 X 1) = (`-**53**) = RECIPROCAL = (`-**35**)!!!~'

(37 (-) 26) = (`-**11**) = SHE DIED (`-**11**) DAYS BEFORE HER NEXT BIRTHDAY!!!~'

(37 + 26) = (`-**63**)!!!~'

(252 + 153) = (`-**405**)!!!~'

(252 (-) 153) = (`-**99**)!!!~'

(405 (-) 99) = (`-**306**) = (30 + 6) = (`-**36**) = RECIPROCAL = (`-**63**)!!!~' (36 + 63) = (`-**99**)!!!~'

`-1962 = (62 (-) 19) = (`-**43**)!!!~'

`-2019 = (20 + 19) = (`-**39**)!!!~

(43 + 39) = (`-**82**) = 2(8's) = (`-**88**) = (**35** + **53**)!!!~'

(43 (-) 39) = (`-**4**)!!!~'

(82 (-) 4) = (`-**78**) = **"The `-DEATH # `-NUMBER for (`-2019)"**!!!~'

(`-13) YEAR BATTLE with `-CANCER!!!~'

81

DIED within `-HER (`-**57**ᵗʰ) YEAR of EXISTING!!!~' (`-**57**) = RECIPROCAL = (`-**75**) = **COKIE ROBERTS & DIED the VERY SAME DAY as COKIE ROBERTS!!!~'**

AMERICAN BUSINESS MAGNATE BARRON HILTON (**91**) (BIRTH: OCTOBER **23**, 1927) (DEATH: SEPTEMBER **19**, 2019)

DIED on a (`-**19**) in (`-20**19**)!!!~'

`-**19** = RECIPROCAL = `-**91** = **DAY of `-DEATH (`-19) is the `-RECIPROCAL of `-AGE of `-DEATH (`-91)!!!~'**

DAY of `-DEATH = (9/19/19) = RECIPROCAL-SEQUENCING-NUMEROLOGY-RSN!!!~'

BIRTHDAY # `-NUMBER = (10 + 23 + 19 + 27) = **79**

DEATH/DAY # `-NUMBER = (9 + 19 + 20 + 19) = **67**

DEATH/DAY # NUMBER = (`-**67**) = RECIPROCAL = (`-**76**) = AGE of `-DEATH of `-HIS `-WIFE MARILYN JUNE HAWLEY!!!~'

MARRIED to MARILYN JUNE HAWLEY for (`-**56**) YEARS!!!~' MARRIED from (19**47** to 2004)!!!~'

(79 (-) 67) = (`-**12**) = RECIPROCAL = (`-**21**)!!!~'

(79 + 67) = (`-1**46**) = (46 + 1) = (`-**47**) = RECIPROCAL = (`-**74**)!!!~'

WAS MARRIED in (`-19**47**)!!!~'

HE DIED (`-**34**) DAYS BEFORE HIS NEXT BIRTHDAY!!!~'

(365 (-) 34) = (`-331)!!!~' (31 x 3) = (`-**93**) = RECIPROCAL = (`-**39**)!!!~'

HE DIED AT THE `-AGE of (`-**91**)!!!~'

(91 + 76) = (`-1**67**) = (67 x 1) = (`-**67**) = RECIPROCAL = (`-**76**)!!!~'

OCTOBER 23 = (10 x 23) = (`-230) = (23 + 0) = (`-**23**) = -**a PROPHETIC NUMBER!!!~'**

SEPTEMBER 19 = (9 x 19) = (`-171) = (71 x 1) = (`-**71**)!!!~'

(230 (-) 171) = (`-**59**) = RECIPROCAL = (`-**95**)!!!~'

OCTOBER 23, 1927 = (1 + 0 + 2 + 3 + 1 + 9 + 2 + 7) = (`-**25**)!!!~'

SEPTEMBER 19, 2019 = (9 + 1 + 9 + 2 + 0 + 1 + 9) = (`-**31**) = RECIPROCAL = (`-**13**)!!!~'

(25 + 31) = (`-**56**) = MARRIED to MARILYN JUNE HAWLEY for (`-**56**) YEARS!!!~'

(`-1927) = (19 + 27) = (`-**46**) = (23 x 2) = DAY of `-BIRTH (`-**23**ʳᵈ)!!!~'

(`-2019) = (20 + 19) = (`-**39**)!!!~'

(46 + 39) = (**85**) = (8 + 5) = (`-**13**) = **"A VERY PIVOTAL NUMBER"!!!~'**

(46 (-) 39) = (**7**) = (3 + 4) = (`-**34**) = **HE DIED (`-34) DAYS BEFORE HIS NEXT BIRTHDAY!!!~'**

(85 (-) 7 = (`-**78**) = **"The `-DEATH # `-NUMBER for (`-2019)"!!!~'**

BARRON HILTON'S WIFE MARILYN JUNE HAWLEY (**76**) (BIRTH: FEBRUARY **11**, 1928) (DEATH: MARCH **11**, 2004)

MARRIED to BARRON HILTON for (`-**56**) YEARS!!!~' MARRIED from (19**47** to 2004)!!!~'

WAS `-BORN on an (`-**11**th) & `-DIED on an (`-**11**th)!!!~'

BIRTHDAY # `-NUMBER = (2 + 11 + 19 + 28) = **60**

DEATH/DAY # `-NUMBER = (3 + 11 + 20 + 04) = **38**

AGE OF DEATH (`-**76**) is the `-RECIPROCAL of HER HUSBAND'S DEATH/DAY # `-NUMBER (`-**67**)!!!~'

(60 (-) 38) = (`-**22**) = WAS `-BORN on an (`-**11**<sup>th</sup>) & `-DIED on an (`-**11**<sup>th</sup>)!!!~' (11 + 11) = (`-**22**)!!!~'

(60 + 38) = (`-**98**) = RECIPROCAL = (`-**89**)!!!~'

SHE DIED (`-**28**) DAYS AFTER HER LAST BIRTHDAY!!!~'

(365 (-) 28) = (`-**337**)!!!~' (37 x 3) = (`-**111**)!!!~'

(365 (-) 28) = (`-**337**)!!!~' (33 x 7) = (`-**231**) = (23 x 1) = (`-**23**) = -a **PROPHETIC NUMBER!!!~'**

SHE DIED AT THE `-AGE of (`-**76**)!!!~' (7 + 6) = (`-**13**)!!!~'

FEBRUARY 11 = (2 x 11) = (`-**22**)!!!~'

MARCH 11 = (3 x 11) = (`-**33**)!!!~'

(33 (-) 22) = (`-**11**)!!!~' WAS `-BORN on an (`-**11**<sup>th</sup>) & `-DIED on an (`-**11**th)!!!~'

(22 + 33) = (`-**55**) = (23 + 32) = -**THESE ARE PROPHETIC NUMBERS!!!~'**

FEBRUARY 11, 1928 = (2 + 1 + 1 + 1 + 9 + 2 + 8) = (`-**24**)!!!~'

MARCH 11, 2004 = (3 + 1 + 1 + 2 + 0 + 0 + 4) = (`-**11**)!!!~'

(24 (-) 11) = (`-**13**) = **"A VERY PIVOTAL NUMBER"**!!!~'

(24 + 11) = (`-**35**) = RECIPROCAL = (`-**53**)!!!~'

(`-1928) = (19 + 28) = (`-**47**) = WAS MARRIED in (`-19**47**)!!!~'

YEAR of `-DEATH** = (`-2**00**4**) = (20 + 04) = (`-**24**) = FEBRUARY 11, 1928 = (`-**24**) = `**-HER `-BIRTH!!!~'**

(47 (-) 24) = (`-**23**) = -a **PROPHETIC NUMBER!!!~'**

(47 + 24) = (`-**71**) = **SEPTEMBER 19**th = **HUSBAND'S DAY of `-DEATH!!!~'**

AMERICAN RESTAURATEUR & CELEBRITY CHEF CARL RUIZ (**44**) (BIRTH: **APRIL 4**, 1975) (DEATH: SEPTEMBER 21, 2019)

WAS `-BORN on (4/4) & `-DIED at (`-44) YEARS of `-AGE!!!~'

BIRTHDAY # `-NUMBER = (4 + 4 + 19 + 75) = **102**

DEATH/DAY # `-NUMBER = (9 + 21 + 20 + 19) = **69**

(102 (-) 69) = (`-**33**)!!!~'

(102 + 69) = (`-1**71**) = (71 x 1) = (`-**71**) = RECIPROCAL = (`-**17**) = **BARRON & MARILYN HILTON!!!~'**

HE DIED (`-**17**0) DAYS AFTER HIS LAST BIRTHDAY!!!~' (170 = (17 + 0) = (`-**17**))!!!~'

(365 (-) 170) = (`-**195**)!!!~' (19 x 5) = (`-**95**) = RECIPROCAL = (`-**59**)!!!~'

HE DIED AT THE `-AGE of (`-**44**)!!!~'

APRIL 4 = (4 x 4) = (`-**16**) = RECIPROCAL = (`-**61**)!!!~'

(61 (-) 16) = (`-**45**) = RECIPROCAL = (`-**54**)!!!~'

SEPTEMBER 21 = (9 x 21) = (`-**189**) = (89 + 1) = (`-**90**)!!!~'

(189 (-) 16) = (`-**173**) = (73 + 1) = (`-**74**) = RECIPROCAL = (`-**47**)!!!~'

APRIL 4, 1975 = (4 + 4 + 1 + 9 + 7 + 5) = (`-**30**)!!!~'

SEPTEMBER 21, 2019 = (9 + 2 + 1 + 2 + 0 + 1 + 9) = (`-**24**) = FEBRUARY 11, 1928 = (`-**24**) = MARILYN JUNE HAWLEY'S BIRTHDAY!!!~'

(30 + 24) = (`-**54**) = RECIPROCAL = (`-**45**)!!!~'

(`-1975) = (75 (-) 19) = (`-**56**)!!!~' BARRON & MARILYN JUNE HAWLEY HILTON were MARRIED for (`-**56**) YEARS!!!~'

(`-2019) = (20 + 19) = (`-**39**)!!!~'

(56 + 39) = (`-**95**) = RECIPROCAL = (`-**59**) = (`-1**95**) **DAYS from NEXT `-BIRTHDAY in `-DEATH!!!~'**

(56 (-) 39) = (`-**17**)!!!~'

(95 (-) 17) = (`-**78**) = **"The `-DEATH # `-NUMBER for (`-2019)"**!!!~'

AMERICAN SINGER/SONGWRITER ROBERT HUNTER LYRICIST FOR "THE GRATEFUL DEAD" (**78**) (BIRTH: JUNE 23, 1941) (DEATH: SEPTEMBER 23, 2019)

BORN on a (`-**23**$^{RD}$); and, **DIED** on a (`-**23**RD)!!!~'

BIRTHDAY # `-NUMBER = (6 + 23 + 19 + 41) = **89**

DEATH/DAY # `-NUMBER = (9 + 23 + 20 + 19) = **71**

(89 (-) 71) = (`-**18**) = RECIPROCAL = (`-**81**)!!!~'

(89 + 71) = (`-**16**0) = (60 + 1) = (`-**61**) = RECIPROCAL = (`-**16**)!!!~'

HE DIED (`-**92**) DAYS AFTER HIS LAST BIRTHDAY!!!~' (`-**92**) = (**23** x **4**)!!!~'

(365 (-) 92) = (`-**273**)!!!~' (73 x 2) = (`-**146**) = (46 X 1) = (`-**46**) = (**23** x **2**)!!!~'

(365 (-) 92) = (`-**273**)!!!~' (27 x 3) = (`-**81**)!!!~'

HE DIED AT THE `-AGE of (`-**78**)!!!~' (7 X 8) – (`-**56**)!!!~'

JUNE 23 = (6 x 23) = (`-**138**) = (38 X 1) = (`-**38**) = **"A DEATH # `-NUMBER"**!!!~' (`-38) = **RECIPROCAL = (`-83)**!!!~'

(83 (-) 38) = (`-**45**) = RECIPROCAL = (`-**54**)!!!~'

SEPTEMBER 23 = (9 x 23) = (`-**207**) = (27 + 0) = (`-**27**) = RECIPROCAL = (`-**72**)!!!~'

(207 (-) 138) = (`-**69**) = (**23** x **3**)!!!~'

JUNE 23, 1941 = (6 + 2 + 3 + 1 + 9 + 4 + 1) = (`-**26**)!!!~'

SEPTEMBER 23, 2019 = (9 + 2 + 3 + 2 + 0 + 1 + 9) = (`-**26**)!!!~'

JUNE 23, 1941 (`-**26**) = SEPTEMBER 23, 2019 (`-**26**) (**!!!**)~'

`-**BORN** on a (`-**26**) & `-**DIED** on a (`-**26**)!!!~'

(26 + 26) = (`-**52**) = RECIPROCAL = (`-**25**)!!!~'

(`-1941) = (41 + 19) = (`-**60**)!!!~'

(`-2019) = (20 + 19) = (`-**39**)!!!~'

(60 + 39) = (`-**99**)!!!~'

(60 (-) 39) = (`-**21**)!!!~'

(99 (-) 21 = (`-**78**) = `-**AGE** of `-**DEATH** of **AMERICAN SINGER/ SONGWRITER ROBERT HUNTER LYRICIST FOR "THE GRATEFUL DEAD"!!!~'**

((`-**23**) x (**1,2,3,4**)) = **PROPHETIC-LINEAR-PROGRESSION-PLP** = (`-**23**), (`-**46**), (`-**69**), (`-**92**) = `-**PROPHETIC NUMBERS!!!~'**

FORMER PRESIDENT OF FRANCE JACQUES CHIRAC (86) (BIRTH: NOVEMBER 29, 1932) (DEATH: SEPTEMBER 26, 2019)

BIRTHDAY # `-NUMBER = (11 + 29 + 19 + 32) = **91**

DEATH/DAY # `-NUMBER = (9 + 26 + 20 + 19) = **74** = **"INDEPENDENCE DAY"!!!~'**

(91 (-) 74) = (`-**17**) = RECIPROCAL = (`-**71**)!!!~'

(91 + 74) = (`-**165**) = (65 x 1) = (`-**65**) = RECIPROCAL = (`-**56**)**!!!~'**

HE DIED (`-**64**) DAYS BEFORE HIS NEXT BIRTHDAY!!!~'
(`-**64**) = RECIPROCAL = (`-**46**)!!!~'

(365 (-) 64) = (`-**301**)!!!~' (30 +1) = (`-**31**) = RECIPROCAL = (`-**13**)!!!~'

HE DIED AT THE `-AGE of (`-**86**)!!!~' (8 X 6) = (`-**48**)!!!~'

NOVEMBER 29 = (11 x 29) = (`-**319**) = (19 X 3) = (`-**57**) = RECIPROCAL = (`-**75**)!!!~'

(57 + 75) = (`-**132**) = (32 X 1) = (`-**32**) = "YEAR JACQUES CHIRAC WAS `-BORN" (`-**32**) = **-a PROPHET NUMBER!!!!~'**

SEPTEMBER 26 = (9 x 26) = (`-**234**) = (34 X 2) = (`-**68**) = RECIPROCAL = (`-**86**) = **`-AGE of `-DEATH of JACQUES CHIRAC (`-86)!!!~'**

(319 (-) 234) = (`-**85**) = RECIPROCAL = (`-**58**)!!!~'

NOVEMBER 29, 1932 = (1 + 1 + 2 + 9 + 1 + 9 + 3 + 2) = (`-**28**)!!!~'

SEPTEMBER 26, 2019 = (9 + 2 + 6 + 2 + 0 + 1 + 9) = (`-**29**)!!!~'

(28 + 29) = (`-**57**) = RECIPROCAL = (`-**75**)!!!~'

(`-1932) = (19 + 32) = (`-**51**)!!!~'

(`-2019) = (20 + 19) = (`-**39**)!!!~'

(51 + 39) = (`-**90**)!!!~'

(51 (-) 39) = (`-**12**)!!!~'

(90 (-) 12 = (`-**78**) = `-**AGE** of `-**DEATH** of **AMERICAN SINGER/ SONGWRITER ROBERT HUNTER LYRICIST FOR "THE GRATEFUL DEAD"**!!!~'

(1129 (-) 926) = (`-**203**) = (23 + 0) = (`-**23**) = RECIPROCAL = (`-**32**) = **"YEAR JACQUES CHIRAC WAS `-BORN"** (`-19**32**) = -**a PROPHET NUMBER**!!!!~'

AMERICAN DIPLOMAT AMBASSADOR JOSEPH C. WILSON (**69**) (BIRTH: NOVEMBER 6, 1949) (DEATH: SEPTEMBER 27, 2019)

BIRTHDAY # `-NUMBER = (11 + 6 + 19 + 49) = **85**

DEATH/DAY # `-NUMBER = (9 + 27 + 20 + 19) = **75**

(85 (-) 75) = (`-**10**) = RECIPROCAL = (`-**01**)!!!~'

(85 + 75) = (`-**160**) = (60 + 1) = (`-**61**) = RECIPROCAL = (`-**16**)!!!~'

HE DIED (`-**40**) DAYS BEFORE HIS NEXT BIRTHDAY!!!~'
(`-**40**) = RECIPROCAL = (`-**04**)!!!~'

(365 (-) 40) = (`-**325**)!!!~' (32 x 5) = (`-**160**) = (16 + 0) = (`-**16**) = RECIPROCAL = (`-**61**)!!!~'

HE DIED AT THE `-AGE of (`-**69**)!!!~' (6 X 9) = (`-**54**)!!!~' (`-**54**) = RECIPROCAL = (`-**45**) = **MARRIED for (`-45) YEARS!!!~'**

NOVEMBER 6 = (11 x 6) = (`-**66**)!!!~'

SEPTEMBER 27 = (9 x 27) = (`-**243**) = (24 X 3) = (`-**72**) = RECIPROCAL = (`-**27**)!!!~'

SEPTEMBER 27 = (9 x 27) = (`-**243**) = (43 X 2) = (`-**86**) = `-**AGE of `-DEATH of JACQUES CHIRAC (`-86**)!!!~'

(243 (-) 66) = (`-**177**) = (77 X 1) = (`-**77**) = 2(7's) = (`-**27**)!!!~'

NOVEMBER 6, 1949 = (1 + 1 + 6 + 1 + 9 + 4 + 9) = (`-**31**)!!!~'

SEPTEMBER 27, 2019 = (9 + 2 + 7 + 2 + 0 + 1 + 9) = (`-**30**)!!!~'

(31 + 30) = (`-**61**) = RECIPROCAL = (`-**16**)!!!~'

(`-1949) = (49 (-) 19) = (`-**30**) = `-**DEATH DAY = SEPTEMBER 27, 2019!!!~'**

(`-1949) = (49 + 19) = (`-**68**) = RECIPROCAL = (`-**86**) = `-**AGE of `-DEATH of JACQUES CHIRAC (`-86**)!!!~'

(`-2019) = (20 + 19) = (`-**39**)!!!~'

(30 + 39) = (`-**69**) = `-**AGE of `-DEATH of AMERICAN DIPLOMAT AMBASSADOR JOSEPH C. WILSON (`-69**)!!!~'

(39 (-) 30) = (`-**9**)!!!~'

(69 + 9) = (`-**78**) = `-**AGE** of `-**DEATH** of **AMERICAN SINGER/ SONGWRITER ROBERT HUNTER LYRICIST FOR "THE GRATEFUL DEAD"!!!~'**

(927 (-) 116) = (`-**811**) = **TWO DAYS AWAY from WIFE VALERIE PLAME'S BIRTHDAY of (8/13)!!!**~'

VALERIE PLAME (AUGUST 13, 1963) (56) = (`-13) YEARS YOUNGER THAN SPOUSE AMERICAN DIPLOMAT AMBASSADOR JOSEPH C. WILSON!!!~'

AUGUST 13, 1963 = (8 + 13 + 19 + 63) = (`-103) = (13 + 0) = (`-13) = "A VERY PIVOTAL NUMBER"!!!~'

AUGUST 13, 1963 = (8 + 1 + 3 + 1 + 9 + 6 + 3) = (`-31) = RECIPROCAL = (`-13)!!!~'

(1963) = (63 + 19) = (`-82) = (`-8(1 + 1)) = (`-811)!!!~'

`-12 = RECIPROCAL = `-21!!!~'

MARRIED to VALERIE PLAME for (`-21) YEARS (1998 - 2019)!!!~'

MARRIED to JACQUELINE WILSON for (`-12) YEARS (1986 - 1998)!!!~'

MARRIED to SUSAN OTCHIS WILSON for (`-12) YEARS (1974 - 1986)!!!~'

(98 / 2) = (`-49) = `-BIRTH/YEAR of AMERICAN DIPLOMAT AMBASSADOR JOSEPH C. WILSON!!!~'

INTERNATIONAL OPERA STAR JESSYE NORMAN (**74**) (BIRTH: SEPTEMBER 15, 1945) (DEATH: SEPTEMBER 30, 2019)

BIRTHDAY # `-NUMBER = (9 + 15 + 19 + 45) = **88**

DEATH/DAY # `-NUMBER = (9 + 30 + 20 + 19) = **78**

(88 (-) 78) = (`-**10**) = RECIPROCAL = (`-**01**)!!!~'

(88 + 78) = (`-1**66**) = (66 + 1) = (`-**67**) = RECIPROCAL = (`-**76**)!!!~'

SHE DIED (`-**15**) DAYS AFTER HER LAST BIRTHDAY!!!~'

(365 (-) 15) = (`-350)!!!~' (50 x 3) = (`-150) = (50 + 1) = (`-**51**)!!!~' (`-**15**) = RECIPROCAL = (`-**51**)!!!~'

SHE DIED AT THE `-AGE of (`-**74**)!!!~' (7 + 4) = (`-**11**)!!!~'

SEPTEMBER 15, 1945 = (9 + 1 + 5 + 1 + 9 + 4 + 5) = (`-**34**)!!!~'

SEPTEMBER 30, 2019) = (9 + 3 + 0 + 2 + 0 + 1 + 9) = (`-**24**)!!!~'

(34 + 24) = (`-**58**)!!!~' (5 X 8) = (`-**40**) = RECIPROCAL = (`-**04**)!!!~'

SEPTEMBER 15 = (9 + 15) = (`-**24**) = **`-DEATH/DAY** = SEPTEMBER 30, 2019 (`-**24**)!!!~' (24 + 24) = (`-**48**) = (4 X 8) = (`-**32**) = **-a PROPHETIC NUMBER!!!~'**

SEPTEMBER 15 = (9 X 15) = (`-**135**) = (35 X 1) = (`-**35**) = RECIPROCAL = (`-**53**)!!!~'

SEPTEMBER 30 = (9 + 30) = (`-**39**)!!!~'

SEPTEMBER 30 = (9 X 30) = (`-**270**)!!!~' (27 + 0) = (`-**27**) = RECIPROCAL = (`-**72**)!!!~'

(39 (-) 24) = (`-**15**) = SHE DIED (`-**15**) DAYS AFTER HER LAST BIRTHDAY!!!~'

(39 + 24) = (`-**63**)!!!~'

(135 + 270) = (`-**405**)!!!~'

`-A `-MIRROR `-COPY of AMERICAN TELEVISION HOST & ACTRESS SUZANNNE WHANG!!!~'

(270 (-) 135) = (`-**135**) = (35 X 1) = (`-**35**) = RECIPROCAL = (`-**53**)!!!~'

(405 (-) 135) = (`-**270**) = (27 + 0) = (`-**27**) = RECIPROCAL = (`-**72**)!!!~' (72 + 27) = (`-**99**)!!!~'

(405 (-) 63) = (`-**342**) = (34 X 2) = (`-**68**) = **MARK of the BEAST `-DEATH # `-NUMBER!!!~'**

(405 (-) 63) = (`-**342**) = (42 X 3) = (`-**126**)!!!~'

`-1945 = (45 (-) 19) = (`-**26**)!!!~'

`-2019 = (20 + 19) = (`-**39**)!!!~

(26 + 39) = (`-**65**) = RECIPROCAL = (`-**56**) = **`-AGE of `-DEATH of AMERICAN TELEVISION HOST & ACTRESS SUZANNNE WHANG!!!~'**

(39 (-) 26) = (`-**13**)!!!~'

(65 + 13) = (`-**78**) = **"The `-DEATH # `-NUMBER for (`-2019)"**!!!~'

(930 (-) 915) = (`-**15**) = **SHE DIED (`-15) DAYS AFTER HER LAST BIRTHDAY!!!~'**

ECCLESIASTES 3:2 (-) "a time to be born, and a time to die; a time to plant, and a time to pluck up that which is planted; -(**ENGLISH REVISED EDITION - 1885)-**

"MUFFS" FRONTWOMAN & FORMER PIXIES BASSIST KIM SHATTUCK (**56**) (BIRTH: **JULY 17**, 19**63**) (DEATH: OCTOBER 2, 2019)

BIRTHDAY # `-NUMBER = (7 + 17 + 19 + 63) = **106**

DEATH/DAY # `-NUMBER = (10 + 2 + 20 + 19) = **51**

(106 (-) 51) = (`-**55**)!!!~'

(106 + 51) = (`-1**57**) = (57 (-) 1) = (`-**56**) = `-**AGE of `-DEATH!!!~'**

SHE DIED (`-**77**) DAYS AFTER HER LAST BIRTHDAY!!!~'

(365 (-) 77) = (`-**288**)!!!~' (88 x 2) = (`-**176**) = (76 + 1) = (`-**77**)!!!~'

SHE DIED AT THE `-AGE of (`-**56**)!!!~' (5 + 6) = (`-**11**)!!!~'

JULY 17, 1963 = (7 + 1 + 7 + 1 + 9 + 6 + 3) = (`-**34**)!!!~' (`-**17**) = RECIPROCAL = (`-**71**)!!!~'

OCTOBER 2, 2019) = (1 + 0 + 2 + 2 + 0 + 1 + 9) = (`-**15**)!!!~'

(34 + 15) = (`-**49**)!!!~' (4 X 9) = (`-**36**) = RECIPROCAL = (`-**63**)!!!~' (**7** X **7**) = (`-**49**)!!!~'

JULY 17 = (7 + 17) = (`-**24**)!!!~'

JULY 17 = (7 X 17) = (`-**119**)!!!~'

OCTOBER 2 = (10 + 2) = (`-**12**)!!!~'

OCTOBER 2 = (10 X 2) = (`-**20**)!!!~'

(24 (-) 12) = (`-**12**)!!!~'

(24 + 12) = (`-**36**) = RECIPROCAL = (`-**63**) = `-YEAR of `-BIRTH (`-**63**)!!!~'

(119 + 20) = (`-**139**)!!!~'

(119 (-) 20) = (`-**99**)!!!~'

`-1963 = (63 (-) 19) = (`-**44**)!!!~'

`-2019 = (20 + 19) = (`-**39**)!!!~

(44 + 39) = (`-**83**) = RECIPROCAL = (`-**38**) = "THE `-DEATH # `-NUMBERS"!!!~'

(44 (-) 39) = (`-**5**)!!!~'

(83 (-) 5) = (`-**78**) = "The `-DEATH # `-NUMBER for (`-2019)"!!!~'

(717 (-) 102) = (`-**615**) = (65 x 1) = (`-**65**) = RECIPROCAL = (`-**56**) = `-AGE of `-DEATH of "MUFFS" FRONTWOMAN & FORMER PIXIES BASSIST KIM SHATTUCK!!!~'

NOTICE that `-THEIR `-AGE # `-NUMBERS (5 + 6) `-add up TO `-ELEVEN (`-11)!!!~'

AMERICAN ACTRESS DIAHANN CARROLL (**84**) (BIRTH: **JULY 17, 19<u>35</u>**) (DEATH: OCTOBER 4, 2019)

BIRTHDAY # `-NUMBER = (7 + 17 + 19 + 35) = **78**

DEATH/DAY # `-NUMBER = (10 + 4 + 20 + 19) = **53** = RECIPROCAL = (`-**35**) = **"DEATH/DAY # `-NUMBER `-EQUALS `-RECIPROCAL `-YEAR of `-BIRTH (`-35)"!!!~'**

(78 (-) 53) = (`-**25**) = RECIPROCAL = (`-**52**)!!!~'

(78 + 53) = (`-1**31**) = (31 + 1) = (`-**32**) = RECIPROCAL = (`-**23**)!!!~'

SHE DIED (`-**79**) DAYS AFTER HER LAST BIRTHDAY!!!~'

(365 (-) 79) = (`-**286**)!!!~' (86 x 2) = (`-**172**) = (72 + 1) = (`-**73**) = RECIPROCAL = (`-**37**)!!!~'

SHE DIED AT THE `-AGE of (`-**84**)!!!~' (8 X 4) = (`-**32**) = **-a PROPHETIC NUMBER!!!~'**

JULY 17, 1935 = (7 + 1 + 7 + 1 + 9 + 3 + 5) = (`-**33**)!!!~'

OCTOBER 4, 2019) = (1 + 0 + 4 + 2 + 0 + 1 + 9) = (`-**17**)!!!~'

(33 + 17) = (`-**50**)!!!~'

JULY 17 = (7 + 17) = (`-**24**)!!!~'

JULY 17 = (7 X 17) = (`-**119**)!!!~'

OCTOBER 4 = (10 + 4) = (`-**14**)!!!~'

OCTOBER 4 = (10 X 4) = (`-**40**)!!!~'

(24 (-) 14) = (`-**10**)!!!~'

(24 + 14) = (`-**38**) = RECIPROCAL = (`-**83**) = **"THE `-DEATH # `-NUMBERS"!!!~'**

(119 + 40) = (`-**159**)!!!~'

(119 (-) 40) = (`-**79**)!!!~'

`-1935 = (19 + 35) = (`-**54**)!!!~'

`-2019 = (20 + 19) = (`-**39**)!!!~

(54 + 39) = (`-**93**) = RECIPROCAL = (`-**39**) = (`-**2019**)!!!~'

(717 (-) 104) = (`-**613**) = (63 x 1) = (`-**63**) = `-YEAR of `-BIRTH of **"MUFFS" FRONTWOMAN & FORMER PIXIES BASSIST KIM SHATTUCK (`-63)!!!~'**

AMERICAN ACTRESS DIAHANN CARROLL & "MUFFS" FRONTWOMAN & FORMER PIXIES BASSIST KIM SHATTUCK were `-BOTH `-BORN on `-(7/17)-'!!!~'

CO-FOUNDER & DRUMMER of the MUSICAL GROUP "CREAM" PETER EDWARD "GINGER" BAKER (**80**) (BIRTH: AUGUST 19, 1939) (DEATH: **OCTOBER 6, 2019**)

BIRTHDAY # `-NUMBER = (8 + 19 + 19 + 39) = **85**

DEATH/DAY # `-NUMBER = (10 + 6 + 20 + 19) = **55** = (**23 + 32**)!!!~'

(85 (-) 55) = (`-**30**) = RECIPROCAL = (`-**03**)!!!~'

$(85 + 55) = (`-\underline{\textbf{140}}) = (14 + 0) = (`-\underline{\textbf{14}}) = \text{RECIPROCAL} = (`-\underline{\textbf{41}})$**!!!~'**
$(14 + 41) = (`-\underline{\textbf{55}}) = (\underline{\textbf{32}} + \underline{\textbf{23}})$!!!~'

HE DIED (`-**48**) DAYS AFTER HIS LAST BIRTHDAY!!!~' (`-**48**) = RECIPROCAL = (`-**84**) = **AMERICAN COMEDIAN & ACTOR RIP TAYLOR (`-84)!!!~'**

$(365 \; (\text{-}) \; 48) = (`-\underline{\textbf{317}})$!!!~' $(17 \times 3) = (`-\underline{\textbf{51}}) = \text{RECIPROCAL} = (`-\underline{\textbf{15}})$!!!~'

HE DIED AT THE `-AGE of (`-**80**)!!!~'

AUGUST 19 = $(8 \times 19) = (`-\underline{\textbf{152}}) = (52 + 1) = (`-\underline{\textbf{53}})$!!!~'

OCTOBER 6 = $(10 \times 6) = (`-\underline{\textbf{60}}) = (\text{RECIPROCAL} = (`-\underline{\textbf{06}}))$!!!~'

$(152 \; (\text{-}) \; 60) = (`-\underline{\textbf{92}}) = \text{RECIPROCAL} = (`-\underline{\textbf{29}})$!!!~'

AUGUST 19, 1939 = $(8 + 1 + 9 + 1 + 9 + 3 + 9) = (`-\underline{\textbf{40}})$!!!~'

OCTOBER 6, 2019 = $(1 + 0 + 6 + 2 + 0 + 1 + 9) = (`-\underline{\textbf{19}})$!!!~'

$(40 + 19) = (`-\underline{\textbf{59}}) = \text{RECIPROCAL} = (`-\underline{\textbf{95}})$!!!~'

$(`-1939) = (39 \; (\text{-}) \; 19) = (`-\underline{\textbf{20}})$!!!~'

$(`-2019) = (20 + 19) = (`-\underline{\textbf{39}})$!!!~'

$(20 + 39) = (`-\underline{\textbf{59}}) - \text{RECIPROCAL} - (`-\underline{\textbf{95}})$!!!~'

$(39 \; (\text{-}) \; 20) = (`-\underline{\textbf{19}})$!!!~'

$(59 + 19) = (`-\underline{\textbf{78}}) = $ `-**AGE** of `-**DEATH** of **AMERICAN SINGER/ SONGWRITER ROBERT HUNTER LYRICIST FOR "THE GRATEFUL DEAD"!!!~'**

(819 (-) 106) = (`-**713**) = (71 x 3) = (`-**213**) = (23 x 1) = (`-**23**) = -a **PROPHET NUMBER!!!~'**

(819 (-) 106) = (`-**713**) = RECIPROCAL = (`-**317**) = `-**DEATH `-DAYS `-AWAY FROM `-BIRTHDAY!!!~'**

AMERICAN COMEDIAN & ACTOR RIP TAYLOR (**84**) (BIRTH: JANUARY 13, 1935) (DEATH: **OCTOBER 6, 2019**)

BIRTHDAY # `-NUMBER = (1 + 13 + 19 + 35) = **68** = (6 x 8) = (`-**48**) = **CO-FOUNDER & DRUMMER of the MUSICAL GROUP "CREAM" PETER EDWARD "GINGER" BAKER (`-48)!!!~'**

DEATH/DAY # `-NUMBER = (10 + 6 + 20 + 19) = **55** = (**23** + **32**)!!!~'

(68 (-) 55) = (`-**13**) = **"DAY of `-BIRTH"** = RECIPROCAL = (`-**31**)!!!~'

(68 + 55) = (`-**123**) = (23 x 1) = (`-**23**) = RECIPROCAL = (`-**32**)!!!~'

HE DIED (`-**99**) DAYS BEFORE HIS NEXT BIRTHDAY!!!~'

(365 (-) 99) = (`-**266**)!!!~' (66 x 2) = (`-**132**) = (32 x 1) = (`-**32**) = -a **PROPHETIC NUMBER!!!~'**

HE DIED AT THE `-AGE of (`-**84**)!!!~'

JANUARY 13 = (1 x 13) = (`-**13**) = RECIPROCAL = (`-**31**)!!!~'

OCTOBER 6 = (10 x 6) = (`-**60**) = (RECIPROCAL = (`-**06**)!!!~'

(60 + 13) = (`-**73**) = RECIPROCAL = (`-**37**)!!!~' CO-FOUNDER & DRUMMER of the MUSICAL GROUP "CREAM" PETER EDWARD "GINGER" BAKER (`-**713**) = RECIPROCAL = (`-**317**)!!!~'

(60 (-) 13) = (`-**47**) = RECIPROCAL = (`-**74**)!!!~'

JANUARY 13, 1935 = (1 + 1 + 3 + 1 + 9 + 3 + 5) = (`-**23**)!!!~'

OCTOBER 6, 2019 = (1 + 0 + 6 + 2 + 0 + 1 + 9) = (`-**19**)!!!~'

(23 + 19) = (`-**42**) = RECIPROCAL = (`-**24**)!!!~'

(`-1935) = (35 (-) 19) = (`-**16**)!!!~'

(`-2019) = (20 + 19) = (`-**39**)!!!~'

(16 + 39) = (`-**55**) = (23 + 32)!!!~'

(39 (-) 16) = (`-**23**) = -a PROPHETIC NUMBER!!!~'

(55 + 23) = (`-**78**) = `-**AGE** of `-**DEATH** of **AMERICAN SINGER/ SONGWRITER ROBERT HUNTER LYRICIST FOR "THE GRATEFUL DEAD"!!!~'**

(113 + 106) = (`-**219**) = (19 x 2) = (`-**38**) = **"THE `-DEATH # `-NUMBERS"!!!~'**

GINGER & RIP `-DIED on the very same `-DAY!!!~'

AMERICAN ACTOR ROBERT FORSTER (78) (BIRTH: **JULY 13**, **1941**) (DEATH: OCTOBER 11, 2019)

BIRTHDAY # `-NUMBER = (7 + 13 + 19 + 41) = **80**

DEATH/DAY # `-NUMBER = (10 + 11 + 20 + 19) = **60** = **(19 + 41) = "YEAR OF `-BIRTH OF AMERICAN ACTOR ROBERT FORSTER"!!!~'**

(80 (-) 60) = (`-**20**) = RECIPROCAL = (`-**02**)!!!~'

(80 + 60) = (`-**140**) = (14 + 0) = (`-**14**) = RECIPROCAL = (`-**41**)!!!~'
(14 + 41) = (`-**55**) = (**32** + **23**)!!!~' `-**EQUALS = CO-FOUNDER & DRUMMER of the MUSICAL GROUP "CREAM" PETER EDWARD "GINGER" BAKER WHO `-DIED AT** (`-**80**)!!!~'

HE DIED (`-**90**) DAYS AFTER HIS LAST BIRTHDAY!!!~'

(365 (-) 90) = (`-**275**)!!!~' (75 x 2) = (`-**150**) = RECIPROCAL = (`-**051**)!!!~'

HE DIED AT THE `-AGE of (`-**78**)!!!~' (7 x 8) = (`-**56**)!!!~' (78 x 2) = (`-**156**)!!!~'

JULY 13 = (7 x 13) = (`-**91**) = RECIPROCAL = (`-**19**)!!!~'

OCTOBER 11 = (10 x 11) = (`-**110**) = (RECIPROCAL = (`-**011**)!!!~'

(110 (-) 91) = (`-**19**) = RECIPROCAL = (`-**91**)!!!~'

JULY 13, 1941 = (7 + 1 + 3 + 1 + 9 + 4 + 1) = (`-**26**)!!!~'

OCTOBER 11, 2019 = (1 + 0 + 1 + 1 + 2 + 0 + 1 + 9) = (`-**15**)!!!~'

(26 + 15) = (`-**41**) = `-**YEAR AMERICAN ACTOR ROBERT FORSTER WAS `-BORN!!!~'**

(`-**1941**) = (41 (-) 19) = (`-**22**)!!!~'

(`-2019) = (20 + 19) = (`-**39**)!!!~'

(22 + 39) = (`-**61**) = RECIPROCAL = (`-**16**)!!!~'

(39 (-) 22) = (`-**17**) = RECIPROCAL = (`-**71**)!!!~'

(61 + 17) = (`-**78**) = `-**AGE** of `-**DEATH** of **AMERICAN SINGER/ SONGWRITER ROBERT HUNTER LYRICIST FOR "THE GRATEFUL DEAD" & AMERICAN ACTOR ROBERT FORSTER (`-78)!!!~'**

(1011 (-) **713**) = (`-**298**) = (29 x 8) = (`-**232**) = **RECIPROCAL-SEQUENCING-NUMEROLOGY-RSN!!!~'**

(1011 (-) **713**) = (`-**298**) = (9(-)2) 8) = (`-**78**) = **"AGE of `-DEATH for AMERICAN ACTOR ROBERT FORSTER"!!!~'**

(1011 + 713) = (`-1724) = (17 + 24) = (`-41) = `-YEAR AMERICAN ACTOR ROBERT FORSTER WAS `-BORN (`-41)!!!~'

(`-713) = CO-FOUNDER & DRUMMER of the MUSICAL GROUP "CREAM" PETER EDWARD "GINGER" BAKER (`-713)!!!~'

IF A OUIJA BOARD CAN `-CONTROL `-YOU; THEN YOU CAN BE CONTROLLED BY THE `-DEMONS & `-SATAN!!!~' IF THEY CAN `-CONTROL YOU; THEN HOW ARE YOU MAKING DECISIONS ON YOUR OWN FOR WHAT YOU YOURSELF WILL BE JUDGED HEAVILY AGAINST & FOR!!!~' WOULD THAT TRULY BE A JUST & DUE DILIGENT

ARRANGEMENT OF AFFAIRS FOR A CLEAR & PRESENT JUDGEMENT `-DAY???~' **WOULD THAT BE `-FAIR!!!~'**

SOUTH KOREAN SINGER-SONGWRITER "SULLI" (CHOI JIN-RI) (**25**) (BIRTH: MARCH 29, 1994) (DEATH: OCTOBER 14, 2019)

BIRTHDAY # `-NUMBER = (3 + 29 + 19 + 94) = **145**

DEATH/DAY # `-NUMBER = (10 + 14 + 20 + 19) = **63**

(145 (-) 63) = (`-**82**)!!!~'

(145 + 63) = (`-**208**) = (28 + 0) = (`-**28**) = RECIPROCAL = (`-**82**)!!!~'

SHE DIED (`-**166**) DAYS BEFORE HER NEXT BIRTHDAY!!!~'

(365 (-) 166) = (`-**199**)!!!~' (99 x 1) = (`-**99**)!!!~'

SHE DIED AT THE `-AGE of (`-**25**)!!!~'

MARCH 29, 1994 = (3 + 2 + 9 + 1 + 9 + 9 + 4) = (`-**37**)!!!~' (`-**37**) = RECIPROCAL = (`-**73**)!!!~'

OCTOBER 14, 2019) = (1 + 0 + 1 + 4 + 2 + 0 + 1 + 9) = (`-**18**)!!!~'

(37 + 18) = (`-**55**)!!!~' (5 X 5) = (`-**25**) = `-**AGE of `-DEATH for SOUTH KOREAN SINGER-SONGWRITER "SULLI" (CHOI JIN-RI)** (`-**25**)!!!~'

MARCH 29 = (3 + 29) = (`-**32**) = -a **PROPHETIC NUMBER!!!~'**

MARCH 29 = (3 X 29) = (`-**87**)!!!~' (8 X 7) = (`-**56**)!!!~'

OCTOBER 14 = (10 + 14) = (`-**24**)!!!~'

OCTOBER 14 = (10 X 14) = (`-**140**)!!!~'

(32 (-) 24) = (`-**8**)!!!~'

(32 + 24) = (`-**56**) = RECIPROCAL = (`-**65**)!!!~' **(BIRTH) (MARCH 29) + (DEATH) (OCTOBER 14) = (3 + 29 + 10 + 14) = (`-56)!!!~'**

(140 + 87) = (`-**227**)!!!~' (27 (-) 2) = (`-**25**) = `-**AGE of `-DEATH for SOUTH KOREAN SINGER-SONGWRITER "SULLI" (CHOI JIN-RI) (`-25)!!!~'**

(140 (-) 87) = (`-**53**)!!!~'

`-1994 = (94 + 19) = (`-**113**)!!!~'

(113 (-) 39) = (`-74) = **"INDEPENDENCE DAY"!!!~'**

`-1994 = (94 (-) 19) = (`-**75**)!!!~' (`-**75**) = RECIPROCAL = (`-**57**) = `-**HEIGHT was (`-5' 7")!!!~'**

`-2019 = (20 + 19) = (`-**39**)!!!~

(75 + 39) = (`-**114**)!!!~' **ADD a `-ZERO (1014) = `-DAY of `-DEATH for SOUTH KOREAN SINGER-SONGWRITER "SULLI" (CHOI JIN-RI)!!!~'**

(75 (-) 39) = (`-**36**) = RECIPROCAL = (`-**63**)!!!~' (36 + 63) = (`-**99**)!!!~' **DIED (`-199) DAYS AWAY from BIRTHDAY!!!~' (`-63) = `-DEATH/DAY # `-NUMBER!!!~'**

(114 (-) 36) = (`-**78**) = **"The `-DEATH # `-NUMBER for (`-2019)"!!!~'**

105

(1014 (-) 329) = (`-**685**) = (68 x 5) = (`-**340**)!!!~'

(1014 + 329) = (`-**1343**) = 1(343) = (343 X 1) = (`-**343**) = **RECIPROCAL-SEQUENCING-NUMEROLOGY-RSN!!!~'**

DO `-YOU EVER HAVE `-IT TO WHERE `-YOU JUST CAN'T REMEMBER SOMETHING; AND, THEN AFTER A WHILE `-IT JUST COMES TO `-YOU!!!~' WHERE DO YOU THINK THAT COMES `-FROM!!!~'

U.S. REPRESENTATIVE ELIJAH CUMMINGS (**68**) (BIRTH: JANUARY 18, 1951) (DEATH: OCTOBER 17, 2019)

BIRTHDAY # `-NUMBER = (1 + 18 + 19 + 51) = **89**

DEATH/DAY # `-NUMBER = (10 + 17 + 20 + 19) = **66**

(89 (-) 66) = (`-**23**) = -a **PROPHETIC NUMBER!!!~'**

(89 + 66) = (`-**155**) = (55 + 1) = (`-**56**) = RECIPROCAL = (`-**65**)!!!~'

HE DIED (`-**93**) DAYS BEFORE HIS NEXT BIRTHDAY!!!~'

CAN ANYONE `-SEE the `-PATTERN of `-PRESIDENTS & `-GOVERNMENT `-OFFICIALS `-HERE!!!~'

(365 (-) 93) = (`-**272**)!!!~' (72 + 2) = (`-**74**) = **INDEPENDENCE DAY!!!~'**

HE DIED AT THE `-AGE of (`-**68**)!!!~' (6 x 8) = (`-**48**) = RECIPROCAL = (`-**84**)!!!~'

NEW BOOK /||\ REAL MESSAGES OF `-GOD I, II; & III-!!!~' /||\

JANUARY 18 = (1 x 18) = (`-**18**) = RECIPROCAL = (`-**81**)!!!~'

OCTOBER 17 = (10 x 17) = (`-**170**) = (RECIPROCAL = (`-**071**)!!!~'

(170 (-) 18) = (`-**152**) = (52 + 1) = (`-**53**) = **"WAR of the `-WORLDS"!!!~'**

JANUARY 18, 1951 = (1 + 1 + 8 + 1 + 9 + 5 + 1) = (`-**26**)!!!~'
EQUALS = AMERICAN ACTOR ROBERT FORSTER (`-**78**)
= **JULY 13**, 1941 = (7 + 1 + 3 + 1 + 9 + 4 + 1) = (`-**26**)!!!~' (26 + 26 + 26) = (`-**78**)!!!~'

(`-713) = CO-FOUNDER & DRUMMER of the MUSICAL GROUP "CREAM" PETER EDWARD "GINGER" BAKER** (`-713**)!!!~'

OCTOBER 17, 2019 = (1 + 0 + 1 + 7 + 2 + 0 + 1 + 9) = (`-**21**)!!!~'

(26 + 21) = (`-**47**) = RECIPROCAL = (`-**74**) = **INDEPENDENCE DAY!!!~'**

(`-1951) = (51 (-) 19) = (`-**32**) = **-a PROPHETIC NUMBER!!!~'**

(`-2019) = (20 + 19) = (`-**39**)!!!~'

(32 + 39) = (`-**71**) = RECIPROCAL = (`-**17**) = **`-DAY of `-DEATH** (`-**17**)**!!!~'**

(39 (-) 32) = (`-**7**)!!!~'

(71 + 7) = (`-**78**) = **`-AGE of `-DEATH of AMERICAN SINGER/ SONGWRITER ROBERT HUNTER LYRICIST FOR "THE GRATEFUL DEAD" & AMERICAN ACTOR ROBERT FORSTER** (`-**78**)**!!!~'**

(1017 + <u>118</u>) = (`-1135) = (11 + 35) = (`-<u>46</u>) = (23 x 2)!!!~'

(1017 (-) <u>118</u>) = (`-<u>899</u>) = (89 x 9) = (`-<u>801</u>) = (81 + 0) = (`-<u>81</u>) = RECIPROCAL = (`-<u>18</u>)!!!~'

(`-<u>89</u>) = BIRTHDAY # `-NUMBER!!!~'

(1017) = (17 + 1 + 0) = (`-<u>18</u>)!!!~'

(1017 / 118) = (0 + (7 x 1 x 1) = (`-<u>7</u>) / (8 x 1 x 1) = (`-<u>8</u>) / = (`-<u>78</u>) = AMERICAN ACTOR ROBERT FORSTER (`-<u>78</u>)!!!~'

U.S. REPRESENTATIVE ELIJAH CUMMINGS SERVED AS A DEMOCRAT FOR MARYLAND'S (7th CONGRESSIONAL DISTRICT) for (`-<u>23</u>) YEARS; SINCE, 19<u>96</u>!!!~' (`-<u>96</u>) = RECIPROCAL = (`-<u>69</u>)!!!~'

(<u>1017</u>) OCTOBER 17th / 19<u>89</u> LOMA PRIETA EARTHQUAKE!!!~'

(<u>1017</u>) = (10 + 17) = (`-<u>27</u>) = RECIPROCAL = (`-<u>72</u>)!!!~'

(`-<u>89</u>) = (8 x 9) = (`-<u>72</u>) = (`-19<u>06</u>) / `-EARTHQUAKE of SAN FRANCISCO!!!~'

LOMA PRIETA MAGNITUDE = (`-<u>6.9</u>)!!!~' MW (<u>6.9</u>).MS (<u>7.2</u>)!!!~' (`-<u>6.9</u>) MAGNITUDE `-HIT the `-HAYWARD `-FAULT in (`-18<u>68</u>)!!!~' (68 + 18) = (`-<u>86</u>)!!!~' THE "PROPHET'S" (DWAYNE W. ANDERSON'S) GRANDFATHER was BORN in / (`-19<u>06</u>) / `-EARTHQUAKE of SAN FRANCISCO (`-<u>7.9</u>) MAGNITUDE (`-<u>5.12</u>AM) (APRIL 18th)!!!~'

(`-<u>5.12</u>) = (12 x 5) = (`-<u>60</u>) / APRIL 18th = (4 x 18) = (`-<u>72</u>)

(60 + 72) = (`-**132**) = (32 x 1) = (`-32) = **-a PROPHETIC NUMBER!!!~'**

(`-**7**.**9**) = (7 x 9) = (`-**63**)!!!~'

NORTHRIDGE EARTHQUAKE (`-**94**) = (9 x 4) = (`-**36**) = RECIPROCAL = (`-**63**)!!!~'

(**04**.**18**.19.**06**) = (04 + 18 + 19 + 06) = (`-**47**) = (`-**1906**) **SAN FRANCISCO # `-NUMBER!!!~'** (47 + 47) = (`-**94**) = **NORTHRIDGE EARTHQUAKE!!!~'**

LOMA PRIETA (`-**5**:0**4**PM) PST/ (`-**63**) **KILLED!!!~'**

(`-**6**.**9**) MAGNITUDE = (6 x 9) = (`-**54**) = (`-**5**:0**4**PM) **PST!!!~'**

(`-**3757**) `-INJURED!!!~' (37 + 57) = (`-**94**) = **NORTHRIDGE EARTHQUAKE!!!~'**

SAN FRANCISCO BAY AREA!!!~'

THE `-PROPHET (**DWAYNE W. ANDERSON**) WAS CALLED OFF OF HIS JOB; AND, WAS ASSIGNED FOR DISASTER RECOVERY THAT VERY EVENING SOON AFTER THE EARTHQUAKE TRAVELING IN PITCH BLACK DARKNESS BY VEHICLE OVER CRATERS & ELEVATED DROP CHANGES WITHIN AND FROM THESE ASPHALT ROADS!!!~' THE `-PROPHET WAS THERE IN SANTA CRUZ, WATSONVILLE, HOLLISTER FOR (`-3) MONTHS STRAIGHT!!!~'

(`-**10**) = **RECIPRICAL** = (`-**01**)!!!~'

LOMA PRIETA **_RECIPROCAL_** (**0117**) **JANUARY** 17th / 19**94**
NORTHRIDGE EARTHQUAKE!!!~'

MAGNITUDE = (`-**6.7**)!!!~' (`-6.9) + (`-6.7) = (`-**13.6**) = (36 x 1) =
(`-**36**) = RECIPROCAL = (`-**63**)!!!~' LOMA PRIETA (`-**5**:0**4**PM)
/ (`-**63**) **KILLED!!!**~'

NORTHRIDGE (`-**8700**) `-INJURED!!!~' (87 + 0 + 0) = (`-**87**) =
(8 x 7) = (`-56)!!!~'

NORTHRIDGE (`-**4**:**30**:**55**AM) **PST**/ (`-**57**) **KILLED!!!**~' (`-**57**)
= (5 x 7) = (`-**35**)!!!~'

TIME of `-NORTHRIDGE = (4 + 30 + 55) = (`-**89**) = **LOMA
PRIETA EARTHQUAKE!!!**~'

(**10.17.20.19**) = (10 + 17 + 20 + 19) = (`-**66**) = **TODAY'S #**
`-**NUMBER!!!**~'

(35 + 31) = (`-**66**)!!!~'

LOMA PRIETA (`-**5**:0**4**PM) = (5 + 4 + 0) = (`-**9**)!!!~' PLUS (+) (`-
89) = (`-**98**)!!!~'

(98 + 89) = (`-**187**) = (87 x 1) = (`-**87**) = (`-**8700**) **INJURED at
NORTHRIDGE EARTHQUAKE!!!**~'

(`-**89**) = RECIPROCAL = (`-**98**)!!!~'

(**10.17.**19.**89**) = (10 + 17 + 19 + 89) = (`-**135**) = **LOMA PRIETA #**
`-**NUMBER!!!**~'

(**01.17.**19.**94**) = (01 + 17 + 19 + 94) = (`-**131**) = **NORTHRIDGE #**
`-**NUMBER!!!**~'

(135 + 131) = (`-**266**)!!!~'

(`-**266**) = (26 x 6) = (`-**156**) = (56 + 1) = (`-57) `-KILLED!!!~'

(`-**266**) = (66 x 2) = (`-**132**) = (32 x 1) = (`-32) = -a PROPHETIC NUMBER!!!~'

(`-**266**) = (26 + 6) = (`-**32**) = -a PROPHETIC NUMBER!!!~'

(`-**266**) = (66 + 2) = (`-**68**) = "THE `-MARK of the `-BEAST"!!!~'

THE SAN FERNANDO VALLEY REGION OF THE COUNTY OF LOS ANGELES!!!~'

THE `-PROPHET (**DWAYNE W. ANDERSON**) WAS CALLED OFF OF HIS JOB; AND, WAS ASSIGNED FOR DISASTER RECOVERY THAT VERY EVENING SOON AFTER THE EARTHQUAKE!!!~' THE `-PROPHET WAS THERE IN NORTHRIDGE FOR (`-3) MONTHS STRAIGHT JUST AS WELL!!!~'

LOMA PRIETA **(10/17)** to NORTHRIDGE **(01/17)** = (`-**92**) DAYS IN-BETWEEN!!!~'

NORTHRIDGE **(01/17)** to (`-**1906**) SAN FRANCISCO **(04/18)** = (`-**91**) DAYS IN-BETWEEN!!!~' **LEAP YEAR (`-INCLUDED + 1)** = (`-**92**)!!!~'

(92 + 92) = (`-**184**) = **RECIPROCAL (SWIPE 1) – (418)** = (`-**1906** SAN FRANCISCO **(4/18)** EARTHQUAKE!!!~'

MARK V. HURD / AMERICAN BUSINESSMAN WHO SERVED AS CO-CEO & AS A MEMBER OF THE BOARD

OF DIRECTORS FOR THE **"ORACLE"** CORPORATION (**62**) (BIRTH: JANUARY 01, 1957) (DEATH: OCTOBER 18, 2019)

BIRTHDAY # `-NUMBER = (1 + 1 + 19 + 57) = **78**

DEATH/DAY # `-NUMBER = (10 + 18 + 20 + 19) = **67**

(`-**1957**) = (57 + 19) = (`-**76**) = RECIPROCAL = (`-**67**) = `-**DEATH/ DAY # `-NUMBER!!!~'**

(78 (-) 67) = (`-**11**)**!!!~'**

(78 + 67) = (`-**145**) = (45 + 1) = (`-**46**) = RECIPROCAL = (`-**64**)**!!!~'**

HE DIED (`-**75**) DAYS BEFORE HIS NEXT BIRTHDAY!!!~'

(365 (-) 75) = (`-**290**)!!!~' (90 x 2) = (`-**180**)**!!!~'**

HE DIED AT THE `-AGE of (`-**62**)!!!~' (`-**62**) = RECIPROCAL = (`-**26**) = (**"EARTHQUAKES"**)**!!!~'**

JANUARY 1 = (1 x 1) = (`-**1**)!!!~'

OCTOBER 18 = (10 x 18) = (`-**180**) = (RECIPROCAL = (`-**081**)!!!~'

(180 (-) 1) = (`-**179**) = (79 (-) 1) = (`-**78**) = `-**BIRTHDAY # `-NUMBER!!!~'**

JANUARY 1, 1957 = (1 + 1 + 1 + 9 + 5 + 7) = (`-**24**)!!!~'

OCTOBER 18, 2019 = (1 + 0 + 1 + 8 + 2 + 0 + 1 + 9) = (`-**22**)!!!~'

(24 + 22) = (`-**46**) = RECIPROCAL = (`-**64**)**!!!~'**

(`-1957) = (57 (-) 19) = (`-**38**)**!!!~'**

(`-2019) = (20 + 19) = (`-**39**)!!!~'

(38 + 39) = (`-**77**)!!!~'(39 (-) 38) = (`-**1**)!!!~'

(77 + 1) = (`-**78**) = **EQUALS `-BIRTHDAY # `-NUMBER & `-<u>AGE</u> of `-<u>DEATH</u> of AMERICAN SINGER/SONGWRITER ROBERT HUNTER LYRICIST FOR "THE GRATEFUL DEAD" & AMERICAN ACTOR ROBERT FORSTER (`-<u>78</u>)!!!~'**

(1018 + <u>11</u>) = (`-1029) = (10 + 29) = (`-<u>39</u>) = (20 + 19) = (`-2019)!!!~'

(1018 (-) <u>11</u>) = (`-<u>1007</u>) = (10 + 07) = (`-<u>17</u>) = RECIPROCAL = (`-<u>71</u>)!!!~'

(1018) = (18 x 1 + 0) = (`-<u>18</u>)!!!~'

(1018 / 11) = (0 + 8 x 1 x 1) = (`-<u>8</u>) / (1 x 1) = (`-<u>1</u>) / = (`-<u>81</u>)!!!~'

(`-<u>78</u>) = "NOW; A `-DEATH # `-NUMBER!!!~'

THOMAS L. J. D'ALESANDRO III FORMER MAYOR & BROTHER OF NANCY PELOSI (SPEAKER OF THE HOUSE) (90) (BIRTH: JULY 24, 1929) (DEATH: OCTOBER 20, 2019)

BIRTHDAY # `-NUMBER = (7 + 24 + 19 + 29) = **<u>79</u>** = **EARTHQUAKE!!!~'**

DEATH/DAY # `-NUMBER = (10 + 20 + 20 + 19) = **<u>69</u>** = **EARTHQUAKE!!!~'**

(79 (-) 69) = (`-**<u>10</u>**)!!!~'

(79 + 69) = (`-**<u>148</u>**) = (48 + 1) = (`-**<u>49</u>**) = RECIPROCAL = (`-**<u>94</u>**)!!!~'

HE DIED (`-**88**) DAYS AFTER HIS LAST BIRTHDAY!!!~'

(365 (-) 88) = (`-**277**)!!!~' (77 x 2) = (`-**154**) = (54 x 1) = (`-**54**) = **EARTHQUAKE!!!~'**

HE DIED AT THE `-AGE of (`-**90**)!!!~'

JULY 24 = (7 x 24) = (`-**168**)!!!~'

OCTOBER 20 = (10 x 20) = (`-**200**)!!!~'

(200 (-) 168) = (`-**32**) = -a **PROPHETIC NUMBER!!!~'**

JULY 24, 1929 = (7 + 2 + 4 + 1 + 9 + 2 + 9) = (`-**34**)!!!~'

OCTOBER 20, 2019 = (1 + 0 + 2 + 0 + 2 + 0 + 1 + 9) = (`-**15**)!!!~'

(34 + 15) = (`-**49**) = RECIPROCAL = (`-**94**)**!!!~'**

(`-1929) = (29 + 19) = (`-**48**)**!!!~'**

(`-2019) = (20 + 19) = (`-**39**)!!!~'

(48 + 39) = (`-**87**) = RECIPROCAL = (`-**78**) = `-**AGE** of `-**DEATH** of **AMERICAN SINGER/SONGWRITER ROBERT HUNTER LYRICIST FOR "THE GRATEFUL DEAD" & AMERICAN ACTOR ROBERT FORSTER (`-78)!!!~'**

(48 (-) 39) = (`-**9**)!!!~'

(87 (-) 9) = (`-**78**) = `-**AGE** of `-**DEATH** of **AMERICAN SINGER/SONGWRITER ROBERT HUNTER LYRICIST FOR "THE GRATEFUL DEAD" & AMERICAN ACTOR ROBERT FORSTER (`-78)!!!~' !!!~'**

(1020 + **724**) = (`-1744) = (44 (-) 17) = (`-**27**)!!!~'

(1020 (-) **724**) = (`-**296**) = (29 x 6) = (`-**174**) = (74 x 1) = (`-74) = **INDEPENDENCE DAY!!!~'**

(74 (-) 27) = (`-47) = **RECIPROCAL** = (`-74) = **INDEPENDENCE DAY!!!~'**

MAJOR LEAGUE BASEBALL (MLB) UMPIRE ERIC COOPER (52) (BIRTH: DECEMBER 18, 1966) (DEATH: OCTOBER 20, 2019)

BIRTHDAY # `-NUMBER = (12 + 18 + 19 + 66) = **115**

DEATH/DAY # `-NUMBER = (10 + 20 + 20 + 19) = **69** = **EARTHQUAKE!!!~'**

(115 (-) 69) = (`-**46**) = RECIPROCAL = (`-**64**)!!!~'

(115 + 69) = (`-**184**) = (84 x 1) = (`-**84**) = RECIPROCAL = (`-**48**) = **THOMAS L. J. D'ALESANDRO III FORMER MAYOR & BROTHER OF NANCY PELOSI (SPEAKER OF THE HOUSE)!!!~'**

HE DIED (`-**59**) DAYS BEFORE HIS NEXT BIRTHDAY!!!~'

(365 (-) 59) = (`-**306**)!!!~' (30 x 6) = (`-**180**)!!!~'

HE DIED AT THE `-AGE of (`-**52**)!!!~'

DECEMBER 18 = (12 x 18) = (`-**216**)!!!~'

OCTOBER 20 = (10 x 20) = (`-**200**)!!!~'

(216 (-) 200) = (`-**16**)!!!~'

DECEMBER 18, 1966 = (1 + 2 + 1 + 8 + 1 + 9 + 6 + 6) = (`-**34**) = JULY 24, 1929 = (7 + 2 + 4 + 1 + 9 + 2 + 9) = (`-**34**) = **THOMAS L. J. D'ALESANDRO III FORMER MAYOR & BROTHER OF NANCY PELOSI (SPEAKER OF THE HOUSE)!!!~'**

OCTOBER 20, 2019 = (1 + 0 + 2 + 0 + 2 + 0 + 1 + 9) = (`-**15**)!!!~'

(34 + 15) = (`-**49**) = RECIPROCAL = (`-**94**)!!!~'

(`-1966) = (66 (-) 19) = (`-**47**)!!!~'

(`-2019) = (20 + 19) = (`-**39**)!!!~'

(47 + 39) = (`-**86**) = RECIPROCAL = (`-**68**)!!!~'

(47 (-) 39) = (`-**8**)!!!~'

(86 (-) 8) = (`-**78**) = `-**AGE** of `-**DEATH** of **AMERICAN SINGER/ SONGWRITER ROBERT HUNTER LYRICIST FOR "THE GRATEFUL DEAD" & AMERICAN ACTOR ROBERT FORSTER (`-78)!!!~' !!!~'**

(1218 + **1020**) = (`-2238) = (38 (-) 22) = (`-**16**)!!!~'

(1218 (-) **1020**) = (`-**198**) = (19 x 8) = (`-**152**) = (52 x 1) = (`-52) = **AGE** of `-**DEATH** for **MAJOR LEAGUE BASEBALL (MLB) UMPIRE ERIC COOPER (`-52)!!!~'**

(52 + 16) = (`-68) = RECIPROCAL = (`-86) = "THE `-MARK"!!!~'

HALL OF FAME CORNERBACK FOOTBALL PLAYER FROM
THE OAKLAND RAIDERS WILLIE BROWN (**78**) (BIRTH:
DECEMBER 2, 1940) (DEATH: OCTOBER 22, 2019)

BIRTHDAY # `-NUMBER = (12 + 2 + 19 + 40) = **73**

DEATH/DAY # `-NUMBER = (10 + 22 + 20 + 19) = **71**

(73 (-) 71) = (`-**2**)!!!~'

(73 + 71) = (`-**144**) = (44 x 1) = (`-**44**)!!!~'

HE DIED (`-**41**) DAYS BEFORE HIS NEXT BIRTHDAY!!!~'

(365 (-) 41) = (`-**324**)!!!~' (24 x 3) = (`-**72**)!!!~' (72 x 2) = (`-**144**)!!!~'

HE DIED AT THE `-AGE of (`-**78**) = (7 x 8) = (`-**56**)!!!~'

DECEMBER 2 = (12 x 2) = (`-**24**)!!!~'

OCTOBER 22 = (10 x 22) = (`-**220**)!!!~'

(220 (-) 24) = (`-**196**)!!!~'

DECEMBER 2, 1940 = (1 + 2 + 0 + 2 + 1 + 9 + 4 + 0) = (`-**19**)!!!~'

OCTOBER 22, 2019 = (1 + 0 + 2 + 2 + 2 + 0 + 1 + 9) = (`-**17**)!!!~'

(19 + 17) = (`-**36**) = RECIPROCAL = (`-**63**)!!!~'

(`-1940) = (40 (-) 19) = (`-**21**)!!!~'

(`-2019) = (20 + 19) = (`-**39**)!!!~'

(21 + 39) = (`-**60**)!!!~'

$(39 (-) 21) = (`-\underline{18})!!!\sim'$

$(60 + 18) = (`-\underline{78}) = `-\underline{AGE}$ of `-$\underline{DEATH}$ of AMERICAN SINGER/ SONGWRITER ROBERT HUNTER LYRICIST FOR "THE GRATEFUL DEAD" & AMERICAN ACTOR ROBERT FORSTER (`-$\underline{78}$) & HALL OF FAME FOOTBALL PLAYER WILLIE BROWN (`-$\underline{78}$)!!!~'

$(1202 + \underline{1022}) = (`-2224) = (24 + 22) = (`-4\underline{6})!!!\sim'$

$(1202 (-) \underline{1022}) = (`-\underline{180}) = (80 \times 1) = (`-\underline{80})!!!\sim'$

$(80 (-) 46) = (`-34) \times 2 = (`-68) = RECIPROCAL = (`-86) = "THE$ `-MARK"!!!~'

$(80 + 46) = (`-126) = (26 \times 1) = (`-\underline{26}) = EARTHQUAKES!!!\sim'$

HALL OF FAME INDUCTION = (`-1984)!!!~'

AMERICAN FILM PRODUCER ROBERT EVANS (**89**) (BIRTH: **JUNE 29**, 1930) (DEATH: OCTOBER 2**6**, **20**1**9**)

OCTOBER (`-10) = RECIPROCAL = (`-01) /|\\ NOT `-UNDERLINED = (10 (2) 01)

`-HIS `-BIRTHDAY is ALMOST a `-RECIPROCAL of `-HIS `-DEATH/DAY!!!~' (629) / 6210)!!!~'

BIRTHDAY # `-NUMBER = (6 + 29 + 19 + 30) = **84**

DEATH/DAY # `-NUMBER = (10 + 26 + 20 + 19) = **75**

$(84 (-) 75) = (`-\underline{9})!!!\sim'$

(84 + 75) = (`-**159**) = (59 + 1) = (`-**60**) = RECIPROCAL = (`-**06**)**!!!~'**

HE DIED (`-**119**) DAYS AFTER HIS LAST BIRTHDAY!!!~'

(365 (-) 119) = (`-**246**)!!!~' (46 + 2) = (`-**48**) = RECIPROCAL = (`-**84**) = **BIRTHDAY # `-NUMBER!!!~'**

HE DIED AT THE `-AGE of (`-**89**)!!!~' (8 x 9) = (`-**72**)!!!~'

JUNE 29 = (6 x 29) = (`-**174**)!!!~'

OCTOBER 26 = (10 x 26) = (`-**260**) = (RECIPROCAL = (`-**062**)!!!~'

(260 (-) 174) = (`-**86**) = RECIPROCAL = (`-**68**)**!!!~'**

JUNE 29, 1930 = (6 + 2 + 9 + 1 + 9 + 3 + 0) = (`-**30**)!!!~'

OCTOBER 26, 2019 = (1 + 0 + 2 + 6 + 2 + 0 + 1 + 9) = (`-**21**)!!!~'

(**3**0 + **2**1) = (`-**51**)**!!!~'**

(`-1930) = (30 (-) 19) = (`-**11**)**!!!~'**

(`-2019) = (20 + 19) = (`-**39**)!!!~'

(11 + 39) = (`-**50**) = RECIPROCAL = (`-**05**)**!!!~'**

(39 ( ) 11) = (`-**28**)!!!~'

(50 + 28) = (`-**78**) = `-**AGE** of `-**DEATH** of **AMERICAN SINGER/ SONGWRITER ROBERT HUNTER LYRICIST FOR "THE GRATEFUL DEAD" & AMERICAN ACTOR ROBERT FORSTER (`-78) & HALL OF FAME FOOTBALL PLAYER WILLIE BROWN (`-78)!!!~'**

(1026 + **629**) = (`-1655) = (16 + 55) = (`-**71**)!!!~'

(1026 (-) **629**) = (`-**397**)!!!~'

(397 (-) 71) = (`-**326**) = (26 x 3) = (`-**78**) = `-**AGE** of `-**DEATH** of **AMERICAN SINGER/SONGWRITER ROBERT HUNTER LYRICIST FOR "THE GRATEFUL DEAD" & AMERICAN ACTOR ROBERT FORSTER (`-78) & HALL OF FAME FOOTBALL PLAYER WILLIE BROWN (`-78)!!!~'**

FORMER U.S. REPRESENTATIVE JOHN CONYERS (**90**) (BIRTH: **MAY 16**, 19**29**) (DEATH: OCTOBER 27, **20**1**9**)

WAS `-MARRIED to MONICA CONYERS for (`-**29**) YEARS & WAS `-BORN in (`-19**29**)!!!~' MARRIED SINCE (`-19**90**)!!!~' WAS `-MARRIED in (`-19**90**) & DIED AT THE `-AGE OF (`-**90**)!!!~'

BIRTHDAY # `-NUMBER = (5 + 16 + 19 + 29) = **69**

DEATH/DAY # `-NUMBER = (10 + 27 + 20 + 19) = **76**

(76 (-) 69) = (`-**7**)!!!~'

(76 + 69) = (`-**145**) = (45 + 1) = (`-**46**) = RECIPROCAL = (`-**64**)!!!~'

HE DIED (`-**201**) DAYS BEFORE HIS NEXT BIRTHDAY!!!~'

KAY HAGAN DIED (`-**210**) DAYS BEFORE HER NEXT BIRTHDAY!!!~'

(365 (-) 201) = (`-**164**)!!!~' (64 + 1) = (`-**65**) = RECIPROCAL = (`-**56**)!!!~'

HE DIED AT THE `-AGE of (`-**90**)!!!~'

MAY 16 = (5 x 16) = (`-**80**) = RECIPROCAL = (`-**08**)!!!~'

OCTOBER 27 = (10 x 27) = (`-**270**) = (RECIPROCAL = (`-**072**)!!!~'

(270 (-) 80) = (`-**190**) = (90 + 1) = (`-**91**) = RECIPROCAL = (`-**19**)**!!!~'**

MAY 16, 1929 = (5 + 1 + 6 + 1 + 9 + 2 + 9) = (`-**33**)!!!~'

OCTOBER 27, 2019 = (1 + 0 + 2 + 7 + 2 + 0 + 1 + 9) = (`-**22**)!!!~'

(33 + 22) = (`-**55**) = (23 + 32)**!!!~'**

(`-1929) = (29 (-) 19) = (`-**10**)**!!!~'**

(`-2019) = (20 + 19) = (`-**39**)!!!~'

(10 + 39) = (`-**49**) = RECIPROCAL = (`-**94**)**!!!~'**

(39 (-) 10) = (`-**29**)!!!~'

(49 + 29) = (`-**78**) = `-**AGE** of `-**DEATH** of **AMERICAN SINGER/ SONGWRITER ROBERT HUNTER LYRICIST FOR "THE GRATEFUL DEAD" & AMERICAN ACTOR ROBERT FORSTER (`-78) & HALL OF FAME FOOTBALL PLAYER WILLIE BROWN (`-78)!!!~'**

(1027 + 516) = (`-1543) = (15 + 43) = (`-58)!!!~'

(1027 (-) 516) = (`-511) = (11 x 5) = (`-55) = (23 + 32)!!!~'

(58 + 55) = (`-**113**) = (13 x 1) = (`-**13**) = **"A VERY PIVOTAL # `-NUMBER"!!!~'**

(`-**67**) /""|""\ (`-**68**)

JOHN CONYERS `-BIRTH (**MAY 16**<sup>th</sup>) - `-DEATH (**27**th) / KAY HAGAN `-BIRTH (**MAY 26**<sup>th</sup>) - `-DEATH (**28**th)

(27 + 28) = (`-**55**) = (`-**23** + `-**32**)!!!~'

MAY 6 = (`-**56**) = (7 x 8)!!!~'

(DEATH/AGE/**CONYERS** (`-**90**) + DEATH/AGE/**HAGAN** (`-**66**)) = (`-**156**) = (56 x 1) = (`-**56**) = `-**BIRTHDAYS!!!~'**

FORMER UNITED STATES SENATOR KAY HAGAN (**66**) (BIRTH: **MAY 26**, 19**53**) (DEATH: OCTOBER 28, 2019)

MARRIED TO CHIP HAGAN SINCE (`-19**77**) for (`-**42**) YEARS!!!~'

BIRTHDAY # `-NUMBER = (5 + 26 + 19 + 53) = **103** = (13 + 0) = (`-**13**) = **"A VERY PIVOTAL # `-NUMBER"!!!~'**

DEATH/DAY # `-NUMBER = (10 + 28 + 20 + 19) = **77** = "WAS MARRIED in (`-**77**)"!!!~'

(103 (-) 77) = (`-**26**) = "WAS `-BORN on a (`-**26**th)!!!~'

(103 + 77) = (`-**180**) = (80 + 1) = (`-**81**) = RECIPROCAL = (`-**18**)!!!~'

SHE DIED (`-**210**) DAYS BEFORE HER NEXT BIRTHDAY!!!~'

JOHN CONYERS DIED (`-**201**) DAYS BEFORE HIS NEXT BIRTHDAY!!!~'

(365 (-) 210) = (`-**155**)!!!~' (55 + 1) = (`-**56**) = RECIPROCAL = (`-**65**)!!!~'

SHE DIED AT THE `-AGE of (`-**66**)!!!~' (6 x 6) = (`-**36**)!!!~'

MAY 26, 1953 = (5 + 2 + 6 + 1 + 9 + 5 + 3) = (`-**31**)!!!~' (`-**31**) = RECIPROCAL = (`-**13**)!!!~'

OCTOBER 28, 2019) = (1 + 0 + 2 + 8 + 2 + 0 + 1 + 9) = (`-**23**)!!!~'

(31 + 23) = (`-**54**) = **EARTHQUAKE!!!~'**

MAY 26 = (5 + 26) = (`-**31**)**!!!~'**

MAY 26 = (5 x 26) = (`-**130**)!!!~' (13 + 0) = (`-**13**) = RECIPROCAL = (`-**31**)!!!~'

OCTOBER 28 = (10 + 28) = (`-**38**)!!!~'

OCTOBER 28 = (10 x 28) = (`-**280**)!!!~'

(38 (-) 31) = (`-**7**)!!!~'

(38 + 31) = (`-**69**) = RECIPROCAL = (`-**96**)!!!~'

(280 + 130) = (`-**410**)!!!~'

(280 (-) 130) = (`-**150**)!!!~'

(410 + 150) = (`-**560**) = (56 + 0) = (`-**56** = **"BIRTHDAYS"!!!~'**

`-1953 = (53 (-) 19) = (`-**34**)!!!~'

`-2019 = (20 + 19) = (`-**39**)!!!~

(34 + 39) = (`-**73**)!!!~'

(39 (-) 34) = (`-**5**)!!!~'

(73 + 5) = (`-**78**) = `-**AGE** of `-**DEATH** of **AMERICAN SINGER/ SONGWRITER ROBERT HUNTER LYRICIST FOR "THE GRATEFUL DEAD" & AMERICAN ACTOR ROBERT FORSTER (`-78) & HALL OF FAME FOOTBALL PLAYER WILLIE BROWN (`-78)!!!~'**

(1028 (-) 526) = (`-**502**) = (50 x 2) = (`-**100**)!!!~'

(1028 + 526) = (`-**1554**) = (15 + 54) = (`-**69**)!!!~'

(100 (-) 69) = (`-**31**) = RECIPROCAL = (`-**13**) = **"A VERY PIVOTAL # `-NUMBER"!!!~'**

(`-**67**) /""|""\ (`-**68**)

JOHN CONYERS `-BIRTH (**MAY 16**th) - `-DEATH (**27**th) / KAY HAGAN `-BIRTH (**MAY 26**th) - `-DEATH (**28**th)

(27 + 28) = (`-**55**) = (`-**23** + `-**32**)!!!~'

MAY 6 = (`-**56**) = (7 x 8)!!!~'

(DEATH/AGE/**CONYERS** (`-**90**) + DEATH/AGE/**HAGAN** (`-**66**)) = (`-**156**) = (56 x 1) = (`-**56**) = `-**BIRTHDAYS!!!~'**

AMERICAN ACTOR JOHN WITHERSPOON (**77**) (BIRTH: JANUARY **27**, 1942) (DEATH: OCTOBER **29**, **2019**)

BIRTHDAY # `-NUMBER = (1 + 27 + 19 + 42) = **89**

DEATH/DAY # `-NUMBER = (10 + 29 + 20 + 19) = **78** = `-**AGE** of `-**DEATH** of **AMERICAN SINGER/SONGWRITER ROBERT HUNTER LYRICIST FOR "THE GRATEFUL DEAD" & AMERICAN ACTOR ROBERT FORSTER (`-78) & HALL OF FAME FOOTBALL PLAYER WILLIE BROWN (`-78)!!!~'**

(89 (-) 78) = (`-**11**)!!!~'

(89 + 78) = (`-**167**) = (67 + 1) = (`-**68**) = RECIPROCAL = (`-**86**)!!!~'

HE DIED (`-**90**) DAYS BEFORE HIS NEXT BIRTHDAY!!!~'

(365 (-) 90) = (`-**275**)!!!~' (75 + 2) = (`-**77**) = **"AGE of `-DEATH"!!!~'**

HE DIED AT THE `-AGE of (`-**77**)!!!~' (7 x 7) = (`-**49**)!!!~'

JANUARY 27 = (1 x 27) = (`-**27**) = **2(7's)** = (`-**77**) = **"AGE of `-DEATH"!!!~'**

OCTOBER 29 = (10 x 29) = (`-**290**) = (RECIPROCAL = (`-**092**)!!!~'

(290 (-) 27) = (`-**263**) = (63 x 2) = (`-**126**)!!!~'

JANUARY 27, 1942 = (1 + 2 + 7 + 1 + 9 + 4 + 2) = (`-**26**)!!!~'

OCTOBER 29, 2019 = (1 + 0 + 2 + 9 + 2 + 0 + 1 + 9) = (`-**24**)!!!~'

(**26** + **24**) = (`-**50**)!!!~'

(`-1942) = (42 (-) 19) = (`-**23**) = -a PROPHETIC NUMBER!!!~'

(`-2019) = (20 + 19) = (`-**39**)!!!~'

(23 + 39) = (`-**62**) = RECIPROCAL = (`-**26**)!!!~'

(39 (-) 23) = (`-**16**)!!!~'

(62 + 16) = (`-**78**) = `-**AGE** of `-**DEATH** of **AMERICAN SINGER/ SONGWRITER ROBERT HUNTER LYRICIST FOR "THE GRATEFUL DEAD" & AMERICAN ACTOR ROBERT FORSTER (`-78) & HALL OF FAME FOOTBALL PLAYER WILLIE BROWN (`-78)!!!~'**

(1029 + 127) = (`-1156) = (11 + 56) = (`-67)!!!~'

(1029 (-) 127) = (`-902) = (90 x 2) = (`-180)!!!~'

(1029 (-) 127) = (`-902) = (9 x 02) = (`-18)!!!~'

(180 (-) 67) = (`-**113**) = (13 x 1) = (`-**13**) = **"A VERY PIVOTAL NUMBER"!!!~'**

(`-**13**) = RECIPROCAL = (`-**31**)

WAS `-MARRIED to ANGELA ROBINSON-WITHERSPOON for (`-31) YEARS SINCE (`-1988)!!!~'

(67 (-) 18) = (`-**49**) = (7 x 7) = 2(7's) = (`-**77**) = **"AGE of `-DEATH FOR AMERICAN ACTOR JOHN WITHERSPOON (77)"!!!~'**

PUERTO RICAN ASTROLOGER WALTER MERCADO SALINAS (**87**) (BIRTH: **MARCH 9**, 19**32**) (DEATH: NOVEMBER 2, **2019**)

`-**87** = RECIPROCAL = `-**78** = `-**AGE** of `-**DEATH** of **AMERICAN SINGER/SONGWRITER ROBERT HUNTER LYRICIST FOR "THE GRATEFUL DEAD" & AMERICAN ACTOR ROBERT**

FORSTER (`-78) & HALL OF FAME FOOTBALL PLAYER WILLIE BROWN (`-78)!!!~'

BIRTHDAY # `-NUMBER = (3 + 9 + 19 + 32) = **63**

DEATH/DAY # `-NUMBER = (11 + 2 + 20 + 19) = **52**

(63 (-) 52) = (`-**11**)!!!~'

(63 + 52) = (`-**115**) = (15 + 1) = (`-**16**) = RECIPROCAL = (`-**61**)!!!~'

HE DIED (`-**127**) DAYS BEFORE HIS NEXT BIRTHDAY!!!~'
HIS `-BIRTHDAY `-EQUALS (`-27) = (3 X 9)!!!~'

(365 (-) 127) = (`-**238**)!!!~' (38 X 2) = (`-**76**)!!!~'

HE DIED AT THE `-AGE of (`-**87**)!!!~' (8 x 7) = (`-**56**)!!!~'

MARCH 9 = (3 x 9) = (`-**27**) = **2(7's)** = (`-**77**) = **"AGE of `-DEATH of AMERICAN ACTOR JOHN WITHERSPOON (`-77)"!!!~'**

NOVEMBER 2 = (11 x 2) = (`-**22**)!!!~'

(27 + 22) = (`-**49**) = RECIPROCAL = (`-**94**)!!!~'

MARCH 9, 1932 = (3 + 9 + 1 + 9 + 3 + 2) = (`-**27**) = `-**BIRTHDAY!!!~'**

NOVEMBER 2, 2019 = (1 + 1 + 2 + 2 + 0 + 1 + 9) = (`-**16**)!!!~'

(**27** + **16**) = (`-**43**)!!!~'

(`-1932) = (32 (-) 19) = (`-**13**) = **"A VERY PIVOTAL # `-NUMBER"!!!~'**

(`-2019) = (20 + 19) = (`-**39**)!!!~'

(13 + 39) = (`-**52**) = "DEATH/DAY # `-NUMBER"!!!~'

(39 (-) 13) = (`-**26**)!!!~'

(52 + 26) = (`-**78**) = `-**AGE** of `-**DEATH** of **AMERICAN SINGER/ SONGWRITER ROBERT HUNTER LYRICIST FOR "THE GRATEFUL DEAD" & AMERICAN ACTOR ROBERT FORSTER (`-78) & HALL OF FAME FOOTBALL PLAYER WILLIE BROWN (`-78)!!!~'**

(1102 + **39**) = (`-1141) = (11 + 41) = (`-**52**) = "DEATH/DAY # `-NUMBER"!!!~'

(1102 (-) **39**) = (`-**1063**) = (10 + 63) = (`-**73**)!!!~'

(52 + 73) = (`-**125**) = (25 X 1) = (`-**25**) = RECIPROCAL = (`-**52**) = "DEATH/DAY # `-NUMBER"!!!~'

(73 (-) 52) = (`-**21**)!!!~'

(125 + 21) = (`-**146**) = (46 X 1) = (`-**46**) = (**23 X 2**)!!!~'

(`-**23**) = RECIPROCAL = (`-**32**) = "YEAR of `-BIRTH"!!!~'

WALTER MERCADO SALINAS WAS `-BORN on (3/9); and, `-DIED within the `-YEAR of (3/9) = (`-39) = (20 + 19)!!!~'

COLUMBIA SPORTSWEAR "MATRIARCH" GERT BOYLE (**95**) (BIRTH: MARCH 6, 1924) (DEATH: NOVEMBER 3, 2019)

BIRTHDAY # `-NUMBER = (3 + 6 + 19 + 24) = **52**

DEATH/DAY # `-NUMBER = (11 + 3 + 20 + 19) = **53**

(53 (-) 52) = (`-**1**)!!!~'

(53 + 52) = (`-**105**) = (5 + 1) = (`-**6**)!!!~'

SHE DIED (`-**123**) DAYS BEFORE HER NEXT BIRTHDAY!!!~'

(365 (-) 123) = (`-**242**)!!!~' (42 X 2) = (`-**84**)!!!~'

SHE DIED AT THE `-AGE of (`-**95**)!!!~' (9 x 5) = (`-**45**)!!!~'

MARCH 6 = (3 x 6) = (`-**18**)!!!~'

NOVEMBER 3 = (11 x 3) = (`-**33**)!!!~'

(33 + 18) = (`-**49**) = RECIPROCAL = (`-**94**)!!!~'

MARCH 9, 1932 = (3 + 9 + 1 + 9 + 3 + 2) = (`-**27**) = `-**BIRTHDAY!!!~'**

NOVEMBER 2, 2019 = (1 + 1 + 2 + 2 + 0 + 1 + 9) = (`-**16**)!!!~'

(**27** + **16**) = (`-**51**)!!!~'

(`-1924) = (24 (-) 19) = (`-**5**)!!!~'

(`-2019) = (20 + 19) = (`-**39**)!!!~'

(5 + 39) = (`-**44**)!!!~' (39 (-) 5 = (`-**34**)!!!~'

(44 + 34) = (`-**78**) = `-**AGE** of `-**DEATH** of **AMERICAN SINGER/ SONGWRITER ROBERT HUNTER LYRICIST FOR "THE GRATEFUL DEAD" & AMERICAN ACTOR ROBERT FORSTER (`-78) & HALL OF FAME FOOTBALL PLAYER WILLIE BROWN (`-78)!!!~'**

(1103 + **36**) = (`-**1139**) = (11 + 39) = (`-**50**)!!!~'

(1103 (-) **36**) = (`-**1067**) = (10 + 67) = (`-**77**)!!!~'

(50 + 77) = (`-**127**) = (27 X 1) = (`-**27**) = RECIPROCAL = (`-**72**)!!!~'
(**72** (-) 27) = (`-**45**)!!!~'

(77 (-) 50) = (`-**27**)!!!~'

(127 + 27) = (`-**154**) = (54 X 1) = (`-**54**) = RECIPROCAL = (`-**45**) = (9 X 5) = (`-**95**) = "**AGE of** `-**DEATH for COLUMBIA SPORTSWEAR "MATRIARCH" GERT BOYLE** (`-**95**)"!!!~'

(50, 51, 52, 53, 54) = **PROPHETIC-LINEAR-PROGRESSION-PLP**!!!~'

#38/PRESIDENT GERALD FORD `-DIED on (**12/26**) & #33/ PRESIDENT HARRY S. TRUMAN `-DIED on (**12/26**)!!!~' (12 + 26) = (`-**38**)!!!~' FIRST LADY BETTY FORD WAS `-BORN on (**4/8**) & `-DIED on (**7/8**) = (48) + (78) = (`-**126**) (ALL-IN-ONE # `-NUMBER) = `-**DEATH/DAYS of the** `-**PRESIDENTS**!!!~' (**12/26**) + (**12/26**) = (12 + 26 + 12 + 26) = (`-**76**)!!!~' (`-**76**) = RECIPROCAL = (`-**67**)!!!~' FIRST LADY BESS TRUMAN was `-BORN in (`-**1885**) = (85 (-) 18) = (`-**67**)!!!~' FIRST LADY BETTY FORD was `-BORN on an (`-**8**ᵗʰ) & `-DIED on an (`-**8**ᵗʰ) = (`-**88**) = "**AGE of** `-**DEATH for #33/PRESIDENT HARRY S. TRUMAN** (`-**88**)!!!~' HARRY S. TRUMAN was `-**BORN** on **MAY 8, 1884** = 3(**8**'s) = (`-**38**) = PRESIDENT GERALD FORD!!!~' **MAY 8, 1884** = (84 (-) 18 (-) 8 (-) 5) = (`-**53**) = **PRESIDENT HARRY S. TRUMAN**!!!~' HARRY S. TRUMAN `-**DIED** in (`-**1972**) = (72 (-) 19) = (`-**53**)!!!~' WAS `-MARRIED to FIRST LADY BESS TRUMAN for (`-**53**) YEARS & SHE AS FIRST LADY FINISHED HER DUTIES IN (`-**1953**)!!!~' FIRST LADY BESS TRUMAN `-**DIED** on **OCTOBER 18, 1982** = (82 (-) 19 (-) 18 (-) 10) = (`-**35**)

= RECIPROCAL = (`-**53**)!!!~' **JULY 14, 1913** = (7 + 14 + 19 + 13) = (`-**53**) = **PRESIDENT GERALD FORD'S BIRTHDAY # `-NUMBER!!!~'** FIRST LADY BETTY FORD was `-**BORN** in (`-**1918**) & `-**DIED** in (`-**2011**) = (19 + 18 + 20 + 11) = (`-**68**) = **"THE `-MARK of the `-BEAST"!!!~'** PRESIDENT HARRY S. TRUMAN was **BORN** on an (`-**8**<sup>th</sup>) & FIRST LADY BESS TRUMAN `-**DIED** on an (`-**18**<sup>th</sup>) = (8 + 18) = (`-**26**) = **"DAY of `-DEATH for `-HER `-HUSBAND #33/PRESIDENT HARRY S. TRUMAN!!!~'** (**2** x **6**) = (`-**12**)!!!~' PRESIDENT GERALD FORD `-**AGE of `-DEATH** = (`-**93**) & FIRST LADY BETTY FORD'S `-**AGE of `-DEATH** = (`-**93**) = (93 + 93) = (`-**186**)!!!~' PRESIDENT HARRY S. TRUMAN'S `-**AGE of `-DEATH** = (`-**88**) & FIRST LADY BESS TRUMAN'S `-**AGE of `-DEATH** = (`-**97**) = (88 + 97) = (`-**185**)!!!~' (**186** + **185**) = (`-**371**) = (71 x 3) = (`-**213**) = `-**EQUALS** = **FIRST LADY BESS TRUMAN'S `-BIRTHDAY (FEBRUARY 13**th/`-**213**)!!!~' **DEATH/DAY of the TWO `-PRESIDENTS** (**12** x **26**) = (`-**312**) = RECIPROCAL = (`-**213**)!!!~' (#**38**/PRESIDENT + #**33**/PRESIDENT = (38 + 33) = (`-**71**)!!!~' #38/PRESIDENT GERALD FORD `-DIED on a (`-**26**) in (`-**2**00**6**) = (20 + 06) = (`-**26**)!!!~' (26 + 26) = (`-**52**)!!!~' FIRST LADY BESS TRUMAN'S BIRTH was on **FEBRUARY 13, 1885** = (85 (-) 18 (-) 13 (-) 2) = (`-**52**)!!!~' PRESIDENT GERALD FORD'S `-**DEATH** = **DECEMBER 26, 2006** = (12 + 26 + 20 + 06) = (`-**64**)!!!~' (`-**64**) = RECIPROCAL = (`-**46**)!!!~' FIRST LADY BETTY FORD'S `-**DEATH** = **JULY 8, 2011** = (7 + 8 + 20 + 11) = (`-**46**)!!!~' (`-**RECIPROCALS-')!!!~'** PRESIDENT HARRY S. TRUMAN'S `-**DEATH** = **DECEMBER 26, 1972** = (12 + 26 + 19 + 72) = (`-**129**)!!!~' FIRST LADY BESS TRUMAN'S `-**DEATH** = **OCTOBER 18, 1982** = (10 + 18 + 19 + 82) = (`-**129**) = **"EXACT # `-NUMBER AS TO `-HER `-HUSBAND HARRY S. TRUMAN"** (`-**129**)!!!~' (12 x 9) = (`-**108**) = **FIRST LADY BESS TRUMAN'S `-DEATH/DAY (ALL-IN-ONE # `-NUMBER)!!!~'** (64 + 46) = (`-**110**) / (`-129 (-) 110) = (`-**19**)!!!~' 64 (-) 46) = (`-**18**)!!!~' (`-**1918**) = `-**BIRTH YEAR OF FIRST LADY BETTY**

FORD!!!~' PRESIDENT GERALD FORD'S BIRTHDAY (**7**/**14**) & FIRST LADY BETTY FORD'S BIRTHDAY (**4**/**8**) were `-**MARRIED** in (`-**48**) = (714 (-) 48) = (`-**666**) = **"THE `-MARK of the `-BEAST"!!!~'**

`-MY `-INVENTION /|\ `-MY `-DISCOVERY /|\ AUTHOR: DWAYNE W. ANDERSON!!!~'

`-PRESS RELEASE-'

This IS JUST the `-TIP of the `-ICEBERG!!!~'

JOE JACKSON (MICHAEL JACKSON'S FATHER) BIRTH = **JULY 26**, 19**28** & DEATH = **JUNE 27**, 2018!!!~' (`-**726** = *MIRROR the # `-NUMBERS* = `-**627**)!!!~' `-**BORN** in (`-**28**) & `-**DIED** in (`-**28**)!!!~'

#35/PRESIDENT JOHN F. KENNEDY `-**DIED** at the `-**AGE** of (`-**46**) & FIRST LADY JACQUELINE KENNEDY `-**DIED** at the `-**AGE** of (`-**64**)!!!~' (`-**RECIPROCALS-'**)!!!~' **#36**/PRESIDENT LYNDON B. JOHNSON `-**DIED** at the `-**AGE** of (`-**64**)!!!~'

#35/JOHN F. KENNEDY `-**BIRTH** = (5 + 29 + 19 + 17) = **70** / JOHN F. KENNEDY `-**DEATH** (11 + 22 + 19 + 63) = **115**!~' (115 (-) 70 = **45**!~' JACQUELINE KENNEDY `-**BIRTH** = (7 + 28 + 19 + 29) = **83** / JACQUELINE KENNEDY `-**DEATH** = (5 + 19 + 19 + 94) = **137**!~' (137 (-) 83) = **54**!~ (`-**RECIPROCALS-'!!!'**) (`-**45** = RECIPROCAL = `-**54**)!!!~'

#38/PRESIDENT GERALD FORD'S `-**DEATH** = **DECEMBER 26, 2006** = (12 + 26 + 20 + 06) = (`-**64**)!!!~' (`-**64**) = RECIPROCAL

= (`-**46**)!!!~' FIRST LADY BETTY FORD'S `-**DEATH** = **JULY 8, 2011** = (7 + 8 + 20 + 11) = (`-**46**)!!!~' (`-**RECIPROCALS**-')!!!~'

#33/PRESIDENT HARRY S. TRUMAN'S `-**DEATH** = **DECEMBER 26, 1972** = (12 + 26 + 19 + 72) = (`-**129**)!!!~' FIRST LADY BESS TRUMAN'S `-**DEATH** = **OCTOBER 18, 1982** = (10 + 18 + 19 + 82) = (`-**129**) = "**EXACT #** `-**NUMBER AS TO** `-**HER** `-**HUSBAND HARRY S. TRUMAN**" (`-**129**)!!!~' (12 x 9) = (`-**108**) = **FIRST LADY BESS TRUMAN'S** `-**DEATH/DAY (ALL-IN-ONE #** `-**NUMBER)!!!~' (29 x 2) = (`-**58**)!!!~'

#16/PRESIDENT ABRAHAM LINCOLN `-**BIRTH** = FEBRUARY 12, 1809 = (2 + 12 + 18 + 09) = (`-**41**)!!!~' **#16**/PRESIDENT ABRAHAM LINCOLN `-**DEATH** = APRIL 15, 18**65** = (4 + 15 + 18 + **65**) = (`-**102**)!!!~' (102 (-) 41) = (`-**61**)!!!~' FIRST LADY MARY TODD LINCOLN `-**BIRTH** = DECEMBER 13, 1818 = (12 + 13 + 18 + 18) = (`-**61**)!!!~' FIRST LADY MARY TODD LINCOLN `-**DEATH** = JULY 16, 1882 = (7 + 16 + 18 + 82) = (`-**123**)!!!~' (BIRTHDAY (1**2**/1**3**) = DEATH/DAY # `-NUMBER (`-**123**))!!!~' (82 (-) 18 (-) 16 (-) 7) = (`-**41**)!!!~' **ALL** `-**INTERTWINED IN TIME!!!~' FIRST LADY MARY TODD LINCOLN WAS** (`-**46**) `-**YEARS of** `-**AGE for WHEN #16/PRESIDENT ABRAHAM LINCOLN WAS** `-**ASSASSINATED!!!~'** (`-**16**) = RECIPROCAL = (`-**61**)!!!~' (7 + 16) = (`-**23**) = **MARRIED** `-**TOGETHER FOR** (`-**23**) **YEARS!!!~'** (`-**23**) = RECIPROCAL = (`-**32**)!!!~' (`-**232**) = (23 x 2) = (`-**46**)!!!~'

#1/PRESIDENT GEORGE WASHINGTON `-**BIRTH** = FEBRUARY 22, 17**32** = (2 + 22 + 17 + **32**) = (`-**73**)!!!~' **#1**/PRESIDENT GEORGE WASHINGTON `-**DEATH** = DECEMBER 14, 1799 = (12 + 14 + 17 + 99) = (`-**142**)!!!~' (142 (-) 73) = (`-**69**)!!!~' (99 (-) 17 (-) 14 (-) 12) = (`-**56**) = **#16**/PRESIDENT ABRAHAM LINCOLN'S `-**AGE of** `-**DEATH!!!~'** FIRST LADY MARTHA WASHINGTON `-**BIRTH** = JUNE 13, 17**31** = (6 + 13 + 17 + 31)

= (`-**67**) = #1/PRESIDENT GEORGE WASHINGTON'S `-**AGE of** `-**DEATH!!!**-' FIRST LADY MARTHA WASHINGTON `-**DEATH** = MAY 22, 1802 = (5 + 22 + 18 + 02) = (`-**47**)!!!-' (67 + 47) = (`-**114**) = (14 X 1) = (`-**14**) = **"DAY of `-DEATH of `-HER `-HUSBAND #1/PRESIDENT GEORGE WASHINGTON"!!!**-' (`-**14**) = RECIPROCAL = (`-**41**)!!!-'

#41/PRESIDENT GEORGE H. W. BUSH `-**BIRTH** = JUNE 12, 1924 = (6 + 12 + 19 + 24) = (`-**61**)!!!-' #41/PRESIDENT GEORGE H. W. BUSH `-**DEATH** = NOVEMBER 30, 2018 = (11 + 30 + 20 + 18) = (`-**79**)!!!-' (79 + 61) = (`-**140**)!!!-' FIRST LADY BARBARA BUSH `-**BIRTH** = JUNE 8, 1925 = (6 + 8 + 19 + 25) = (`-**58**)!!!-' FIRST LADY BARBARA BUSH `-**DEATH** = APRIL 17, 2018 = (**4** + 1**7** + 20 + 18) = (`-**59**)!!!-' (59 + 58) = (`-**117**)!!!-' (140 (-) 117) = (`-**23**)!!!-' (140 + 117) = (`-**257**) = (57 x 2) = (`-**114**)!!!-'

#37/PRESIDENT RICHARD M. NIXON `-**BIRTH** = JANUARY 9, 1913 = (1 + 9 + 19 + 13) = (`-**42**)!!!-' `-**DIED** on (**42**/2)!!!-' #37/PRESIDENT RICHARD M. NIXON `-**DEATH** = APRIL 22, 1994 = (4 + 22 + 19 + 94) = (`-**139**)!!!-' (139 (-) 42) = (`-**97**) = **"AGE of `-DEATH of `-FIRST LADY BESS TRUMAN (`-97)"!!!**-' (94 (-) 19 (-) 22 (-) 4) = (`-**49**) = RECIPROCAL = (`-**94**) = **"THE `-YEAR `-HE `-DIED `-WITHIN (`-94)"!!!**-' FIRST LADY PAT NIXON `-**BIRTH** = MARCH 16, 1912 = (3 + 16 + 19 + 12) = (`-**50**)!!!-' FIRST LADY PAT NIXON `-**DEATH** = JUNE 22, 1993 = (6 + 22 + 19 + 93) = (`-**140**)!!!-' (140 (-) 97) = (`-**43**)!!!-' (140 + 97) = (`-**237**) = (**37** x 2) = (`-**74**)!!!-'

#36/PRESIDENT LYNDON B. JOHNSON `-**BIRTH** = AUGUST 27, 1908 = (8 + 27 + 19 + 08) = (`-**62**)!!!-' #36/PRESIDENT LYNDON B. JOHNSON `-**DEATH** = JANUARY 22, 19**73** = (1 + 22 + 19 + **73**) = (`-**115**)!!!-' (115 (-) 62) = (`-**53**) = RECIPROCAL = (`-**35**) = **#35/PRESIDENT JOHN F. KENNEDY `-SHARES THE `-EXACT SAME `-DEATH/DAY # `-NUMBER AS #36/**

PRESIDENT LYNDON B. JOHNSON (`-115)!!!~' (73 (-) 19 (-) 22 (-) 1) = (`-**31**) = RECIPROCAL = (`-**13**) = **"A VERY PIVOTAL # `-NUMBER"!!!~'** FIRST LADY LADY BIRD JOHNSON `-**BIRTH** = DECEMBER 22, 1912 = (12 + 22 + 19 + 12) = (`-**65**) = **"YEAR #16/PRESIDENT ABRAHAM LINCOLN WAS `-ASSASSINATED"!!!~'** FIRST LADY LADY BIRD JOHNSON `-**DEATH** = JULY 11, 2007 = (7 + 11 + 20 + 07) = (`-**45**)!!!~' (65 (-) 45) = (`-**20**)!!!~' (53 + 20) = (`-**73**)!!!~' (65 + 45) = (`-**110**)!!!~' (110 + 53) = (`-**163**) = (63 x 1) = (`-**63**) = **"YEAR #35/PRESIDENT JOHN F. KENNEDY WAS `-ASSASSINATED"!!!~'**

#34/PRESIDENT DWIGHT D. EISENHOWER `-**BIRTH** = OCTOBER 14, 1890 = (10 + 14 + 18 + 90) = (`-**132**)!!!~' (90 (-) 18 (-) 14 (-) 10) = (`-48)!!!~' **#34**/PRESIDENT DWIGHT D. EISENHOWER `-**DEATH** = MARCH 28, 1969 = (3 + 28 + 19 + 69) = (`-**119**)!!!~' (132 (-) 119) = (`-**13**) = **#35/PRESIDENT JOHN F. KENNEDY** = `-**EQUALS** = (`-**313**)!!!~' (69 (-) 19 (-) 28 (-) 3) = (`-**19**)!!!~' FIRST LADY MAMIE EISENHOWER `-**BIRTH** = NOVEMBER 14, 1896 = (11 + 14 + 18 + 96) = (`-**139**)!!!~' (96 (-) 18 (-) 14 (-) 11) = (`-**53**)!!!~' FIRST LADY MAMIE EISENHOWER `-**DEATH** = NOVEMBER 1, 1979 = (11 + 1 + 19 + 79) = (`-**110**)!!!~' (139 (-) 110) = (`-**29**) = **"PART of the `-DEATH # `-NUMBERS for THE `-PREVIOUS PRESIDENT & FIRST LADY"!!!~'** (139 + 110) = (`-**249**) = (49 x 2) = (`-**98**)!!!~' (79 (-) 19 (-) 1 (-) 11) = (`-**48**)!!!~' (98 + 48) = (`-**146**)!!!~' (`-**79**) = RECIPROCAL = (`-**97**) = **"THE YEAR THE `-NEXT FIRST LADY DIED `-EQUALS THE (`-RECIPROCAL-') `-AGE of `-DEATH of THE `-PREVIOUS `-FIRST `-LADY"!!!~'**

#32/PRESIDENT FRANKLIN DELANO ROOSEVELT!!!~'

(82 (-) 18) = (`-**64**)!!!~' /|\ (19 + 45) = (`-**64**)!!!~' **BIRTH `-EQUALS** = `-**DEATH!!!~'** (64 + 64) = (`-**128**)!!!~' (64/2) = (`-**32**) = **FOR THE `-32nd PRESIDENT of the UNITED STATES of AMERICA!!!~'**

#32/PRESIDENT FRANKLIN D. ROOSEVELT `-**BIRTH** = JANUARY 30, 1882 = (1 + 30 + 18 + 82) = (`-**131**)!!!~' (82 (-) 18 (-) 30 (-) 1) = (`-**33**)!!!~' **#32**/PRESIDENT FRANKLIN D. ROOSEVELT `-**DEATH** = APRIL 12, 1945 = (4 + 12 + 19 + 45) = (`-**80**)!!!~' (131 (-) 80) = (`-**51**)!!!~' FIRST LADY ELEANOR ROOSEVELT `-**BIRTH** = OCTOBER 11, 1884 = (10 + 11 + 18 + 84) = (`-**123**)!!!~' **#32**/ PRESIDENT FRANKLIN D. ROOSEVELT WAS (`-**23**) **YEARS of** `-**AGE for WHEN** `-**THEY** `-**GOT** `-**MARRIED!!!~'** (84 (-) 18 (-) 11 (-) 10) = (`-**45**) = **"THE `-YEAR THAT `-HER HUSBAND #32/PRESIDENT FRANKLIN D. ROOSEVELT HAD `-DIED (`-19_45_)"!!!~'** FIRST LADY ELEANOR ROOSEVELT `-**DEATH** = NOVEMBER 7, 1962 = (11 + 7 + 19 + 62) = (`-**99**)!!!~' (123 + 99) = (`-**222**) = **"EQUALS THE `-BIRTHDAY OF #1/ PRESIDENT GEORGE WASHINGTON (`-222)"!!!~'** (62 (-) 19 (-) 7 (-) 11) = (`-**25**)!!!~' (222 (-) 25) = (`-**197**) = (97 x 1) = (`-**97**) = **"AGE of `-DEATH of `-NEXT FIRST LADY BESS TRUMAN (`-97)"!!!~'** **#32**/PRESIDENT FRANKLIN D. ROOSEVELT HAD `-DIED (`-**72**) DAYS AFTER HIS LAST `-**BIRTHDAY;** WHILE, HIS `-WIFE FIRST LADY ELEANOR ROOSEVELT HAD `-DIED (`-**27**) DAYS AFTER HER LAST **BIRTHDAY**!!!~' (`-**RECIPROCALS**-')!!!~' (`-**72**) (-) (`-**27**) = (`-**45**) = `-**YEAR of** `-**DEATH of** `-**HUSBAND #32/PRESIDENT FRANKLIN DELANO ROOSEVELT!!!~'** (365 (-) 72) = (`-**293**) = (29 x 3) = (`-**87**) = RECIPROCAL = (`-**78**) = **"AGES of** `-**DEATH of** FIRST LADY **EDITH ROOSEVELT** & `-**HIS** `-**WIFE** FIRST LADY **ELEANOR ROOSEVELT**"!!!~' (93 x 2) = (`-**186**) = (86 x 1) = (`-**86**) = RECIPROCAL = (`-**68**) = **"THE `-MARK of the `-BEAST"!!!~'**

#31/PRESIDENT HERBERT HOOVER `-**BIRTH** = AUGUST 10, 1874 = (8 + 10 + 18 + 74) = (`-**110**)!!!~' (74 (-) 18 (-) 10 (-) 8) = (`-**38**)!!!~' **#31**/PRESIDENT HERBERT HOOVER `-**DEATH** = OCTOBER 20, 1964 = (10 + 20 + 19 + 64) = (`-**113**)!!!~' (110 + 113) = (`-**223**) = (23 x 2) = (`-**46**)!!!~' FIRST LADY LOU HENRY HOOVER `-**BIRTH** = MARCH **29**, 18**74** = (3 + **29** + 18 + **74**) =

(`-**124**)!!!~' (24 (-) 1) = (`-**23**)!!!~' (74 (-) 18 (-) 29 (-) 3) = (`-**24**)!!!~'
FIRST LADY LOU HENRY HOOVER `-**DEATH** = JANUARY
7, 1944 = (1 + 7 + 19 + 44) = (`-**71**)!!!~' (124 (-) 71) = (`-**53**)!!!~' THEY
WERE `-MARRIED FROM (`-1899 to `-1944) = (`-**45**) YEARS
= **"EQUALS the `-YEAR the `-VERY `-NEXT `-PRESIDENT
`-DIES #32/PRESIDENT FRANKLIN DELANO ROOSEVELT
(`-1945)"!!!~'**

#30/PRESIDENT CALVIN COOLIDGE `-**BIRTH** = JULY 4,
1872 = (7 + 4 + 18 + 72) = (`-**101**)!!!~' (72 (-) 18 (-) 4 (-) 7) = (`-**43**)!!!~'
#30/PRESIDENT CALVIN COOLIDGE `-**DEATH** = JANUARY
5, 1933 = (1 + 5 + 19 + 33) = (`-**58**)!!!~' (101 (-) 58) = (`-**43**)!!!~' FIRST
LADY GRACE COOLIDGE `-**BIRTH** = JANUARY 3, 1879 = (1
+ 3 + 18 + 79) = (`-**101**) = **"SAME `-BIRTHDAY # `-NUMBER as
`-HER HUSBAND #30/PRESIDENT CALVIN COOLIDGE
(`-101)"!!!~'** **REVERSE** `-BIRTHDAY # `-NUMBER = (79 (-)
18 (-) 3 (-) 1) = (`-**57**) = **"YEAR of `-HER `-OWN `-DEATH for
`-FIRST LADY GRACE COOLIDGE" (`-57)"!!!~'** (57 + 43) = (`-
100)!!!~' FIRST LADY GRACE COOLIDGE `-**DEATH** = **JULY
8**, 19**57** = (**7** + **8** + 19 + 57) = (`-**91**)!!!~' (101 + 91) = (`-**192**) = (92
X 1) = (`-**92**) = RECIPROCAL = (`-**29**)!!!~' **REVERSE** `-**DEATH/
DAY # `-NUMBER** = (57 (-) 19 (-) 8 (-) 7) = (`-**23**)!!!~'

#29/PRESIDENT WARREN G. HARDING `-**BIRTH** =
NOVEMBER 2, 1865 = (11 + 2 + 18 + 65) = (`-**96**) = (32 X 3)!!!~'
(65 (-) 18 (-) 2 (-) 11) = (`-**34**)!!!~' #29/PRESIDENT WARREN
G. HARDING `-**DEATH** = AUGUST 2, 19**23** = (8 + 2 + 19 +
23) = (`-**52**)!!!~' (96 (-) 52) = (`-**44**)!!!~' FIRST LADY FLORENCE
HARDING `-**BIRTH** = AUGUST 15, 1860 = (8 + 15 + 18 +
60) = (`-**101**) = **"SAME BIRTHDAY # `-NUMBER as #30/
PRESIDENT CALVIN COOLIDGE & FIRST LADY GRACE
COOLIDGE (`-101)"!!!~'** (60 (-) 18 (-) 15 (-) 8) = (`-**19**)!!!~' FIRST
LADY FLORENCE HARDING `-**DEATH** = NOVEMBER 21,
1924 = (11 + 21 + 19 + 24) = (`-**75**)!!!~' (`-**75**) = RECIPROCAL =

(`-**57**)!!!~' (101 (-) 57) = (`-**44**)!!!~' (101 + 75) = (`-**176**)!!!~' (101 (-) 75) = (`-**26**)!!!~'

#40/PRESIDENT RONALD REAGAN `-**BIRTH** = **FEBRUARY 6**, 1911 = (**2** + **6** + 19 + 11) = (`-**38**)!!!~' #40/PRESIDENT RONALD REAGAN `-**DEATH** = JUNE 5, 20**04** = (6 + 5 + 20 + **04**) = (`-**35**) = RECIPROCAL = (`-**53**)!!!~' (38 + 35) = (`-**73**)!!!~' FIRST LADY NANCY REAGAN `-**BIRTH** = **JULY 6**, 1921 = (**7** + **6** + 19 + 21) = (`-**53**) = **"NANCY & RONALD are `-RECIPROCALS in `-BIRTH & `-DEATH"**!!!~' FIRST LADY NANCY REAGAN `-**DEATH** = MARCH 6, 2016 = (3 + 6 + 20 + 16) = (`-**45**)!!!~' (53 + 45) = (`-**98**) = (98 / 3) = (`-**32.666**)!!!~' **THEY** WERE `-**MARRIED** IN (`-**1952**); AND, **FOLLOWING RONALD'S DEATH** in (`-**2004**); THAT'S (`-**52**) YEARS `-**LATER!!!~'** (`-**04**) = RECIPROCAL = (`-**40**) = "THE (`-**40**th) PRESIDENT `-**DIES** in `-HIS `-**RECIPROCAL** `-**YEAR** of `-LIFE (`-**04**)"!!!~'

(`-**46**) = **RECIPROCAL** = (`-**64**)!!!~'

#45/PRESIDENT DONALD TRUMP `-**BIRTH** = **JUNE** 14, 19**46** = (**6** + 1**4** + 19 + **46**) = (`-**85**) = RECIPROCAL = (`-**58**)!!!~' FIRST LADY MELANIA TRUMP `-**BIRTH** = **APRIL** 26, 1970 = (**4** + 2**6** + 19 + 70) = (`-**119**) = RECIPROCAL = (`-**911**)!!!~'

#44/PRESIDENT BARACK OBAMA `-**BIRTH** = AUGUST 4, 19**61** = (8 + 4 + 19 + **61**) = (`-**92**) = RECIPROCAL = (`-**29**)!!!~' FIRST LADY MICHELLE OBAMA `-**BIRTH** = JANUARY 17, 19**64** = (1 + 17 + 19 + **64**) = (`-**101**) = **"ANOTHER `-ONE"**!!!~'

#43/PRESIDENT GEORGE W. BUSH `-**BIRTH** = **JULY 6**, 19**46** = (**7** + **6** + 19 + **46**) = (`-**78**) = RECIPROCAL = (`-**87**)!!!~' FIRST LADY LAURA BUSH `-**BIRTH** = NOVEMBER 4, 19**46**) = (11 + 4 + 19 + **46**) = (`-**80**) = RECIPROCAL = (`-**08**)!!!~'

#42/PRESIDENT BILL CLINTON `-**BIRTH** = AUGUST 19, 19**46** = (8 + 19 + 19 + **46**) = (`-**92**) = RECIPROCAL = (`-**29**)!!!~' FIRST LADY HILLARY CLINTON `-**BIRTH** = OCTOBER 26, 19**47** = (10 + 26 + 19 + **47**) = (`-**102**) = RECIPROCAL = (`-**201**)!!!~'

#39/PRESIDENT JIMMY CARTER `-**BIRTH** = OCTOBER 1, 1924 = (10 + 1 + 19 + 24) = (`-**54**) = RECIPROCAL = (`-**45**)!!!~' FIRST LADY ROSALYNN CARTER `-**BIRTH** = AUGUST 18, 19**27** = (8 + 18 + 19 + **27**) = (`-**72**) = RECIPROCAL = (`-**27**)!!!~' (72 (-) 27) = (`-**45**) = RECIPROCAL = (`-**54**)!!!~' (`-**RECIPROCALS**-')!!!~' **MARRIED** in (`-19**46**)!!!~'

NOTE HOW CLOSE #44 & #42 ARE IN `-BIRTHDAY # `-NUMBERS!!!~' (44 + 42) = (`-86) = RECIPROCAL = (`-68) = "THE `-MARK of the `-BEAST"!!!~'

NOTE **#43** (78 + 80) = (`-**158**) = (58 x 1) = (`-**58**) = RECIPROCAL = (`-**85**)!!!~' NOTE **#45** = (119 (-) 85) = (`-**34**) = RECIPROCAL = (`-**43**)!!!~'

#28/PRESIDENT WOODROW WILSON `-**BIRTH** = **DECEMBER 28**, 18**56** = (**12** + **28** + 18 + **56**) = (`-**114**)!!!~' **#28/**PRESIDENT WOODROW WILSON `-**DEATH** = **FEBRUARY 3**, 1924 = (**2** + **3** + 19 + 24) = (`-**48**)!!!~' (114 (-) 48) = (`-**66**)!!!~' FIRST LADY EDITH WILSON `-**BIRTH** = OCTOBER 15, 18**72** = (10 + 15 + 18 + **72**) = (`-**115**) = **"ANOTHER ONE"**!!!~' FIRST LADY EDITH WILSON `-**DEATH** = **DECEMBER 28**, 19**61** = (12 + 28 + 19 + **61**) = (`-**120**)!!!~' (115 + 120) = (`-**235**) = (35 x 2) = (`-**70**)!!!~' (23 x 5) = (`-**115**)!!!~' (235 + 66) = (`-**301**) = (31 + 0) = (`-**31**) = RECIPROCAL = (`-**13**) = **"A VERY PIVOTAL # `-NUMBER"**!!!~' THIS `-FIRST `-LADY EDITH WILSON `-**DIED** on `-HER `-HUSBAND'S **#28/PRESIDENT WOODROW WILSON'S `-BIRTHDAY (DECEMBER 28TH)** for the (`-**28TH**) **PRESIDENT!!!~'** `-FIRST `-LADY **EDITH**

WILSON was `-**BORN** in (`-**72**); and, `-**DIED** at the `-**AGE** of (`-**89**) = (8 x 9) = (`-**72**)!!!~' /|||\ FIRST LADY ELLEN AXSON WILSON `-**BIRTH** = MAY 15, 1**86**0 = (5 + 15 + 1**8** + **6**0) = (`-**98**)!!!~' FIRST LADY ELLEN AXSON WILSON `-**DEATH** = **AUGUST 6**, 1914 = (**8** + **6** + 19 + 14) = (`-**47**)!!!~' (98 + 47) = (`-**145**) = (45 X 1) = (`-**45**) = RECIPROCAL = (`-**54**) = `-**AGE** of `-**DEATH** of FIRST LADY ELLEN AXSON WILSON!!!~' THEY WERE `-MARRIED FROM (1885 TO 1914) FOR SOME (`-**29**) YEARS - (`-**28**) **YEARS LIE-IN-BETWEEN!!!~'** FIRST LADY EDITH WILSON & FIRST LADY ELLEN AXSON WILSON'S `-WEDDING `-DATES WERE (`-**188**) DAYS APART!!!~' (`-**188**) = (88 X 1) = (`-**88**) = 2(**8**'s) = (`-**28**) for the (`-**28**ᵀᴴ) PRESIDENT #28/WOODROW WILSON!!!~' FIRST LADY ELLEN AXON WILSON'S; **HER** `-**DEATH/DAY** (**8/6**)/**AUGUST 6**TH = `-EQUALS `-EXACTLY = **"THE `-BIRTHDAY OF FIRST LADY EDITH KERMIT ROOSEVELT (8/6)/AUGUST 6TH"!!!~'** (86 + 86) = (`-**172**) = (72 X 1) = (`-**72**) = RECIPROCAL = (`-**27**)!!!~'

#27/PRESIDENT WILLIAM HOWARD TAFT `-**BIRTH** = SEPTEMBER 15, 1857 = (9 + 15 + 18 + 57) = (`-**99**)!!!~' #27/ PRESIDENT WILLIAM HOWARD TAFT `-**DEATH** = MARCH 8, 1930 = (3 + 8 + 19 + 30) = (`-**60**)!!!~' (9**9** (-) **6**0) = (`-**39**)!!!~' FIRST LADY HELEN HERRON TAFT `-**BIRTH** = JUNE 2, 18**61** = (6 + 2 + 18 + **61**) = (`-**87**) = **"AGE of `-DEATH** of the `-**PREVIOUS** FIRST LADY EDITH ROOSEVELT (`-**87**)"!!!~'** (61 (-) 18 (-) 2 (-) 6) = (`-**35**) = RECIPROCAL = (`-**53**)!!!~' FIRST LADY HELEN HERRON TAFT `-**DEATH** = MAY 22, 19**43** = (5 + 22 + 19 + **43**) = (`-**89**) = **"AGE of `-DEATH** of the `-**NEXT FIRST LADY EDITH WILSON (`-89**)"!!!~'** (87 + 89) = (`-**176**)!!!~' (76 + 1) = (`-**77**) = 2(**7**'s) = (`-**27**) = RECIPROCAL = (`-**72**)!!!~' THE (`-**27**TH) PRESIDENT `-**DIED** at the `-**AGE** of (`-**72**)!!!~' THE **TAFT'S** WERE MARRIED ON **JUNE** 1**9**, 18**86**!!!~' FIRST LADY HELEN HERRON TAFT `-**DIED** in

(`-**43**) & WAS `-**MARRIED** for (`-**43**) **YEARS**!!!~' (43 + 43) = (`-**86**) = "**YEAR** of `-**MARRIAGE** (`-**86**)"!!!~'

#**26**/PRESIDENT THEODORE ROOSEVELT `-**BIRTH** = OCTOBER 27, 18**58** = (10 + 27 + 18 + **58**) = (`-**113**) = (13 X 1) = (`-**13**) = "**A VERY PIVOTAL # `-NUMBER**"!!!~' #**26**/PRESIDENT THEODORE ROOSEVELT `-**DEATH** = JANUARY 6, 1919 = (1 + 6 + 19 + 19) = (`-**45**)!!!~' (113 (-) 45) = (`-**68**) = RECIPROCAL = (`-**86**) = "**THE `-MARK of the `-BEAST**"!!!~' FIRST LADY **EDITH** KERMIT ROOSEVELT `-**BIRTH** = **AUGUST 6**, 18**61** = (**8** + **6** + 1**8** + **6**1) = (`-**93**) = RECIPROCAL = (`-**39**)!!!~' (**61** (-) 1**8** (-) **6** (-) **8**) = (`-**29**)!!!~' (48 (-) 19) = (`-**29**)!!!~' (29 + 29) = (`-**58**) = "**YEAR** of `-**BIRTH** for #**26**/PRESIDENT THEODORE ROOSEVELT"!!!~' BIRTH/YEAR for THEODORE (`-**1858**) = (18 + 58) = (`-**76**) = RECIPROCAL = (`-**67**) = (19 + 48) = (`-**1948**) = **DEATH/YEAR** of `-**WIFE FIRST LADY EDITH ROOSEVELT**!!!~' FIRST LADY **EDITH** KERMIT ROOSEVELT `-**DEATH** = **SEPTEMBER 3**0, **1948** = (**9** + **3**0 + 19 + 48) = (`-**106**) = (16 + 0) = (`-**16**) = RECIPROCAL = (`-**61**) = **WAS `-BORN in** (`-**61**)!!!~' `-BIRTHDAY # `-NUMBER (`-**93**) = `-EQUALS = `-DEATH/DAY (**93**/0) & `-**DEATH/DAY # `-NUMBER** (10**6**) = `-**EQUALS** (`-**RECIPROCAL**-') = `-BIRTH YEAR of `-**LIFE** (`-**61**)!!!~' THE ROOSEVELT'S WERE `-**MARRIED** on DECEMBER 2, 18**86**!!!~' **THEY** were `-**MARRIED** for (`-**32**) **YEARS**!!!~' HER `-**BIRTHDAY** (**8**/**6**) = `-**EQUALS** = "**THE `-YEAR `-SHE was `-MARRIED** (`-**86**)"!!!~' THE `-**TAFT'S** & ROOSEVELT'S `-**WEDDINGS** were (`-**199**); OR, (`-**166**) DAYS `-**AWAY** from `-**EACH** `-**OTHER**!!!~' (`-**96**) = (**32** x **3**)!!!~'

"THE `-**BUCK** STOPS `-**HERE**"!!!~'

(`-**RECIPROCAL**-`) =

"The `-MIRRORED `-IMAGE of the `-PRECEDING # `-NUMBER"!!!~'

`-**CREATOR** = AUTHOR: DWAYNE W. ANDERSON!!!~'

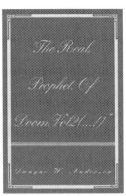

NEW BOOK /||\ REAL MESSAGES OF `-GOD I, II; & III-!!!~' /||\

The `-END!!!~'

AMERICAN SNOWBOARDER JAKE BURTON CARPENTER (65) (BIRTH: APRIL 29, 1954) (DEATH: NOVEMBER 20, 2019)

(54 (-) 19 (-) 29 (-) 4) = (`-2) = `-DIED on a (`-20ᵗʰ)!!!~'

BIRTHDAY # `-NUMBER = (4 + 29 + 19 + 54) = **106**

DEATH/DAY # `-NUMBER = (11 + 20 + 20 + 19) = **70**

(106 (-) 70) = (`-**36**) = RECIPROCAL = (`-**63**)!!!~'

(106 + 70) = (`-**176**) = (76 + 1) = (`-**77**)!!!~'

HE DIED (`-**160**) DAYS BEFORE HIS NEXT BIRTHDAY!!!~'
SWIPE 1 = `-BIRTHDAY # `-NUMBER (`-106)!!!~'

(365 (-) 160) = (`-**205**)!!!~' (5 + 2) = (`-**7**)!!!~'

HE DIED AT THE `-AGE of (`-**65**)!!!~' (6 x 5) = (`-**30**)!!!~'

APRIL 29 = (4 x 29) = (`-**116**)!!!~'

NOVEMBER 20 = (11 x 20) = (`-**220**) = (RECIPROCAL = (`-**022**)!!!~'

(220 (-) 116) = (`-**104**) = (4 x 1) = (`-**4**)!!!~'

APRIL 29, 1954 = (4 + 2 + 9 + 1 + 9 + 5 + 4) = (`-**34**)!!!~'

NOVEMBER 20, 2019 = (1 + 1 + 2 + 0 + 2 + 0 + 1 + 9) = (`-**16**)!!!~'

$(\underline{34} + \underline{16}) = (`-\underline{50})!!!\_`$

$(`-1954) = (54 (-) 19) = (`-\underline{35})!!!\_`$

$(`-2019) = (20 + 19) = (`-\underline{39})!!!\_`$

$(35 + 39) = (`-\underline{74}) = RECIPROCAL = (`-\underline{47})!!!\_`$

$(39 (-) 35) = (`-\underline{4})!!!\_`$

$(74 + 4) = (`-\underline{78}) = `-\underline{AGE}$ of `-**DEATH** of **AMERICAN SINGER/ SONGWRITER ROBERT HUNTER LYRICIST FOR "THE GRATEFUL DEAD" & AMERICAN ACTOR ROBERT FORSTER** (`-\underline{78}) **& HALL OF FAME FOOTBALL PLAYER WILLIE BROWN** (`-\underline{78})!!!\_`

$(\mathbf{1120} + \underline{\mathbf{429}}) = (`-\mathbf{1549}) = (15 + 49) = (`-\underline{\mathbf{64}}) = (32 \times 2)!!!\_`$

$(\mathbf{1120} (-) \underline{\mathbf{429}}) = (`-\underline{\mathbf{691}}) = (91 \times 6) = (`-\underline{\mathbf{546}}) = (46 \times 5) = (`-\underline{\mathbf{230}})!!!\_`$

$(230 (-) 64) = (`-\underline{\mathbf{166}}) = (16 \times 6) = (`-96) = (\underline{\mathbf{32}} \times \underline{\mathbf{3}})!!!\_`$

K-POP STAR/ARTIST GOO HARA (28) (BIRTH: JANUARY 13, 1991) (DEATH: NOVEMBER 24, 2019)

$(91 (-) 19 (-) 13 (-) 1) = (`-\underline{\mathbf{58}}) = (5 + 8) = (`-\underline{\mathbf{13}}) = `-\underline{\mathbf{DAY}}$ of `-**BIRTH** **for K-POP STAR/ARTIST GOO HARA!!!**_`

`-**19** = RECIPROCAL = `-**91** = `-**BORN** in (`-**91**) & `-**DIED** in (`-**19**)!!!_`

BIRTHDAY # `-NUMBER = $(1 + 13 + 19 + 91) = \underline{\mathbf{124}} = (24 \times 1) = (`-\underline{\mathbf{24}}) = `-$**DIED on the** (`-**24**th) **OF THE MONTH!!!**_`

DEATH/DAY # `-NUMBER = (11 + 24 + 20 + 19) = **74**

(124 (-) 74) = (`-**50**)**!!!~'**

(124 + 74) = (`-**198**) = (98 + 1) = (`-**99**)**!!!~'**

SHE DIED (`-**50**) DAYS BEFORE HER NEXT BIRTHDAY!!!~'
EQUALS = "THE `-DIFFERENCE BETWEEN `-BIRTHDAY # `-NUMBER & `-DEATH/DAY # `-NUMBER (`-50)"!!!~'

(365 (-) 50) = (`-**315**)!!!~' (15 X 3) = (`-**45**) = RECIPROCAL = (`-**54**)**!!!~'**

SHE DIED AT THE `-AGE of (`-**28**)!!!~' (2 x 8) = (`-**16**)!!!~'

JANUARY 13 = (1 x 13) = (`-**13**)!!!~'

NOVEMBER 24 = (11 x 24) = (`-**264**)!!!~'

(264 + 13) = (`-**277**)**!!!~'**

JANUARY 13, 1991 = (1 + 1 + 3 + 1 + 9 + 9 + 1) = (`-**25**)**!!!~'**

NOVEMBER 24, 2019 = (1 + 1 + 2 + 4 + 2 + 0 + 1 + 9) = (`-**20**)!!!~'

(**25** + **20**) = (`-**45**)**!!!~'**

(`-1991) = (91 (-) 19) = (`-**72**)**!!!~'**

(`-2019) = (20 + 19) = (`-**39**)!!!~'

(72 + 39) = (`-**111**)**!!!~'** (72 (-) 39 = (`-**33**)!!!~'

(111 (-) 33) = (`-**78**) = `-**AGE** of `-**DEATH** of **AMERICAN SINGER/SONGWRITER ROBERT HUNTER LYRICIST**

FOR "THE GRATEFUL DEAD" & AMERICAN ACTOR ROBERT FORSTER (`-78) & HALL OF FAME FOOTBALL PLAYER WILLIE BROWN (`-78)!!!~'

(1124 + 113) = (`-1237) = (12 + 37) = (`-49)!!!~'

(1124 (-) 113) = (`-1011) = (10 + 11) = (`-21)!!!~'

(49 (-) 21) = (`-28) = `-AGE of `-DEATH for K-POP STAR/ ARTIST GOO HARA (`-28)!!!~'

CANADIAN-TAIWANESE MODEL GODFREY GAO (`-35) (BIRTH: SEPTEMBER 22, 1984) (DEATH: NOVEMBER 27, 2019)

(84 (-) 19 (-) 22 (-) 9) = (`-34) = "BIRTHDAY # `-NUMBER"!!!~'

BIRTHDAY # `-NUMBER = (9 + 22 + 19 + 84) = 134 = (34 + 1) = (`-35) = "AGE OF `-DEATH" (`-35)!!!~'

DEATH/DAY # `-NUMBER = (11 + 27 + 20 + 19) = 77 = 2(7's) = (`-27) = "DAY OF `-DEATH" (`-27)!!!~'

(134 (-) 77) = (`-57) = RECIPROCAL = (`-75)!!!~'

(134 + 77) = (`-211) = (2 x 11) = (`-22) = "DAY OF BIRTH" (`-22)!!!~'

HE DIED (`-66) DAYS AFTER HIS LAST BIRTHDAY!!!~'

(365 (-) 66) = (`-299)!!!~' (99 x 2) = (`-198)!!!~'

HE DIED AT THE `-AGE of (`-35)!!!~' (3 x 5) = (`-15)!!!~'

SEPTEMBER 22 = (9 x 22) = (`-**198**)!!!~'

NOVEMBER 27 = (11 x 27) = (`-**297**) = (RECIPROCAL) = (`-**792**)!!!~'

(297 (-) 198) = (`-**99**)!!!~'

`-*BIRTHDAY* = SEPTEMBER 22, 1984 = (9 + 2 + 2 + 1 + 9 + 8 + 4) = (`-**35**) = "**AGE of `-DEATH**" (`-**35**) & **BIRTHDAY # `-NUMBER** (`-**134**) = (34 + 1) = (`-**35**)!!!~'

NOVEMBER 27, 2019 = (1 + 1 + 2 + 7 + 2 + 0 + 1 + 9) = (`-**23**)!!!~'

(**35** + **23**) = (`-**58**)!!!~'

(`-1984) = (84 (-) 19) = (`-**65**)!!!~'

(`-2019) = (20 + 19) = (`-**39**)!!!~'

(65 + 39) = (`-**104**)!!!~' (65 (-) 39) = (`-**26**)!!!~'

(104 (-) 26) = (`-**78**) = `-**AGE** of `-**DEATH** of **AMERICAN SINGER/SONGWRITER ROBERT HUNTER LYRICIST FOR "THE GRATEFUL DEAD" & AMERICAN ACTOR ROBERT FORSTER** (`-**78**) & **HALL OF FAME FOOTBALL PLAYER WILLIE BROWN** (`-**78**)!!!~'

(1127 + **922**) = (`-2049) = (20 + 49) = (`-**69**) = (**3** x **23**)!!!~'

(1127 (-) 922) = (`-**205**) = (20 x 5) = (`-**100**)!!!~'

(69 +100) = (`-**169**) = (69 x 1) = (`-**69**) = (**3** x **23**)!!!~'

(`-**69**) = (6 x 9) = (`-**54**)!!!~'

SEPTEMBER 22 (**BIRTH**) + NOVEMBER 27 (**DEATH**) = (9 + 22 + 11 + 27) = ('-**69**)!!!~'

#1/PRESIDENT GEORGE WASHINGTON '-**DIED** at the '-**AGE** of ('-**67**) in ('-**1799**)!!!~' ('-1799) = (99 (-) 17) = ('-**82**) = RECIPROCAL = ('-**28**) = "THE ('-**28TH**) PRESIDENT WOODROW WILSON '-**DIED** in the '-**YEAR** of ('-**24**) ONE-HUNDRED & TWENTY-FOUR ('-**124**) YEARS LATER at the '-**AGE** of ('-**67**)!!!~' ONE BEING '-**BORN** & THE OTHER ONE '-**DYING** in the **MONTH** of '-**DECEMBER**; AND, THE '-**OTHER BEING** '-**BORN** & THE OTHER ONE '-**DYING** in the '-**MONTH** of '-**FEBRUARY**!!!~' (**2**) FEBRUARY/(**12**) DECEMBER = ('-**212**) = "THE **BIRTHDAY** of #16/PRESIDENT ABRAHAM LINCOLN WHO at the '-AGE of ('-**56**) DIED in the '-**RECIPROCAL** '-**YEAR** of ('-**65**)!!!~' #16/PRESIDENT ABRAHAM LINCOLN was '-**BORN** on (2/12/1809) = (2 + 12 + 18 + 09) = ('-**41**)!!!~' #16/PRESIDENT ABRAHAM LINCOLN '-**DIED** on (04/15/1865) = (4 + 15 + 18 + 65) = ('-**102**)!!!~' (**102**) DEATH # (-) **41** (BIRTH #) = ('-**61**) = RECIPROCAL = ('-**16**) = FOR THE ('-**16TH**) PRESIDENT ABRAHAM LINCOLN & **THE DEATH DAY** of the '-**PREVIOUS PRESIDENT** #15/PRESIDENT JAMES BUCHANAN who '-**DIED** on (**6/1**) = **JUNE 1st** = (6/1/1868)!!!~' ('-1868) = (18 + 68) = ('-**86**) = RECIPROCAL = ('-**68**) = "THE '-**MARK of the** '-**BEAST**"!!!~'

#14/PRESIDENT FRANKLIN PIERCE **BIRTH** = (11/**23**/18**04**) = (11 + 23 + 18 + 04) = ('-**56**) = ABRAHAM LINCOLN!!!~' #12/PRESIDENT ZACHARY TAYLOR **BIRTH** = (11/**24**/17**84**) = (11 + 24 + 17 + 84) = ('-**136**) = (36 x 1) = ('-**36**) = RECIPROCAL = ('-**63**) = "DAY of '-DEATH" = (7 x 9) = (**JULY 9th**) = **DYING at the** '-**AGE of** ('-**65**) = ABRAHAM LINCOLN!!!~' #12/PRESIDENT ZACHARY TAYLOR **DEATH/DAY** # '-**NUMBER** = (7/9/1850)

= (7 + 9 + 18 + 50) = `-(`-**84**)-` = "**HE WAS `-BORN in (`-84)**"!!!~'
(84 + 84) = (`-**168**)!!!~' (1850) = (50 + 18) = (`-**68**) = "**THE `-MARK of the `-BEAST**"!!!~'

#13/PRESIDENT MILLARD FILLMORE `-**DIED** at the `-AGE of (`-**74**) in (`-**74**)!!!~' #15/PRESIDENT JAMES BUCHANAN was `-BORN in (`-**1791**) = (91 (-) 17) = (`-**74**)!!!~' (74 x 3) = (`-**222**) = "**BIRTHDAY** of #1/PRESIDENT GEORGE WASHINGTON WHO `-DIED on (**12/14**) = (12 x 14) = (`-**168**) = "**THE `-MARK of the `-BEAST**"!!!~' #1/PRESIDENT GEORGE WASHINGTON was `-BORN in (`-**32**); while, #15/PRESIDENT JAMES BUCHANAN & #14/PRESIDENT FRANKLIN PIERCE were `-**BORN** on a (`-**23**rd)!!!~' #28/PRESIDENT WOODROW WILSON `-**DIED** on a (**2/3**) IN (**24**); while, #12/PRESIDENT ZACHARY TAYLOR was `-BORN on a (`-**24**$^{th}$); and, WHEN `-YOU COUNT #12/PRESIDENT ZACHARY TAYLOR'S **BIRTHDAY # `-NUMBER** (`-**BACKWARDS**) `-YOU GET (84 (-) 17 (-) 24 (-) 11) = (`-**32**)!!!~' #14/PRESIDENT FRANKLIN PIERCE **BIRTH** = (11/**23**/18**04**) = (11 + 23 + 18 + 04) = (`-**56**); AND, `-**DEATH** = (10/8/1869) = (10 + 8 + 18 + 69) = (`-**105**)!!!~' (105 + 56) = (`-**161**) (**ALL-IN-ONE # `-NUMBER**) = #**16**/PRESIDENT ABRAHAM LINCOLN & #15/PRESIDENT JAMES BUCHANAN**'S `-DEATH/DAY**!!!~'

#17/PRESIDENT ANDREW JOHNSON'S **BIRTHDAY # `-NUMBER** = (12/29/1808) = (12 + 29 + 18 + 08) = (`-**67**) & `-**DIED** in `-HIS (`-**67TH**) `-**YEAR of `-EXISTENCE** at the `-**AGE** of (`-**66**) = (6 x 6) = (`-**36**) = RECIPROCAL = (`-**63**) = "**AGE of `-DEATH of FIRST LADY MARY TODD LINCOLN**"!!!~' `-**BORN** in (`-**1808**) & `-**DIED** in (`-**1875**)!!!~' (1808) = (18 + 08) = (`-**26**)!!!~' (1875) = (18 + 75) = (`-**93**)!!!~' (93 (-) 26) = (`-**67**) = "**AGE of `-DEATH** of #1/PRESIDENT GEORGE WASHINGTON `-**WHO** was `-**BORN** in (`-**1732**) & `-**DIED** in (`-**1799**)!!!~' #1/PRESIDENT GEORGE WASHINGTON'S **DEATH/DAY #**

`-**NUMBER** in `-**REVERSE** = (99 (-) 17 (-) 14 (-) 12) = (`-**56**) = #16/
PRESIDENT ABRAHAM LINCOLN'S `-**AGE of** `-**DEATH!!!**~'
(1732) = (17 + 32) = (`-**49**) = (4 x 9) = (`-**36**)!!!~' (1799) = (17 + 99)
= (`-**116**) = (**SWIPE 1** = **161**)!!!~' (116 (-) 49) = (`-**67**) = `-**AGE of**
`-**DEATH** of #**28**/PRESIDENT WOODROW WILSON & #**23**/
PRESIDENT BENJAMIN HARRISON **WHOSE** `-**BIRTHDAY**
WAS ON **AUGUST 20**th = (**8**/**2**0) = (8 + 20) = (`-**28**)!!!~' #**23**/
PRESIDENT BENJAMIN HARRISON `-**BIRTH** = (8/20/1833) =
(8 + 20 + 18 + 33) = (`-**79**) = (7 x 9) = #12/PRESIDENT ZACHARY
TAYLOR'S DEATH/DAY = (`-**63**) = RECIPROCAL = (`-**36**)!!!~'
#**23**/PRESIDENT BENJAMIN HARRISON'S `-**DEATH** `-**DAY**
`-**NUMBER** = (03/13/1901) = (03 + 13 + 19 + 01) = "(`-**36**)" =
3(**6**'s) = (`-**666**)!!!~'

#22/#24/PRESIDENT GROVER CLEVELAND `-**BIRTH** =
(03/18/1837) = (03 + 18 + 18 + 37) = (`-**76**) = RECIPROCAL =
(`-**67**)!!!~' THERE were (`-2**67**) DAYS that `-**HE** `-**DIED** before
`-**HIS** `-**NEXT** `-**BIRTHDAY!!!**~' THE (`-**24TH**) PRESIDENT
`-**DIED** on a (`-**24TH**) = (06/**24**/1908) = (06 + 24 + 19 + 08)
= (`-**57**)!!!~' (76 (-) 57) = (`-**19**)!!!~' #25/PRESIDENT WILLIAM
MCKINLEY `-**BIRTH** = (0**1**/2**9**/18**43**) = (01 + 29 + 18 + 43)
= (`-**91**) = RECIPROCAL = (`-**19**) = "**TO THE** `-**PREVIOUS**
`-**PRESIDENT;** `-**AGAIN, #22/#24/ PRESIDENT GROVER
CLEVELAND**"!!!~' #25/PRESIDENT WILLIAM MCKINLEY
`-**DEATH** (`-**ASSASSINATION**) = (09/14/1901) = (09 + 14 + 19
+ 01) = (`-**43**) = `-**DEATH/DAY** # `-**NUMBER** (`-**43**) = "**THE**
`-**YEAR** `-**HE was** `-**BORN** (`-**43**)!!!**~' (43 + 43) = (`-**86**) =
RECIPROCAL = (`-**68**) = "**THE** `-**MARK of the** `-**BEAST**"!!!~'
`-**DEATH/DAY** = (0**9**/1**4**) = (**9** + 1**4**) = (`-**23**)!!!~' (9 x 4) = (`-**36**) = **3**(**6**'s) = (`-**666**)!!!~' (`-**23**) = RECIPROCAL = (`-**32**)!!!~'
THE (`-**26**th) PRESIDENT THEODORE ROOSEVELT was
`-**MARRIED** to `-**HIS** `-**FIRST LADY** `-**EDITH** `-**ROOSEVELT**

for (`-**32**) **YEARS!!!~' `-NOTE** & `-**LOOK** at `-**HOW** `-**MANY** `-**PRESIDENTS** got `-**MARRIED** in (`-**86**)!!!~'"

WHY `-DO `-WE have `-LAWS???~' SO that `-WE can `-REALLY `-ENJOY; A LOT `-MORE, `-OUT of `-EVERYTHING; that `-EXISTS!!!~'

The `-**MARK** (`-**68**)-'

Of the

`-**BEAST**!!!~' (`-**666**)-' = **3**(**6**'s)!!!~'

The `-**PROPHET** `-LOST `-HIS `-**MOTHER** & `-**FATHER** at the `-**AGES** of (`-**63**) & (`-**66**) on the `-**VERY** `-**SAME** `-**DAY** just (`-**4**) **HOURS** `-**APART!!!~'** (63 + 66) = (`-**129**)!!!~' (129 X 4) = (`-**516**) = (56 X 1) = (`-**56**) = "**AGE of `-DEATH** of #16/PRESIDENT ABRAHAM LINCOLN WHOSE `-WIFE FIRST LADY `-MARY TODD LINCOLN `-**DIED** at the `-**AGE** of (`-**63**)"!!!~'

FROM: **#1**-PRESIDENT = GEORGE WASHINGTON `-DAY of `-DEATH – DECEMBER 14th – (12/14) = (12 x 14) = `-**168**!' TO **#2**-PRESIDENT = JOHN ADAMS `-DAY of `-DEATH = JULY 4$^{th}$ = (7/4) = (7 x 4) = `-**28**!' = (`-**163**) `-DAYS!!!~'

AS a `-REMINDER for the `-SIMPLEST of `-CREATION a `-SPERM `-CELL; and, an `-EGG (OOCYTE) `-FORM `-YOU with `-ALL of `-ITS `-MAGNIFICENTS to `-CONTEMPLATE `-EVEN this `-BOOK that `-YOU are ACTUALLY `-READING RIGHT `-NOW!!!~' CAN `-ANYONE `-SEE the `-HAND of `-GOD; `-HERE!!!~'

WITH `-GOD `-STITCHING `-US `-TOGETHER IN `-TIME `-PHYSICALLY & TIMELY; IT JUST `-BOGGLES THE `-MIND!!!~'

`-DEATH `-DATE = <u>APRIL 17</u>, 1790 = $(4 + 17 + 17 + 90) = ($`-**128**$)$ = **BENJAMIN FRANKLIN'S `-DEATH/DAY # `-NUMBER!!!~'** (`-**28**) = RECIPROCAL = (`-**82**)!!!~'

$(41 + 41) = ($`-**82**$)$!!!~' **DEATH/DAY to DEATH/DAY with BENJAMIN FRANKLIN & ALEXANDER HAMILTON = (`-86) DAYS!!!~'** (`-**86**) = RECIPROCAL = (`-**68**) = "THE `-MARK of the `-BEAST"!!!~'**

FROM **ALEXANDER HAMILTON'S** BIRTHDAY = **JANUARY 11** -to- **BENJAMIN FRANKLIN'S** BIRTHDAY = **JANUARY 17** /|\ $(11 + 17) = ($`-**28**$)$!!!~'

BENJAMIN FRANKLIN'S DEATH = <u>APRIL 17</u>th = (4/17) = (47 x 1) = (`-47) = "THE `-AGE of `-DEATH of `-ALEXANDER HAMILTON"!!!~'

`-**DEATH** `-**DATE** = **JULY 12**th, 1<u>804</u> = $(7 + 12 + 18 + 4)$ = `-**41** = **ALEXANDER HAMILTON'S DEATH/DAY # `-NUMBER!!!~'**

`-BORN `-DATE = JANUARY 17ᵗʰ, 1706 = (1 + 17 + 17 + 6) = `-41 = BENJAMIN FRANKLIN'S `-BIRTHDAY # `-NUMBER!!!~'

(JANUARY 17ᵗʰ -to- JULY 12ᵗʰ) = (`-176) DAYS!!!~' THEY are `-ALMOST `-EXACT `-RECIPROCALS of `-EACH `-OTHER = 712 = RECIPROCAL = 217 (117)!!!~'

THIS (1/2); DOES `-IT `-STAND for (FEBRUARY 12ᵗʰ)!!!~'

#16/PRESIDENT ABRAHAM LINCOLN was `-BORN FEBRUARY 12ᵗʰ, 1809 = (2 + 12 + 18 + 09) = `-41!~'

(41 + 41 + 41) = (`-123)!!!~' ALEXANDER HAMILTON'S BIRTHDAY = JANUARY 11ᵗʰ!!!~' FROM `-HIS `-BIRTHDAY to #16/PRESIDENT ABRAHAM LINCOLN'S BIRTHDAY there are (`-32) DAYS!!!~' (`-32) = RECIPROCAL = (`-23)!!!~'

BENJAMIN FRANKLIN'S DEATH/DATE & #16/PRESIDENT ABRAHAM LINCOLN'S DEATH/DATES are (`-363) `-DAYS away FROM EACH `-OTHER!!!~'

#16/PRESIDENT ABRAHAM LINCOLN `-DIED APRIL 15ᵗʰ, 1865 = (4 + 15 + 18 + 65) = `-102!~' (`-102) = (12 + 0) = (`-12) = "THIS MYSTERIOUS #12; `-AGAIN" & "THE BIRTHDAY of the `-PRESIDENT"!!!~'

FROM: ALEXANDER HAMILTON'S DEATH/DATE & #16/PRESIDENT ABRAHAM LINCOLN'S DEATH/DATES /|\ they are (`-88) `-DAYS away FROM EACH `-OTHER!!!~' (8 x 8) = (`-64) = RECIPROCAL = (`-46) = "AGE of FIRST LADY MARY TODD LINCOLN at the `-TIME of `-DEATH of HER

`-HUSBAND #16/PRESIDENT ABRAHAM LINCOLN"!!!~'
(`-**88**) = **2**(**8's**) = (`-**28**)!!!~'

`-**BORN** = (`-**1944**) = (19 + 44) = (`-**63**)!!!~' THE `-**PROPHET'S MOTHER** `-**DIED** at the `-**AGE** of (`-**63**)!!!~'

The `-PROPHET'S `-MOTHER `-PASSED on (**4**/1**6**/2**00**8) = (4 + 16 + 20 + 8) = (`-**48**) = "The `-**MARK**"!!!~' SHE was `-BORN on (11/15/**1944**) = (11 + 15 + **19** + **44**) = (`-**89**) = "The `-**DEATH** `-AGE of** `-**HER** `-**MOTHER** (`-**89**)!!!~'

(**89** (-) **48**) = (`-**41**)!!!~'

`-**HER** `-**SISTER** FRANCES A. ROUGHT `-**PASSED** (`-**81**) DAYS `-LATER on (**7**/**6**/2008) = (7 + 6 + 20 + 08) = (`-**41**)!!!~' SHE was `-BORN on (10/29/1933) = (10 + 29 + 19 + 33) = (`-**91**)!!!~' (91 + 41) = (`-**132**)!!!~' (365 (-) 81) = (`-2**84**) = (2 x 84) = (`-**168**) = (68 x 1) = (`-**68**) = "The `-MARK of the `-BEAST"!!!~' THEIR `-FATHER `-DIED at the `-AGE of (`-**86**)!!!~' (`-**86**) = RECIPROCAL = (`-**68**)!!!~'

(41 + 41) = (`-**82**) = RECIPROCAL = (`-**28**) = "THESE `-SISTERS `-BOTH `-DIED in (`-**2**00**8**)!!!~'

The `-**PROPHET'S BROTHER** was `-**BORN** in (`-**1967**) = (19 + 67) = (`-**86**) = "**AGE** of `-**DEATH** of `-**MATERNAL GRANDFATHER**"!!!~'

The "PROPHET" & the "PROPHET'S" BROTHER are (`-1**89**) DAYS AWAY from EACH OTHER from `-**BIRTH** to `-**BIRTH**!!!~'

THE `-**PROPHET'S** `-**MOTHER LOST** `-**HER** `-**LIFE** at the `-**AGE** of (`-**63**); while, `-**HER** `-**SISTER LOST** `-**HER** `-**LIFE** at the `-**AGE** of (`-**74**)!!!~' (7 x 4) = (`-**28**)!!!~' (6 x 3) = (`-**18**)!!!~' (28 + 18) = (`-**46**) = "**DAY** of `-**DEATH** of the `-**PROPHET'S** `-**MOTHER**"!!!~'

FRANCES A. ROUGHT `-**DIED** (`-**115**) DAYS before `-**HER** `-**NEXT** `-**BIRTHDAY**!!!~' THIS is an (**all-in-one-#**) FOR `-**HER YOUNGER SISTER (THE `-PROPHET'S MOTHER'S)** `-**BIRTHDAY** = (11/15)!!!~'

THE "PROPHET'S" MOTHER `-**DIED** (`-**213**) = (23 x 1) = (`-**23**) = **DAYS** BEFORE `-**HER** `-**NEXT** `-**BIRTHDAY**!!!~'

(213 (-) 115) = (`-**98**) = RECIPROCAL = (`-**89**) = "**AGE of** `-**DEATH** of `-**THEIR** `-**MOTHER (THE "PROPHET'S" GRANDMOTHER)**"!!!~'

FRANCES A. ROUGHT'S HUSBAND JUST PASSED!!!~' HER HUSBAND SELLIVAN ROUGHT `-PASSED on (11/18/2019) = (11 + 18 + 20 + 19) = (`-**68**)!!!~' HE was `-BORN on (6/12/1930) = (6 + 12 + 19 + 30) = (`-**67**) = RECIPROCAL = (`-**76**) = "**HIS** `-**WIFE'S** `-**DAY** of `-**DEATH** (**JULY** 6th)!!!~' HE `-**DIED** at the `-**AGE** of (`-**89**) = "**THE** `-**AGE** of `-**DEATH** of `-**HIS** `-**MOTHER-IN-LAW**"!!!~'

`-HE `-DIED (`-**206**) DAYS BEFORE `-HIS `-NEXT `-BIRTHDAY!!!~' `-BORN (**612**)!!!~' (`-**62**) = RECIPROCAL = (`-**26**)!!!~' (206 (-) 115 (WIFE) = (`-**91**) – "**WIFE'S FRANCES A. ROUGHT'S** `-**BIRTHDAY # `-NUMBER**"!!!~'

FRANCES & SELLIVAN ROUGHT `-**LOST** their `-**SON**; SELLIVAN ANDREW ROUGHT JR. in (`-**2012**) = (20 + 12) = (`-**32**)!!!~' SELLIVAN ANDREW ROUGHT JRS. `-BIRTHDAY = (5/3/19**63**) = (5 + 3 + 19 + **63**) = (`-**90**)!!!~' HIS `-DEATH/DAY = (12/29/2012) = (12 + 29 + 20 + 12) = (`-**73**)!!!~' (90 + 73) = (`-**163**)

= (63 x 1) = (`-**63**) = "**AGE** of `-**DEATH** of `-HIS `-AUNTIE
(THE `-PROPHET'S MOTHER)"!!!~' THE `-**DAYS** `-between
`-**DEATHS** of `-FATHER & `-SON is (`-**41**) DAYS = "HIS
`-MOTHER & `-AUNTIE (`-**41**)"!!!~'

SELLIVAN ANDREW ROUGHT JR. `-**PASSED** at the `-**AGE** of
(`-**49**); which, IS THE `-**CURRENT** `-**AGE** of the `-**PROPHET** for
WHILE I AM WRITING this `-**BOOK** of #'S `-**NUMBERS**!!!~'
HIS `-FATHER was `-BORN in (`-**1930**) = (19 + 30) = (`-**49**)!!!~'
(4 x 9) = (`-**36**) = RECIPROCAL = (`-**63**) = "THE `-PROPHET'S
`-MOTHER & HIS `-YEAR of `-BIRTH; WHICH, (ALSO)
`-MIRRORS HIS `-AUNTIE"!!!~' `-HE `-DIED (`-**125**) DAYS
BEFORE `-HIS `-NEXT `-BIRTHDAY!!!~' (`-**125**) = (25 + 1) =
(`-**26**) = HIS `-FATHER'S # `-NUMBER (**206**)!!!~' (125 + 206) =
(`-**331**) = (33 x 1) = (`-**33**) = "YEAR HIS `-MOTHER FRANCES
A. ROUGHT was `-BORN (`-**33**)"!!!~' SHE was `-**BORN** on a (`-
29th) & `-**HE** `-**DIED** on a (`-**29**th)!!!~' (`-**92**) = RECIPROCAL =
(`-**29**)!!!~' (92 (-) 29) = (`-**63**)!!!~' (2012 (-) 1933) = (`-**79**) = (7 x 9) =
(`-**63**)!!!~' (63 + 63) = (`-**126**) = RECIPROCAL = (`-**621**) = SWIPE
1 = (**612**) = "SELLIVAN ROUGHT SR'S. `-BIRTHDAY (JUNE
12th)"!!!~' (62 + 1) = (`-**63**)!!!~' (61 x 2) = (`-**122**) = (22 + 1) = (`-**23**)
= -a PROPHETIC # `-NUMBER!!!~' (2012 (-) 1930) = (`-**82**) =
RECIPROCAL = (`-**28**) = "HIS `-**MOTHER** & `-**AUNTIE** `-both
`-**DIED** in (`-**2008**)!!!~' (**2008**) = (20 + 08) = (`-**28**)!!!~'

THE `-**PROPHET** was `-**BORN** on (03/20/1970) = (03 + 20) =
(`-**23**)!!!~' (19 + 70) = (`-**89**)!!!~'

(49 + 49) = (`-**98**) = RECIPROCAL = (`-**89**) = "**AGE** of `-**DEATH**
of `-**FATHER** & **GRANDMOTHER** for SELLIVAN ANDREW
ROUGHT JR."!!!~'

SELLIVAN ROUGHT'S `-**YEAR** of `-**BIRTH** = (`-**1930**) = (19 + 30) = (`-**49**) = "**AGE** of `-**DEATH** of `-**HIS** `-**SON** SELLIVAN ANDREW ROUGHT JR. (`-**49**)"!!!~'

THE `-PROPHET'S MOTHER'S `-TWIN `-SISTER `-LOST `-HER `-DAUGHTER at the `-**AGE** of (`-**49**) JUST as `-**WELL**!!!~' SHE was in the `-LAST `-BOOK!!!~'

HER `-NAME is **ANEESHA RENEE HEARD** with a `-BIRTHDAY of (**7**/3**1**/19**68**) = (**7** + **3**1 + 19 + **68**) = (`-**125**) = "HER COUSIN **SELLIVAN ANDREW ROUGHT JR.**"!!!~ HER `-DEATH/DAY = (**3**/1**6**/2**0**18) = (**3** + 1**6** + 2**0** + 18) = (`-**57**)!!!~' (125 + 57) = (`-**182**) = (82 x 1) = (`-**82**) = RECIPROCAL = (`-**28**) = "SHE `-DIED in (`-**2018**)"!!!~' (`-**2018**) = (28 x 1 + 0) = (`-**28**)!!!~' BORN in (`-**68**) = "The `-**MARK**"!!!~' (125 (-) 57) = (`-**68**)!!!~' **DEATH/ DAY** = (**3**/1**6**) = (36 x 1) = (`-**36**) = RECIPROCAL = (`-**63**)!!!~'

SHE `-**DIED** (`-**137**) DAYS BEFORE `-**HER** `-**NEXT** `-**BIRTHDAY**!!!~' HER BIRTHDAY is (**7**/3**1**) = (73 x 1) = (`-**73**) = RECIPROCAL = (`-**37**)!!!~' THIS is a `-**PATTERN** with `-**ALL** of the `-**CELEBRITIES** that the `-**DISTANCE** from **DEATH/ DAY** to **BIRTHDAY** = `-**EQUALS** = "THE `-**RECIPROCAL** of the `-**BIRTHDAY**"!!!~' (`-**137**) = RECIPROCAL (**MIRRORS**) = (`-**731**)!!!~'

HER `-**UNCLE**; and, the `-**ELDEST** of the `-**BROTHER'S** `-**PASSED** ` **AWAY** `-RECENTLY; **Just as WeLL**!!!~' HIS `-NAME is FRANK BYRDWELL JR.!!!~' HIS BIRTHDAY = (0**6**/**3**0/19**37**) = (0**6** + **3**0 + 19 + **37**) = (`-**92**)!!!~' HIS DEATH/DAY = (0**4**/**2**0/2018) = (04 + 20 + 20 + 18) = (`-**62**)!!!~' (92 + 62) = (`-**154**)!!!~' (06 + 30) = (`-**36**) = RECIPROCAL = (`-**63**)!!!~' HE was `-**BORN** in (`-**37**) = "**HIS NIECE ANEESHA RENEE HEARD** (`-**37**/**73**-`)"!!!~' (154 (-) 80) = (`-**74**) = "**HIS** `-**SISTER FRANCES A. ROUGHT**"!!!~'

FRANK BYRDWELL JR. `-**PASSED** `-**AWAY** at the `-**AGE** of (`-**80**); (`-**71**) DAYS BEFORE `-**HIS** `-**NEXT** `-**BIRTHDAY**!!!-` (NIECE (`-**137**) + (`-**71**) = (`-**208**) = (20 + 8) = (`-**28**) = "**BOTH** `-**DIED** in (`-**2018**)"!!!-`

(NIECE (`-**137**) (-) (`-**71**) = (`-**66**)!!!-` ANEESHA RENEE **HEARD** & **FRANK BYRDWELL JR.** from `-**DEATH/ DAY** to `-**DEATHDAY** = (3/16) to (4/20) = (`-**35**) **DAYS**!!!-` ANEESHA RENEE HEARD & FRANK BYRDWELL JR. from `-**BIRTHDAY** to `-**BIRTHDAY** = (6/30) to (7/31) = (`-**31**) **DAYS**!!!-` (35 + 31) = (`-**66**) = (6 x 6) = (`-**36**) = RECIPROCAL = (`-**63**)!!!-` THEIR **BIRTHDAY** (UNCLE) & **DEATH/DAY** (NIECE) are `-**RECIPROCALS** (**MIRRORS**) of `-**EACH** `-**OTHER** = (**6**/**3**0)/\(**3**/1**6**)!!!-` THEY `-**BOTH** are `-**END** of the `-**MONTH** `-**BABIES**!!!-` (66 + 66) = (`-**132**) = (32 x 1) = (`-**32**) = -a PROPHETIC # `-**NUMBER**!!!-`

`-**BORN** = (`-**1944**) = (19 + 44) = (`-**63**)!!!-`

`-**BORN** = (`-**1933**) = (19 + 33) = (`-**52**)!!!-` `-**HUSBAND** & **WIFE** (=)

`-**BORN** = (`-**1930**) = (19 + 30) = (`-**49**)!!!-` (`-**33**) + (`-**30**) = (`-**63**)!!!-`

`-**BORN** = (`-**1963**) = (19 + 63) = (`-**82**)!!!-`

`-**BORN** = (`-**1968**) = (19 + 68) = (`-**87**)!!!-`

`-**BORN** = (`-**1937**) = (19 + 37) = (`-**56**)!!!-`

(63 + 52 + 49 + 82 + 87 + 56) = (`-**3**(**89**))!!!-`

AVERAGE `-DIVIDED by (`-**6**) = (`-**64.83**333)!!!-`

DIVIDED by (`-**2**) = (`-**32.**41**666**)!!!-`

The `-**PROPHET'S BROTHER** was `-**BORN** in (`-**1967**) = (19 + 67) = (`-**86**) = "**AGE** of `-**DEATH** of `-**MATERNAL GRANDFATHER**"!!!~'

The "PROPHET" & the "PROPHET'S" BROTHER are (`-1**89**) DAYS AWAY from EACH OTHER from `-**BIRTH** to `-**BIRTH**!!!~'

The "PROPHET" & the "PROPHET'S" FATHER are (`-1**65**) DAYS AWAY from EACH OTHER from `-**BIRTH** to `-**BIRTH**!!!~'

The "PROPHET" & the "PROPHET'S" MOTHER are (`-**24**0) DAYS AWAY from EACH OTHER from `-**BIRTH** to `-**BIRTH**!!!~'

(89 (-) 24) = (`-**65**) = "**SIMPLE** `-**ARITHMETIC**" = "**ALL** of the `-**FAMILY** `-**ADDS** `-**UP**"!!!~'

(`-**165**) = (65 + 1) = (`-**66**) = "**AGE** of `-**DEATH** of the `-**PROPHET'S FATHER**"!!!~' The "PROPHET'S" FATHER'S `-**FATHER PASSED** at `-AGE (`-**88**)!!!~' (**66/88**) = (`-**68**) = "The `-**MARK**"!!!~'

The "PROPHET'S" FATHER was `-BORN in (9/1/1941) = (9 + 1 + 19 + 41) = (`-**70**) = "THE YEAR the `-PROPHET was `-BORN (`-**70**)"!!!~'

The "PROPHET'S" MOTHER & the "PROPHET'S" FATHER are (`-**75**) DAYS AWAY from EACH OTHER from `-**BIRTH** to `-**BIRTH**!!!~'

The "PROPHET'S" MOTHER & the "PROPHET'S" BROTHER are (`-**51**) DAYS AWAY from EACH OTHER from `-**BIRTH** to `-**BIRTH**!!!~'

The "PROPHET'S" MOTHER & the "PROPHET" are (`-**240**) DAYS AWAY from EACH OTHER from `-**BIRTH** to `-**BIRTH**!!!~'

(75 + 51) = (`-**126**) / 2 = (`-**63**) = "**AGE** of `-**DEATH** of the `-**PROPHET'S** **MOTHER**"!!!~'

(75 + 51 + 240) = (`-**366**) = "*(ALL-IN-ONE-#-NUMBER)* for the `-**DEATHS** of `-**BOTH** of the `-**PROPHET'S** `-**PARENTS**"!!!~'

THEATER ACTRESS SHELLEY MORRISON (**83**) (BIRTH: OCTOBER 26, 19**36**) (DEATH: DECEMBER 1, 2019)

(10 + 26) = (`-**36**) = `-**BIRTHDAY** = "THE `-**YEAR** `-**SHE** was `-**BORN** in (`-**36**)"!!!~'

BIRTHDAY # `-NUMBER = (10 + 26 + 19 + 36) = **91**

DEATH/DAY # `-NUMBER = (12 + 1 + 20 + 19) = **52**

(91 (-) 52) = (`-**39**) = "THE `-**YEAR** that `-**SHE** `-**DIED** (`-**39**) = (**20** + **19**)"!!!~'

(91 + 52) = (`-**143**) = (43 x 1) = (`-**43**)!!!~' (43 x 2) = (`-**86**) = RECIPROCAL = (`-**68**) = "The `-**MARK**"!!!~'

SHE DIED (`-**36**) DAYS AFTER HER LAST BIRTHDAY!!!~'

(365 (-) 36) = (`-**329**)!!!~' (29 + 3) = (`-**32**) = -a PROPHETIC # `-**NUMBER**!!!~'

SHE DIED AT THE `-AGE of (`-**83**)!!!~' (8 x 3) = (`-**24**)!!!~'

OCTOBER 26 = (10 x 26) = (`-**260**)!!!~'

DECEMBER 1 = (12 x 1) = (`-**12**)!!!~'

(260 + 12) = (`-**272**) = **RECIPROCAL-<u>S</u>EQUENCING-<u>N</u>UMEROLOGY-RSN!!!~'**

OCTOBER 26, 1936 = (1 + 0 + 2 + 6 + 1 + 9 + 3 + 6) = (`-**28**)!!!~'

DECEMBER 1, 2019 = (1 + 2 + 1 + 2 + 0 + 1 + 9) = (`-**16**)!!!~'

(**28** + **16**) = (`-**44**)!!!~'

(`-1936) = (36 (-) 19) = (`-**17**)!!!~'

(`-2019) = (20 + 19) = (`-**39**)!!!~'

(17 + 39) = (`-**56**)!!!~' (39 (-) 17) = (`-**22**)!!!~'

(56 + 22) = (`-**78**) = `-**<u>AGE</u>** of `-**<u>DEATH</u>** of **AMERICAN SINGER/ SONGWRITER ROBERT HUNTER LYRICIST FOR "THE GRATEFUL DEAD" & AMERICAN ACTOR ROBERT FORSTER (`-78) & HALL OF FAME FOOTBALL PLAYER WILLIE BROWN (`-78)!!!~'**

(1026 + **121**) = (`-1147) = (47 (-) 11) = (`-**36**) = `-**HER `-BIRTHDAY** (10 + 26) = "**THE `-YEAR `-SHE was `-BORN**" (`-**36**) = "**THE AMOUNT of `-DAYS AFTER `-HER `-BIRTHDAY** that `-**<u>SHE</u> `-<u>DIED</u>** (`-36)!!!~'

(1026 (-) **121**) = (`-**905**) = (90 + 5) = (`-**95**)!!!~'

(95 + 36) = (`-**131**) = (**13 x 1**) = (`-**13**) = "**A VERY PIVOTAL # `-NUMBER**"!!!~'

(`-**36**) = **RECIPROCAL** = (`-**63**)!!!~'

(95 (-) 36) = (`-**59**) = RECIPROCAL = (`-**95**)!!!~'

`-MARRIED to WALTER DOMINGUEZ from (`-19**73** to `-2019)!!!~'

(2019 (-) 19**73**) = (`-**46**) = (`-**23** x **2**) = (`-**232**) = **R**ECIPROCAL-**S**EQUENCING-**N**UMEROLOGY-**RSN**!!!~'

BREAKING NEWS TODAY!!!~'

(200 (-) 122) = (`-**78**)!!!~'

12/**2**/2019!!!~' (**12** + **2** + 20 + 19) = (`-**53**)!!!~' (DAY = **12**/**2** = (`-**122**) = (22 + 1) = (`-**23**)!!!~'

THE `-**SENATE** (`-**53**) **REPUBLICANS** has (`-**23**) `-**SEATS UP** for `-**GRABS** `-**NEXT** `-**YEAR** in (`-**20/20**)!!!~'

(78 + 53) = (`-**131**) = (13 x 1) = (`-**13**) = **"A VERY PIVOTAL #** `-**NUMBER"**!!!~'

THE `-**HOUSE** has (`-**31**) `-**SEATS UP** for `-**GRABS** `-**NEXT** `-**YEAR** in (`-**20/20**)!!!~'

HOUSE REPUBLICANS WRITE **123**-PAGE REPORT DEFENDING TRUMP IN IMPEACHMENT INQUIRY!!!~'

(53 + 123) = (`-**176**) = (76 x 1) = (`-**76**) = RECIPROCAL = (`-**67**) = **"THE `-AMOUNT `-NEEDED in the `-SENATE to `-CONVICT & `-REMOVE from the `-OFFICE of the `-PRESIDENT"**!!!~' **(`-2/3rds) `-MAJORITY**!!!~'

(`-**230**) `-**YEARS** `-**AGO** the `-**IMPEACHMENT** `-**CLAUSE** was `-**THOUGHT** `-**UP**!!!~'

162

HOUSE JUDICIARY COMMITTEE `-VOTES to `-IMPEACH `-PRESIDENT `-TRUMP!!!~'

ARTICLE **1**: (`-**23**) DEMS / (`-**17**) REPS

ARTICLE **2**: (`-**23**) DEMS / (`-**17**) REPS

(17 + 17) = (`-**34**) = `-REPUBLICAN `-VOTES!!!~'

(`-**34**) + (ARTICLE `-**1**, ARTICLE `-**2**) / (`-**12**) = (`-**46**) = `-DEMOCRATIC `-VOTES!!!~'

DATE: (12/18/2019) = (12 x 18) = (`-216)!!!~'

`-SIMPLE `-MAJORITY (`-**216**) **VOTES NEEDED to `-IMPEACH!!!~'** (2 x 16) = (`-**32**)!!!~'

FULL HOUSE ON AGREEING to ARTICLE I of the RESOLUTION

H RES 755

ARTICLE 1 = ABUSE of `-POWER

DEMOCRATIC /|\ REPUBLICAN /|\ INDEPENDENT

TOTALS = YEA (`-**230**) /|\ NAY (`-**197**) /|\ PRESENT (`-**1**) /|\ NOT VOTING (`-**3**)

(230 + 197 + 1 + 3) = (`-**431**) = (43 x 1) = (`-**43**) = RECIPROCAL = (`-**34**)!!!~'

NAY = (`-**197**) = (19 x 7) = (`-**133**) = (33 (-) 1) = (`-**32**) = RECIPROCAL = (`-**23**) = -a PROPHETIC # `-NUMBER!!!~'

FULL HOUSE ON AGREEING to ARTICLE II of the RESOLUTION

H RES 755

ARTICLE 2 = OBSTRUCTION of `-JUSTICE

DEMOCRATIC /|\ REPUBLICAN /|\ INDEPENDENT

TOTALS = YEA (`-**229**) /|\ NAY (`-**198**) /|\ PRESENT (`-**1**) /|\ NOT VOTING (`-**3**)

(229 + 198 + 1 + 3) = (`-**431**) = (43 x 1) = (`-**43**) = RECIPROCAL = (`-**34**)!!!~'

YEA = (`-**229**) = (22 x 9) = (`-**198**) = **NAY!!!~'**

AMERICAN FILM/TELEVISION PRODUCER LEONARD GOLDBERG (85) (BIRTH: JANUARY 24, 1934) (DEATH: DECEMBER 4, 2019)!!!~'

`-BIRTHDAY (`-1/24) = `-DEATH/DAY (`-12/4)!!!~'

BIRTHDAY # `-NUMBER = (1 + 24 + 19 + 34) = **78**

DEATH/DAY # `-NUMBER = (12 + 4 + 20 + 19) = **55**

(78 (-) 55) = (`-**23**) = RECIPROCAL = (`-**32**)!!!~'

(78 + 55) = (`-**133**) = (33 + 1) = (`-**34**) = **"YEAR of `-BIRTH"** (`-**34**)!!!~'

HE DIED (`-**51**) DAYS BEFORE HIS NEXT BIRTHDAY!!!~'

(365 (-) 51) = (`-**314**)!!!~' (34 x 1) = (`-**34**) = **"YEAR of `-BIRTH"** (`-**34**)!!!~'

HE DIED AT THE `-AGE of (`-**85**)!!!~' (8 x 5) = (`-**40**)!!!~'

JANUARY 24 = (1 x 24) = (`-**24**)!!!~'

DECEMBER 4 = (12 x 4) = (`-**48**) = (RECIPROCAL) = (`-**84**)!!!~'

(48 (-) 24) = (`-**24**)!!!~'

JANUARY 24, 1934 = (1 + 2 + 4 + 1 + 9 + 3 + 4) = (`-**24**) = **`-BIRTHDAY (`-24)!!!~'**

DECEMBER 4, 2019 = (1 + 2 + 4 + 2 + 0 + 1 + 9) = (`-**19**)!!!~'

(**24** + **19**) = (`-**43**) = RECIPROCAL = (`-**34**) = **"YEAR of `-BIRTH"** (`-**34**)!!!~'

(`-1934) = (34 (-) 19) = (`-**15**)!!!~'

(`-2019) = (20 + 19) = (`-**39**)!!!~'

(15 + 39) = (`-**54**)!!!~' (39 (-) 15) = (`-**24**)!!!~'

(54 + 24) = (`-**78**) = **`-AGE** of **`-DEATH** of **AMERICAN SINGER/ SONGWRITER ROBERT HUNTER LYRICIST FOR "THE GRATEFUL DEAD" & AMERICAN ACTOR ROBERT FORSTER (`-78) & HALL OF FAME FOOTBALL PLAYER WILLIE BROWN (`-78)!!!~'**

(**124** + **124**) = (`-**248**) = (24 + 8) = (`-**32**)!!!~'

(**124** + **124**) = (`-**248**) = (2 + 4) 8) = (`-**68**)!!!~'

(124 (-) 124) = (`-**0**)!!!~'

(32 + 0) = (`-**32**) = -a PROPHETIC # `-NUMBER!!!~'

JANUARY 24 (**BIRTH**) + DECEMBER 4 (**DEATH**) = (1 + 24 + 12 + 4) = (`-**41**)!!!~'

(34 + 34) = (`-**68**) = "THE `-MARK of the `-BEAST"!!!~'

AMERICAN ACTOR RON LEIBMAN (82) (BIRTH: OCTOBER 11, 1937) (DEATH: DECEMBER 6, 2019)!!!~'

BIRTHDAY # `-NUMBER = (10 + 11 + 19 + 37) = **77**

DEATH/DAY # `-NUMBER = (12 + 6 + 20 + 19) = **57**

(77 (-) 57) = (`-**20**)!!!~'

(77 + 57) = (`-**134**) = (34 + 1) = (`-**35**)!!!~'

HE DIED (`-**56**) DAYS AFTER HIS LAST BIRTHDAY!!!~'

(**365** (-) **56**) = (`-**309**)!!!~' (30 x 9) = (`-**270**) = (27 + 0) = (`-**27**) = **2(7's)** = (`-**77**) = "BIRTHDAY # `-NUMBER"!!!~'

HE DIED AT THE `-AGE of (`-**82**)!!!~' (8 x 2) = (`-**16**)!!!~'

OCTOBER 11 = (10 x 11) = (`-**110**)!!!~'

DECEMBER 6 = (12 x 6) = (`-**72**) = (RECIPROCAL) = (`-**27**)!!!~'

(110 (-) 72) = (`-**38**)!!!~'

OCTOBER 11, 1937 = (1 + 0 + 1 + 1 + 1 + 9 + 3 + 7) = (`-**23**) = RECIPROCAL = (`-**32**)!!!~'

DECEMBER 6, 2019 = (1 + 2 + 6 + 2 + 0 + 1 + 9) = (`-**21**)!!!~'

(**23** + **21**) = (`-**44**)!!!~'

(`-1937) = (37 (-) 19) = (`-**18**)!!!~'

(`-2019) = (20 + 19) = (`-**39**)!!!~'

(18 + 39) = (`-**57**) = "**DEATH/DAY # `-NUMBER**"!!!~'

(39 (-) 18) = (`-**21**)!!!~'

(57 + 21) = (`-**78**) = `-**AGE** of `-**DEATH** of **AMERICAN SINGER/ SONGWRITER ROBERT HUNTER LYRICIST FOR "THE GRATEFUL DEAD" & AMERICAN ACTOR ROBERT FORSTER (`-78) & HALL OF FAME FOOTBALL PLAYER WILLIE BROWN (`-78)**!!!~'

(**1011** + **126**) = (`-**1137**) = (11 + 37) = (`-**48**) = "**MARRIED for a `-TOTAL of (`-48) YEARS = JESSICA WALTER (`-36) - (1983 to 2019) & LINDA LAVIN (`-12) (1969 to 1981)**"!!!~'

(**1011** (-) **126**) = (`-**885**) = (85 x 8) = (`-**680**) = (68 + 0) = (`-**68**) = "**THE `-MARK**"!!!~'

(680 (-) 48) = (`-**632**) = (**63 x 2**) = (`-**126**) = "**DAY of `-DEATH**" = (**12/6**) = "**DECEMBER 6ᵗʰ**"!!!~'

OCTOBER 11 (**BIRTH**) + DECEMBER 6 (**DEATH**) = (10 + 11 + 12 + 6) = (`-**39**) = "**DIES IN (`-39) = (20 + 19)**"!!!~'

FROM `-WIFE'S JESSICA WALTER'S `-BIRTHDAY to `-BIRTHDAY of `-HUSBAND'S AMERICAN ACTOR RON LEIBMAN = (`-112) DAYS!!!~'

(`-112 (/) 2) = (`-**56**) = "HOW MANY DAYS from `-WIFE'S JESSICA WALTER'S `-BIRTHDAY & HER `-HUSBAND'S AMERICAN ACTOR RON LEIBMAN'S `-DEATH/DAY" = (`-**56**) DAYS = "CUT in `-HALF"!!!~'

AGAIN; `-HE DIED (`-56) DAYS AFTER HIS LAST BIRTHDAY & (`-56) DAYS BEFORE HIS WIFE'S NEXT `-BIRTHDAY!!!~'

AT `-TIME of `-DEATH `-WIFE JESSICA WALTER was (`-**78**) & `-**BORN** on (JANUARY 31, 1941) = (1 + 31 + 19 + 41) = (`-**92**)!!!~' (**12/7**/2019) = "(`-**78**ᵗʰ) ANNIVERSARY of `-PEARL HARBOR `-ATTACK (`-19**41**)"!!!~'

AT `-TIME of `-DEATH FORMER `-WIFE LINDA LAVIN was (`-**82**) & `-**BORN** on (OCTOBER 15, 1937) = (10 + 15 + 19 + 37) = (`-**81**)!!!~'

(92 + 81) = (`-**173**) = (73 x 1) = (`-**73**) = RECIPROCAL = (`-**37**) = "AMERICAN ACTOR RON LEIBMAN was `-**BORN** in (`-**37**)"!!!~'

AMERICAN RAPPER JUICE WRLD (JARAD ANTHONY HIGGINS) (21) (BIRTH: DECEMBER 2, 1998) (DEATH: DECEMBER 8, 2019)!!!~' (**31 (-) 8**) = (`-**23**)!!!~'

(98 (-) 19 (-) 2 (-) 12) = (`-**65**) = RECIPROCAL = (`-**56**)!!!~'

BIRTHDAY # `-NUMBER = (12 + 2 + 19 + 98) = **131**

DEATH/DAY # `-NUMBER = (12 + 8 + 20 + 19) = **59**

(131 (-) 59) = (`-**72**)**!!!~'**

(131 + 59) = (`-**190**) = (19 + 0) = (`-**19**) = RECIPROCAL = (`-**91**)**!!!~'**

(91 (-) 19) = (`-**72**)**!!!~'**

HE DIED (`-**6**) DAYS AFTER HIS LAST BIRTHDAY!!!~'

(3**65** (-) **6**) = (`-**359**)!!!~' (59 x 3) = (`-**177**) = (77 x 1) = (`-**77**) = **2**(**7**'**s**) = (`-**27**)**!!!~'**

HE DIED AT THE `-AGE of (`-**21**)!!!~' (**3** x **7**)**!!!~'**

DECEMBER 2 = (12 x 2) = (`-**24**)**!!!~'**

DECEMBER 8 = (12 x 8) = (`-**96**) = (RECIPROCAL) = (`-**69**) = (**3** x **23**)**!!!~'**

(96 (-) 24) = (`-**72**)**!!!~'**

DECEMBER **2**, 1998 = (1 + 2 + 2 + 1 + 9 + 9 + 8) = (`-**32**) = RECIPROCAL = **(`-23)!!!~'**

DECEMBER **8**, 2019 = (1 + 2 + 8 + 2 + 0 + 1 + 9) = (`-**23**) = RECIPROCAL = (`-**32**)**!!!~'**

(**32** + **23**) = (`-**55**)**!!!~'**

BIRTHDAY & DEATH/DAY = EQUAL = <u>RECIPROCALS</u> = (23/32) = "HE has `-ALL of the #'s `-NUMBERS `-HERE"!!!~'

(`-1998) = (98 (-) 19) = (`-**79**)!!!~'

(`-2019) = (20 + 19) = (`-**39**)!!!~'

(79 + 39) = (`-**118**)!!!~' (79 (-) 39) = (`-**40**)!!!~'

(118 (-) 40) = (`-**78**) = `-**AGE** of `-**DEATH** of **AMERICAN SINGER/SONGWRITER ROBERT HUNTER LYRICIST FOR "THE GRATEFUL DEAD" & AMERICAN ACTOR ROBERT FORSTER (`-78) & HALL OF FAME FOOTBALL PLAYER WILLIE BROWN (`-78)!!!~'**

(**128** + **122**) = (`-**250**) = (25 + 0) = (`-**25**)!!!~'

(**128** (-) **122**) = (`-**6**)!!!~'

(25 + 6) = (`-**31**) = RECIPROCAL = (`-**13**) = **"A VERY PIVOTAL # `-NUMBER"!!!~'**

DECEMBER 2 (**BIRTH**) + DECEMBER 8 (**DEATH**) = (12 + 2 + 12 + 8) = (`-**34**)!!!~'

(34 (-) 21 (**AGE of** `-**DEATH**) = (`-**13**) = **"A VERY PIVOTAL # `-NUMBER"!!!~'**

`-**BORN** & `-**DIED** in the `-**MONTH** of `-**DECEMBER** = (`-**12**) = RECIPROCAL = (`-**21**) = **"AGE of `-DEATH"!!!~'**

AMERICAN PUPPETEER for SESAME STREET'S "BIG BIRD & OSCAR the GROUCH" (CAROLL SPINNEY) (**85**) (BIRTH: **DECEMBER 26**, 1933) (DEATH: **DECEMBER 8**, 2019)!!!~' (31 (-) 8) = (`-**23**)!!!~'

BIRTHDAY # `-NUMBER = (12 + 26 + 19 + 33) = **90**

DEATH/DAY # `-NUMBER = (12 + 8 + 20 + 19) = **59**

(90 (-) 59) = (`-**31**) = RECIPROCAL = (`-**13**) = **"A VERY PIVOTAL # `-NUMBER"!!!~'**

(90 + 59) = (`-**149**) = (14 x 9) = (`-**126**) = **(ALL-IN-ONE-#-NUMBER) for `-HIS `-BIRTHDAY (1/_22_/6)!!!~'**

HE DIED (`-**18**) DAYS BEFORE HIS NEXT BIRTHDAY**!!!~'**

(365 (-) 18) = (`-**347**)!!!~' (47 x 3) = (`-**141**) = (14 x 1) = (`-**14**) = **RECIPROCAL** = (`-**41**) = (41 + 14) = (`-**55**) = (23 + 32)**!!!~'**

HE DIED AT THE `-AGE of (`-**85**)!!!~' (**8** x **5**) = (`-**40**) = **"MARRIED to `-HIS `-WIFE DEBRA SPINNEY for (`-40) YEARS from (1979 to 2019)"!!!~'**

DECEMBER 26 = (12 x 26) = (`-**312**) = (32 x 1) = (`-**32**) = **-a PROPHETIC # `-NUMBER!!!~'**

DECEMBER 8 = (12 x 8) = (`-**96**) = (RECIPROCAL) = (`-**69**) = (**3** x **23**)**!!!~'**

(312 (-) 96) = (`-**216**) = (21 x 6) = (`-**126**) = **(ALL-IN-ONE-#-NUMBER) for `-HIS `-BIRTHDAY (1/_22_/6)!!!~'**

DECEMBER **26**, 1933 = (1 + 2 + 2 + 6 + 1 + 9 + 3 + 3) = (`-**27**) = RECIPROCAL = **(`-72)!!!~'**

DECEMBER **8**, 2019 = (1 + 2 + 8 + 2 + 0 + 1 + 9) = (`-**23**) = RECIPROCAL = (`-**32**)**!!!~'**

(**27** + **23**) = (`-**50**)!!!~'

(`-1933) = (33 (-) 19) = (`-**14**)!!!~'

(`-2019) = (20 + 19) = (`-**39**)!!!~'

(14 + 39) = (`-**53**)!!!~' (39 (-) 14) = (`-**25**)!!!~'

(53 + 25) = (`-**78**) = `-<u>AGE</u> of `-<u>DEATH</u> of AMERICAN SINGER/ SONGWRITER ROBERT HUNTER LYRICIST FOR "THE GRATEFUL DEAD" & AMERICAN ACTOR ROBERT FORSTER (`-**78**) & HALL OF FAME FOOTBALL PLAYER WILLIE BROWN (`-**78**)!!!~'

(**1226** + **128**) = (`-**1354**) = (13 + 54) = (`-**67**)!!!~'

(**1226** (-) **128**) = (`-**1098**) = (10 + 98) = (`-**108**)!!!~'

(**1226** (-) **128**) = (`-**1098**) = (98 (-) 10) = (`-**88**)!!!~'

(108 + 67) = (`-**175**) = (1 + 7) 5 = (`-**85**) = "AGE of `-DEATH for AMERICAN PUPPETEER of SESAME STREET'S "BIG BIRD & OSCAR the GROUCH" (CAROLL SPINNEY)(`-**85**)"!!!~'

(88 (-) 67) = (`-**21**) = "AGE of `-DEATH of AMERICAN RAPPER JUICE WRLD (JARAD ANTHONY HIGGINS) (`-**21**)"!!!~'

DECEMBER 26 (**BIRTH**) + DECEMBER 8 (**DEATH**) = (12 + 26 + 12 + 8) = (`-**58**)!!!~'

(`-**58**) = RECIPROCAL = (`-**85**) = "HIS `-<u>BIRTHDAY</u> & `-<u>DEATH/DAY</u> `-<u>ADDED</u> `-<u>UP</u> to `-<u>HIS</u> `-<u>OWN</u> `-<u>AGE</u> of `-<u>DEATH</u> (`-**85**)"!!!~'

`-<u>BORN</u> & `-<u>DIED</u> in the `-MONTH of `-DECEMBER = (`-**12**) = RECIPROCAL = (`-**21**) = (12 + 21) = (`-**33**) = "YEAR of `-BIRTH" (`-**33**)!!!~'

`-DIED (`-**18**) DAYS AWAY from `-BEING (`-**86**) = RECIPROCAL = (`-**68**) = "THE `-**MARK**"!!!~' (86 (-) 18) = (`-**68**)!!!~'

AMERICAN ACTOR of "BENSON" AND "STAR TREK" (RENE AUBERJONOIS) (**79**) (BIRTH: **JUNE 1**, 1940) (DEATH: **DECEMBER 8**, 2019)!!!~' (**31** (-) **8**) = (`-**23**)!!!~'

`-DIED (in-between) a (`-**7**) & a (`-**9**) at the `-**AGE** of (`-**79**)!!!~'

BIRTHDAY # `-NUMBER = (6 + 1 + 19 + 40) = **66** = (6 x 6) = (`-**36**) = RECIPROCAL = (`-**63**) = (7 x 9) = (`-**79**) = "AGE of `-DEATH for AMERICAN ACTOR RENE AUBERJONOIS"!!!~'

DEATH/DAY # `-NUMBER = (12 + 8 + 20 + 19) = **59** = (`-**1940**) = "YEAR of `-BIRTH" = `-EQUALS = "DEATH/DAY # `-NUMBER = (19 + 40) = (`-**59**)!!!~'

(66 (-) 59) = (`-**7**)!!!~'

(66 + 59) = (`-**125**) = (12 x 5) = (`-**60**)!!!~' **BORN** on (`-61)!!!~'

HE DIED (`-**175**) DAYS BEFORE HIS NEXT BIRTHDAY!!!~' (17 x 5) = (`-**85**) = "AGE of `-DEATH for AMERICAN PUPPETEER for SESAME STREET'S "BIG BIRD & OSCAR the GROUCH" (CAROLL SPINNEY) (`-**85**)"!!!~'

(365 (-) 175) = (`-**190**)!!!~' (19 + 0) = (`-**19**) = **RECIPROCAL** = (`-**91**)!!!~'

(91 (-) 19) = (`-**72**)!!!~'

HE DIED AT THE `-AGE of (`-**79**)!!!~' (**7** x **9**) = (`-**63**)!!!~'

JUNE 1 = (6 x 1) = (`-**6**)!!!~'

DECEMBER 8 = (12 x 8) = (`-**96**) = (RECIPROCAL) = (`-**69**) = (**3** x **23**)!!!~'

(96 (-) 6) = (`-**90**)!!!~'

JUNE **1**, 1940 = (6 + 1 + 1 + 9 + 4 + 0) = (`-**21**) = RECIPROCAL = (`-**12**)!!!~'

DECEMBER **8**, 2019 = (1 + 2 + 8 + 2 + 0 + 1 + 9) = (`-**23**) = RECIPROCAL = (`-**32**)!!!~'

(**21** + **23**) = (`-**44**)!!!~'

(`-1940) = (40 (-) 19) = (`-**21**)!!!~'

(`-2019) = (20 + 19) = (`-**39**)!!!~'

(21 + 39) = (`-**60**)!!!~'

(39 (-) 21) = (`-**18**)!!!~'

(60 + 18) = (`-**78**) = `-**AGE** of `-**DEATH** of **AMERICAN SINGER/ SONGWRITER ROBERT HUNTER LYRICIST FOR "THE GRATEFUL DEAD" & AMERICAN ACTOR ROBERT FORSTER (`-78) & HALL OF FAME FOOTBALL PLAYER WILLIE BROWN (`-78)!!!~'**

(**128** + **61**) = (`-**189**) = (1 (-) 8) 9 = (`-**79**) = **"AGE of `-DEATH for AMERICAN ACTOR of "BENSON" AND "STAR TREK" (RENE AUBERJONOIS) (`-79)"!!!~'**

(**128** + **61**) = (`-**189**) = (18 + 9) = (`-**27**)!!!~'

(128 (-) 61) = (`-**67**)!!!~'

(67 + 27) = (`-**94**) = (9 x 4) = (`-**36**) = RECIPROCAL = (`-**63**) = (7 x 9) = (`-**79**) = **"AGE of `-DEATH for AMERICAN ACTOR of "BENSON" AND "STAR TREK" (RENE AUBERJONOIS) (`-79)"!!!~'**

JUNE 1 (**BIRTH**) + DECEMBER 8 (**DEATH**) = (6 + 1 + 12 + 8) = (`-**27**)!!!~'

(79 RENE AUBERJONOIS **(-) 21** JUICE WRLD) = (`-**58**) = RECIPROCAL = (`-**85**) = **"AGE of `-DEATH for AMERICAN PUPPETEER for SESAME STREET'S "BIG BIRD & OSCAR the GROUCH" (CAROLL SPINNEY) (`-85)"!!!~'**

`-ALL (`-**3**) `-THREE `-TIED `-TOGETHER!!!~'

`-DIED in (`-12) & was `-BORN in (`-6) = (`-126) = (ALL-IN-ONE-#-NUMBER) for AMERICAN PUPPETEER of the SESAME STREET'S "BIG BIRD & OSCAR the GROUCH" CAROLL SPINNEY'S `-BIRTHDAY (1/22/6)!!!~'

CAPTAIN of "DEEP SPACE NINE" AVERY BROOKS = `-BIRTHDAY # `-NUMBER = (10/2/1948) = (10 + 2 + 19 + 48) = (`-**79**) = "AGE of `-DEATH of AMERICAN ACTOR of "BENSON" AND "STAR TREK" (RENE AUBERJONOIS) (`-**79**)"!!!~'

ANOTHER "STAR TREK" ACTOR (COLM MEANEY) from "DEEP SPACE NINE" was ` BORN on (5/30/1953)!!!~' (`-53) = RECIPROCAL = (`-35)!!!~'

HUSBAND of STAR TREK ACTRESS MARINA SIRTIS (STAR TREK NEXT GENERATION) (MICHAEL LAMPER) ROCKER & ACTOR on STAR TREK NEXT GENERATION

DIED at the `-**AGE** (`-**61**) (RENE AUBERJONOIS' `-BIRTHDAY **(6/1)** on (12/7/2019) = (12 + 7 + 20 + 19) = (`-**58**) = RECIPROCAL = (`-**85**) = "AGE of `-DEATH for AMERICAN PUPPETEER for SESAME STREET'S "BIG BIRD & OSCAR the GROUCH" (CAROLL SPINNEY) (`-**85**)"!!!~' MR. MICHAEL LAMPER was `-BORN in (`-**58**)!!!~'

FORMER CHAIR (CARTER-REAGAN) of the FEDERAL RESERVE PAUL VOLCKER (92) (BIRTH: SEPTEMBER 5, 1927) (DEATH: DECEMBER 8, 2019)!!!~' **(31 (-) 8) = (`-23)!!!~'**

DECEMBER 8 = (12/8) = (12 x 8) = (`-96) = (32 x 3)!!!~'

(`-**92**) = RECIPROCAL = (`-**29**)!!!~' (92 (-) 29) = (`-**63**)!!!~'

BIRTHDAY # `-NUMBER = (9 + 5 + 19 + 27) = **60**

DEATH/DAY # `-NUMBER = (12 + 8 + 20 + 19) = **59**

(60 (-) 59) = (`-**1**)!!!~'

(60 + 59) = (`-**119**) = (11 x 9) = (`-**99**)!!!~'

HE DIED (`-**94**) DAYS AFTER HIS LAST BIRTHDAY!!!~' (9 x 4) = (`-**36**) = RECIPROCAL = (`-**63**)!!!~'

(365 (-) 94) = (`-**271**)!!!~' (71 x 2) = (`-**142**)!!!~'

HE DIED AT THE `-AGE of (`-**92**)!!!~' (**9** x **2**) = (`-**18**)!!!~'

SEPTEMBER 5 = (9 x 5) = (`-**45**)!!!~'

DECEMBER 8 = (12 x 8) = (`-**96**) = (RECIPROCAL) = (`-**69**) = (**3** x **23**)!!!~'

(96 (-) 45) = (`-**51**)!!!~'

SEPTEMBER **5**, 1927 = (9 + 5 + 1 + 9 + 2 + 7) = (`-**33**)!!!~'

DECEMBER **8**, 2019 = (1 + 2 + 8 + 2 + 0 + 1 + 9) = (`-**23**) = RECIPROCAL = (`-**32**)!!!~'

(**33** + **23**) = (`-**56**)!!!~'

(`-1927) = (27 (-) 19) = (`-**8**)!!!~'

(`-2019) = (20 + 19) = (`-**39**)!!!~'

(8 + 39) = (`-**47**)!!!~'

(39 (-) 8) = (`-**31**)!!!~'

(47 + 31) = (`-**78**) = `-**AGE** of `-**DEATH** of **AMERICAN SINGER/ SONGWRITER ROBERT HUNTER LYRICIST FOR "THE GRATEFUL DEAD" & AMERICAN ACTOR ROBERT FORSTER** (`-**78**) **& HALL OF FAME FOOTBALL PLAYER WILLIE BROWN** (`-**78**)!!!~'

(**128** + **95**) = (`-**223**) = (22 x 3) = (`-**66**) = `-**BIRTHDAY #** `-**NUMBER** of **AMERICAN ACTOR** of **"BENSON" AND "STAR TREK" (RENE AUBERJONOIS)** (`-**66**)!!!~'

(**128** + **95**) = (`-**223**) = (23 x 2) = (`-**46**) = "**YEAR** of `-**BIRTH**" (`-**1927**) = (19 + 27) = (`-**46**)!!!~'

(**128** (-) **95**) = (`-**33**)!!!~'

(46 + 33) = (`-79) = "AGE of `-DEATH for AMERICAN ACTOR of "BENSON" AND "STAR TREK" (RENE AUBERJONOIS) (`-79)"!!!~'

SEPTEMBER 5 (**BIRTH**) + DECEMBER 8 (**DEATH**) = (9 + 5 + 12 + 8) = (`-34)!!!~'

(92 PAUL VOLCKER (-) 34) = (`-58) = RECIPROCAL = (`-85) = "AGE of `-DEATH for AMERICAN PUPPETEER for SESAME STREET'S "BIG BIRD & OSCAR the GROUCH" (CAROLL SPINNEY) (`-85)"!!!~'

STAR TREK'S RENE AUBERJONOIS = JUNE 1 (**BIRTH**) + DECEMBER 8 (**DEATH**) = (6 + 1 + 12 + 8) = (`-27)!!!~'

(34 + 27) = (`-61) = `-BIRTHDAY (6/1) of AMERICAN ACTOR of "BENSON" AND "STAR TREK" (RENE AUBERJONOIS) & `-AGE of `-DEATH of ROCKER/ACTOR MICHAEL LAMPER (`-61)!!!~'

RAPPER JUICE WRLD = DECEMBER 2 (**BIRTH**) + DECEMBER 8 (**DEATH**) = (12 + 2 + 12 + 8) = (`-34)!!!~'

(34 + 34) = (`-68) = "THE `-MARK"!!!~'

`-ALL (`-4) `-FOUR are `-TIED `-TOGETHER!!!~'

`-ALL (`-5) `-FIVE are `-TIED `-TOGETHER!!!~'

`-DIED in (`-12) & was `-BORN in (`-9) = (`-129) = "DAY after `-DEATH"!!!~'

(ALS) ICE BUCKET CHALLENGE FOUNDER /|\ BASEBALL PLAYER PETE FRATES (`-**34**) (BIRTH: DECEMBER 28, 1984) (DEATH: DECEMBER 9, 2019)!!!~'

MARRIED to WIFE JULIE FRATES SINCE (`-**2**01**3**)!!!~' **MARRIED for** (`-**6**) **YEARS!!!~'** (`-**2**01**3**) = (2 + 0 + 1 + 3) = (`-**6**)!!!~'

(`-1984) = (84 + 19) = (`-**103**) = (13 + 0) = (`-**13**) = **"A VERY PIVOTAL # `-NUMBER"!!!~'**

(`-1984) = (84 (-) 19) = (`-**65**) = RECIPROCAL = (`-**56**)!!!~'

(84 (-) 19 (-) 28 (-) 12) = (`-**25**)!!!~'

(103 (-) 65 (-) 25) = (`-**13**) = **"A VERY PIVOTAL # `-NUMBER"!!!~'**

BIRTHDAY # `-NUMBER = (12 + 28 + 19 + 84) = **143** = (43 x 1) = (`-**43**) = RECIPROCAL = (`-**34**) = **"AGE of `-DEATH for ALS ICE BUCKET CHALLENGE FOUNDER /|\ BASEBALL PLAYER PETE FRATES (`-34)"!!!~'**

DEATH/DAY # `-NUMBER = (12 + 9 + 20 + 19) = **60**

(143 (-) 60) = (`-**83**) = **"PART of the `-DEATH # `-NUMBERS"!!!~'**

(143 + 60) = (`-**203**) = (23 + 0) = (`-**23**) = RECIPROCAL = (`-**32**)!!!~'

HE DIED (`-**19**) DAYS BEFORE HIS NEXT BIRTHDAY!!!~'

(365 (-) 19) = (`-**346**)!!!~' (**34** (AGE of -DEATH) (-) **6** (YEARS-OF-MARRIAGE)) = (`-**28**) = `-BIRTHDAY of ALS ICE BUCKET CHALLENGE FOUNDER /|\ BASEBALL PLAYER PETE FRATES!!!~'

HE DIED AT THE `-AGE of (`-**34**)!!!~' (**3** x **4**) = (`-**12**) = `-**BORN** & `-**DIED** in the `-**MONTH** of (`-**12**)!!!~'

DECEMBER 28 = (12 x 28) = (`-**336**)!!!~'

DECEMBER 9 = (12 x 9) = (`-**108**)!!!~'

(336 + 108) = (`-**444**) = `-**ORIGINAL** `-**BOOK** `-**PAGE** `-**COUNT** to "The REAL PROPHET of DOOM (KISMET) - INTRODUCTION - PENDULUM FLOW"!!!~'

DECEMBER 28, 1984 = (1 + 2 + 2 + 8 + 1 + 9 + 8 + 4) = (`-**35**)!!!~'

DECEMBER 9, 2019 = (1 + 2 + 9 + 2 + 0 + 1 + 9) = (`-**24**) = RECIPROCAL = (`-**42**)!!!~'

(**35** + **24**) = (`-**59**)!!!~'

(`-1984) = (84 (-) 19) = (`-**65**)!!!~'

(`-2019) = (20 + 19) = (`-**39**)!!!~'

(65 + 39) = (`-**104**)!!!~'

(65 (-) 39) = (`-**26**)!!!~'

(104 (-) 26) = (`-**78**) = `-**AGE** of `-**DEATH** of **AMERICAN SINGER/SONGWRITER ROBERT HUNTER LYRICIST FOR "THE GRATEFUL DEAD" & AMERICAN ACTOR ROBERT FORSTER (`-78) & HALL OF FAME FOOTBALL PLAYER WILLIE BROWN (`-78)!!!~'

(**1228** + **129**) = (`-**1357**) = (13 + 57) = (`-**70**)!!!~'

(**1228** (-) **129**) = (`-**1099**) = (10 + 99) = (`-**109**)!!!~'

(109 + 70) = (`-**179**) = (79 x 1) = (`-**79**) = "AGE of `-DEATH for AMERICAN ACTOR of "BENSON" AND "STAR TREK" (RENE AUBERJONOIS) (`-**79**)"!!!~'

DECEMBER 28 (**BIRTH**) + DECEMBER 9 (**DEATH**) = (12 + 28 + 12 + 9) = (`-**61**) = `-BIRTHDAY of AMERICAN ACTOR of "BENSON" AND "STAR TREK" (RENE AUBERJONOIS) (`-**6/1**)!!!~'

`-DIED in (`-**12**) & was `-BORN in (`-**12**) = (`-**12/12**) = (12 x 12) = (`-**144**) = `-ADDED this `-MANY `-PAGES to "The REAL PROPHET of DOOM (KISMET) - INTRODUCTION - PENDULUM FLOW"!!!~'

`-BIRTHDAY = (12/28) = (ALL-IN-ONE-#-NUMBER) = (`-**128**) = `-**DIES** the **VERY NEXT** `-**DAY** on (`-**129**)!!!~'

SWEDISH SINGER (of POP/ROCK DUO GROUP ROXETTE) MARIE FREDRIKSSON (`-**61**) (BIRTH: **MAY 30**, 19**58**) (DEATH: DECEMBER 9, 2019)!!!~'

MARRIED to SWEDISH SINGER-SONGWRITER MIKAEL BOLYOS from (1994 to 2019) for (`-25) YEARS!!!~' HIS `-BIRTHDAY # `-NUMBER is (4/6/1957) = (4 + 6 + 19 + 57) = (`-86)!!!~'

AT MARIE'S TIME of `-DEATH `-HER `-HUSBAND'S `-AGE was (`-**62**); while, `-HER `-DAUGHTER'S (INEZ JOSEFIN BOLYOS) `-AGE was (`-**26**)!!!~' (`-**26**) = RECIPROCAL = (`-**62**)!!!~' (62 (-) 26) = (`-**36**)!!!~'

`-HER `-DAUGHTER'S (INEZ JOSEFIN BOLYOS) BIRTHDAY
`-NUMBER is (4/29/1993) = (4 + 29 + 19 + **93**) = (`-**145**) = (45 +
1) = (`-**46**) = **"DAD'S DATE of `-BIRTH (4/6)"!!!~'** (93 (-) 19 (-)
29 (-) 4) = (`-**41**)!!!~'

MARIE FREDRIKSSON'S `-SON OSCAR MIKAEL BOLYOS
`-BIRTHDAY # `-NUMBER is (11/**26**/1996) = (11 + **26** + 19
+ 96) = (`-**152**) = (52 x 1) = (`-**52**) = RECIPROCAL = (`-**25**) =
"PARENTS were `-MARRIED for (`-25) YEARS!!!~' AT the
`-TIME of `-HIS `-MOTHER'S `-DEATH OSCAR was (`-23)
YEARS OLD!!!~'** (96 (-) 19 (-) **26** (-) 11) = (`-**40**)!!!~' (40 + 23) =
(`-**63**) = RECIPROCAL = (`-**36**)!!!~'

BIRTHDAY # `-NUMBER = (5 + 30 + 19 + 58) = **112** =
**"DAUGHTER'S `-YEAR of `-BIRTH (`-1993) = (19 + 93) =
(`-112)"!!!~'**

DEATH/DAY # `-NUMBER = (12 + 9 + 20 + 19) = **60**

(112 (-) 60) = (`-**52**) = RECIPROCAL = (`-**25**) = **"MARRIED for
(`-25) YEARS"!!!~'**

(112 + 60) = (`-**172**) = (17 x 2) = (`-**34**) = RECIPROCAL = (`-**43**)!!!~'

SHE DIED (`-**172**) DAYS BEFORE HER NEXT BIRTHDAY!!!~'

(365 (-) 172) = (`-**193**) = (19 x 3) = (`-**57**) = **"YEAR `-HUSBAND
MIKAEL BOLYOS was `-BORN (`-57)"!!!~'**

(365 (-) 172) = (`-**193**) = (93 x 1) = (`-**93**) = **"DAUGHTER'S `-YEAR
of `-BIRTH = (`-93)"!!!~'**

SHE DIED AT THE `-AGE of (`-**61**)!!!~' (**6** x **1**) = (`-**6**)!!!~'

MAY 30 = (5 x 30) = (`-**150**)!!!~'

DECEMBER 9 = (12 x 9) = (`-**108**)!!!~'

(150 + 108) = (`-**258**)!!!~'

MAY 30, 19**58** = (5 + 3 + 0 + 1 + 9 + 5 + 8) = (`-**31**) = RECIPROCAL = (`-**13**)!!!~'

DECEMBER 9, 2019 = (1 + 2 + 9 + 2 + 0 + 1 + 9) = (`-**24**) = RECIPROCAL = (`-**42**)!!!~'

(**31** + **24**) = (`-**55**) = (23 + 32)!!!~'

(`-1958) = (58 (-) 19) = (`-**39**)!!!~'

(`-2019) = (20 + 19) = (`-**39**)!!!~'

(39 + 39) = (`-**78**)!!!~'

(39 (-) 39) = (`-**0**)!!!~'

(78 + 0) = (`-**78**) = `-**AGE** of `-**DEATH** of **AMERICAN SINGER/ SONGWRITER ROBERT HUNTER LYRICIST FOR "THE GRATEFUL DEAD" & AMERICAN ACTOR ROBERT FORSTER** (`-**78**) **& HALL OF FAME FOOTBALL PLAYER WILLIE BROWN** (`-**78**)!!!~'

(**530** + **129**) = (`-**659**) = (59 + 6) = (`-**65**) = RECIPROCAL = (`-**56**) = "**5' 6**" = HEIGHT of SWEDISH SINGER (of POP/ROCK DUO ROXETTE) MARIE FREDRIKSSON!!!~'

(**530** (-) **129**) = (`-**401**) = (40 (-) 1) = (`-**39**) = "YEAR of `-DEATH" = (`-**39**) = (20 + 19)!!!~'

(65 (-) 39) = (`-**26**) = "AGE of `-DAUGHTER at the `-TIME of `-HER `-DEATH ROXETTE'S MARIE FREDRIKSSON"!!!~'

183

MAY 30 (**BIRTH**) + DECEMBER 9 (**DEATH**) = (5 + 30 + 12 + 9) = (`-**56**`) = "5' 6" = HEIGHT of SWEDISH SINGER (of POP/ROCK DUO ROXETTE) MARIE FREDRIKSSON!!!~'

`-DIED in (`-**12**`) & was `-BORN in (`-**5**`) = (`-**12/5**`) = (12 x 5) = (`-**60**`) = "WAS `-HER `-AGE PRIOR to (`-**193**`) DAYS AGO to `-HER `-LAST `-BIRTHDAY!!!~' (`-**193**`) = (93 x 1) = (`-**93**`) = RECIPROCAL = (`-**39**`) = (20 + 19)!!!~'

MARIE FREDRIKSSON & `-HER `-HUSBAND MIKAEL BOLYOS are (`-**54**`) DAYS AWAY from EACH OTHER from `-BIRTH to `-BIRTH!!!~'

MARIE FREDRIKSSON & `-HER `-DAUGHTER INEZ JOSEFIN BOLYOS are (`-**31**`) DAYS AWAY from EACH OTHER from `-BIRTH to `-BIRTH!!!~'

MARIE FREDRIKSSON & `-HER `-SON OSCAR MIKAEL BOLYOS are (`-**185**`) DAYS AWAY from EACH OTHER from `-BIRTH to `-BIRTH!!!~' (54 + 31) = (`-**85**`) = "SEE the `-PATTERNS"!!!~'

SWEDISH SINGER (of POP/ROCK DUO GROUP ROXETTE) MARIE FREDRIKSSON was `-**BORN** in (`-**58**`) = RECIPROCAL = (`-**85**`)!!!~'

STAR TREK ENCOUNTER same `-BIRTHDAY (**5/30**) at O'BRIEN (COLM MEANEY) & `-AGE of `-DEATH (`-**61**`) the SAME as the `-BIRTHDAY (**6/1**) for AMERICAN ACTOR of "BENSON" AND "STAR TREK" (RENE AUBERJONOIS)!!!~' WAS `-**BORN** in (`-**58**`) & `-**DIED** at the `-**AGE** of (`-**61**`) just as with **MICHAEL LAMPER** (HUSBAND of STAR TREK ACTRESS MARINA SIRTIS from STAR TREK NEXT GENERATION)!!!~' (`-**58**`) = RECIPROCAL = (`-**85**`) = "AGE of `-DEATH for **AMERICAN PUPPETEER** for **SESAME STREET'S "BIG BIRD & OSCAR the GROUCH" (CAROLL SPINNEY)** (`-**85**)"!!!~'

AMERICAN ACTOR from the SITCOM "ALICE" PHILIP ANTHONY MCKEON (`-**55**) (BIRTH: NOVEMBER 11, 1964) (DEATH: DECEMBER 10, 2019)!!!~'

HIS SISTER AMERICAN ACTRESS NANCY MCKEON'S `-BIRTHDAY # `-NUMBER = (4/4/1966) = (4 + 4 + 19 + 66) = (`-93)!!!~' (66 (-) 19 (-) 4 (-) 4) = (`-39) = RECIPROCAL = (`-93)!!!~' SHE'S 5' 6" in `-HEIGHT & was `-MARRIED in (`-2003)!!!~' HER `-AGE at the `-TIME of `-HER `-BROTHER'S `-DEATH was (`-53)!!!~' NANCY MCKEON'S HUSBAND MARC ANDRUS was `-BORN in (`-1965); AND, is `-CURRENTLY (`-54) YEARS of `-AGE!!!~'

BIRTHDAY # `-NUMBER = (11 + 11 + 19 + 64) = **105**

(64 (-) 19 (-) 11 (-) 11) = (`-**23**) = -a **PROPHETIC # `-NUMBER!!!~'**

DEATH/DAY # `-NUMBER = (12 + 10 + 20 + 19) = **61** = **"THIS # `-NUMBER (`-61) has `-MANY `-ATTACHMENTS from the `-PREVIOUS `-WRITINGS"!!!~'**

(105 (-) 61) = (`-**44**) = (4 x 4) = (`-**16**) = RECIPROCAL = (`-**61**)!!!~'

(105 + 61) = (`-**166**) = (66 x 1) = (`-**66**) = **`-HIS `-SISTER'S NANCY MCKEON'S `-YEAR of `-BIRTH (`-66)!!!~'**

HE DIED (`-**29**) DAYS AFTER HIS LAST BIRTHDAY!!!~'

(365 (-) 29) = (`-**336**) = (36 + 3) = (`-**39**) = (20 + 19)**!!!~'**

HE DIED AT THE `-AGE of (`-**55**) = (23 + 32)!!!~'

NOVEMBER 11 = (11 x 11) = (`-**121**)!!!~'

DECEMBER 10 = (12 x 10) = (`-**120**)!!!~'

(121 + 120) = (`-**241**)!!!~'

NOVEMBER 11, 1964 = (1 + 1 + 1 + 1 + 1 + 9 + 6 + 4) = (`-**24**) = RECIPROCAL = (`-**42**)!!!~'

DECEMBER 10, 2019 = (1 + 2 + 1 + 0 + 2 + 0 + 1 + 9) = (`-**16**) = RECIPROCAL = (`-**61**)!!!~'

(**24** + **16**) = (`-**40**)!!!~'

(`-1964) = (64 (-) 19) = (`-**45**)!!!~'

(`-2019) = (20 + 19) = (`-**39**)!!!~'

(45 + 39) = (`-**84**)!!!~'

(45 (-) 39) = (`-**6**)!!!~'

(84 (-) 6) = (`-**78**) = `-**AGE** of `-**DEATH** of **AMERICAN SINGER/ SONGWRITER ROBERT HUNTER LYRICIST FOR "THE GRATEFUL DEAD" & AMERICAN ACTOR ROBERT FORSTER (`-78) & HALL OF FAME FOOTBALL PLAYER WILLIE BROWN (`-78)!!!~'**

(**1210** + **1111**) = (`-**2321**) = (23 + 21) = (`-**44**) = (4 x 4) = (`-**16**) = RECIPROCAL = (`-**61**)!!!~'!!!~'

(**1210** (-) **1111**) = (`-**99**)!!!~'

(99 (-) 44) = (`-**55**) = "**AGE of `-DEATH for AMERICAN ACTOR from SITCOM "ALICE" PHILIP ANTHONY MCKEON** (`-**55**)"!!!~'

NOVEMBER 11 (**BIRTH**) + DECEMBER 10 (**DEATH**) = (11 + 11 + 12 + 10) = (`-**44**)!!!~' SISTER NANCY MCKEON'S `-BIRTHDAY (**4/4**)!!!~' (100 (-) 44) = (`-**56**) = "HIS SISTER NANCY MCKEON has a `-HEIGHT of (**5' 6**")"!!!~' PHILIP ANTHONY MCKEON & HIS SISTER NANCY MCKEON are (`-**144**) DAYS AWAY from EACH OTHER from `-BIRTH to `-BIRTH!!!~'

`-DIED in (`-**12**) & was `-BORN in (`-**11**) = (`-**12/11**) = (12 x 11) = (`-**132**) = (32 x 1) = (`-**32**) = -a PROPHETIC # `-NUMBER!!!~'

`-BIRTHDAY = (11/11) = `-BORN `-BETWEEN (`-**12**) & (`-**10**) = `-HIS `-DEATH/DAY!!!~' (10, 11, 12) = PROPHETIC-LINEAR-PROGRESSION-PLP!!!~'

AMERICAN GANGSTERS!!!~'

BONNIE & CLYDE KNOWN FOR ROBBERY & VIOLENCE WERE SHOT DEAD ON MAY **23**rd, 19**34**!!!~' (5 + **23** + 19 + **34**) = (`-**81**)!!!~' (5 x 23) = (`-**115**)!!!~' (115 (-) 81) = (`-**34**) = "**THERE** were some (`-**134**) **ROUNDS** that `-**KILLED** `-**THEM**"!!!~' (`-**43**)!!!~'

PRETTY BOY FLOYD'S `-BIRTHDAY # `-NUMBER – (**2/3/19**04) = (2 + 3 + 19 + 04) = (`-**28**) = "**HE** was `-**BURIED** on the (`-**28**th) in (`-19**34**)!!!~' (**19** + 04) = (`-**23**) = "HIS `-**DAY** of `-BIRTH or `-BIRTHDAY"!!!~' (19 + 34) = (`-**53**) = "**WAR** of the `-WORLDS"!!!~' HIS `-DEATH/DAY # `-NUMBER = (10/22/1934) = (10 + 22 + 19 + 34) = (`-**85**)!!!~' (10 + 22) = (`-**32**)

= -a PROPHETIC # `-NUMBER!!!~' (85 (-) 28) = (`-**57**)!!!~' (`-**57**) = (`-**23**) + (`-**34**)!!!~' **BURIED** on (10/28/19**34**) = (10 + 28 + 19 + 34) = (`-**91**)!!!~' (91 (-) 57) = (`-**34**)!!!~'

BABY FACE NELSON'S `-**BIRTHDAY** # `-**NUMBER** = (12/6/1908) = (12 + 6 + 19 + 08) = (`-**45**)!!!~' HIS `-**DEATH/DAY** # `-**NUMBER** = (11/27/19**34**) = (11 + 27 + 19 + **34**) = (`-**91**)!!!~' (91 (-) 45) = (`-**46**) = (23 x 2)!!!~' HEIGHT = **5**' **5**" = (`-**55**) = (23 + 32)!!!~'

JOHN DILLINGER'S `-**BIRTHDAY** # `-**NUMBER** = (6/**22**/19**0**3) = (6 + **22** + 1**9** + 0**3**) = (`-**50**)!!!~' (6 x 22) = (`-**132**) = (32 x 1) = (`-**32**) = -a PROPHETIC # `-**NUMBER**!!!~' HIS `-**DEATH/DAY** # `-**NUMBER** = (7/**22**/19**34**) = (7 + **22** + 19 + 34) = (`-**82**)!!!~' (`-**28**) = RECIPROCAL = (`-**82**)!!!~' (82 (-) 50) = (`-**32**) = -a PROPHETIC # `-**NUMBER!!!~' BORN** on a (`-**22**nd) & **DIED** on a (`-**22**nd)!!!~' (22 + 22) = (`-**44**)!!!~' (44 + **34**) = (`-**78**)!!!~' HEIGHT = **5**' **7**" = (`-**57**) = (`-**23**) + (`-**34**)!!!~' (34 + 34) = (`-**68**) = "THE `-**MARK**"!!!~'

(`-**68**) = RECIPROCAL = (`-**86**)!!!~'

JOHN DILLINGER'S EX-WIFE BERYL HOVIOUS `-**BIRTHDAY** # `-**NUMBER** = (**8**/**6**/19**06**) = (**8** + **6** + 1**9** + 0**6**) = (`-**39**)!!!~' BERYL HOVIOUS' `-**DEATH/DAY** # `-**NUMBER** = (11/30/19**93**) = (11 + 30 + 19 + 93) = (`-**153**)!!!~' `-**MARRIED** from (1924 to 1929)!!!~' (29 + 24) = (`-**53**)!!!~' (153 (-) 39) = (`-**114**)!!!~' (114 / 2) = (`-**57**) = (`-**23**) + (`-**34**)!!!~' (**1924**) = (19 + 24) = (`-**43**) = RECIPROCAL = (`-**34**)!!!~' (**1929**) = (19 + 29) = (`-**48**) = RECIPROCAL = (`-**84**)!!!~' (`-**84**) x (`-**2**) = (`-**168**)!!!~' **DIED** in the `-**RECIPROCAL** `-**YEAR** of `-**HER** `-**BIRTHDAY** # `-**NUMBER** (`-**39**) = RECIPROCAL = (`-**93**)!!!~' (`-**1993**) = (93 (-) 19) = (`-**74**) = "THE `-**SECRET** `-**INGREDIENT** in `-**EVERY** `-**EQUATION**"!!!~' **GO** `-**BACK** & `-**GIVE** `-**IT** a `-**TRY!!!~'** (93 (-) 19 (-) 30 (-) 11) = (`-**33**)!!!~' (`-**96**) = (32 x **3**)!!!~'

AMERICAN OFFICIAL MELVIN PERVIS (**FBI AGENT**) `-BIRTHDAY # `-NUMBER = (10/24/19<u>0</u>3) = (10 + 24 + 1<u>9</u> + 0<u>3</u>) = (`-**56**) = "HE `-<u>DIED</u> at the `-<u>AGE</u> of (`-<u>56</u>)"!!!~' `-**BIRTHDAY** = (10/24) = (10 + 24) = (`-**34**)!!!~' HIS `-**DEATH/DAY** # `-**NUMBER** = (2/29/1960) = (2 + 29 + 19 + 60) = (`-<u>110</u>)!!!~' (110 (-) 56) = (`-<u>54</u>) = "HE was <u>5</u>' <u>4</u>" in `-<u>HEIGHT</u> (`-<u>54</u>)"!!!~'

CLYDE BARROW of "**BONNIE & CLYDE**" `-BIRTHDAY # `-**NUMBER** = (<u>3</u>/2<u>4</u>/19<u>0</u><u>9</u>) = (<u>3</u> + 2<u>4</u> + 1<u>9</u> + 0<u>9</u>) = (`-<u>55</u>) = (23 + 32)!!!~' HIS `-**DEATH/DAY** # `-**NUMBER** = (5/2<u>3</u>/193<u>4</u>) = (5 + **23** + 19 + **34**) = (`-**81**)!!!~' (`-**81**) = (<u>9</u> x <u>9</u>) = "**IN** the `-**YEAR** `-**HE** was `-**BORN**"!!!~' (81 (-) 55) = (`-<u>26</u>)!!!~' **HE** was <u>5</u>' <u>7</u>" in `-HEIGHT (`-**57**) = (`-**23**) + (`-**34**)!!!~' HE `-<u>DIED</u> at the `-<u>AGE</u> of (`-<u>25</u>)!!!~'

BONNIE PARKER of "**BONNIE & CLYDE**" `-BIRTHDAY # `-**NUMBER** = (**10**/*1*/*1*9**10**) = (**10** + 1 + 19 + **10**) = (`-<u>4</u>0)!!!~' (9, 10, 11) = (9 + 10 + 11) = (`-<u>3</u>0)!!!~' HER `-**DEATH/DAY** # `-**NUMBER** = (5/2<u>3</u>/193<u>4</u>) = (5 + **23** + 19 + **34**) = (`-**81**)!!!~' (81 (-) 40) = (`-<u>41</u>)!!!~' **SHE** was <u>4</u>' **11**" in "**HEIGHT** (**411**)!!!~' **SHE** `-<u>DIED</u> at the `-<u>AGE</u> of (`-<u>23</u>)!!!~' **BONNIE PARKER** `-**DIED** (`-<u>131</u>); or, (`-<u>234</u>) **DAYS** `-**AWAY** from `-**HER** `-**BIRTHDAY**!!!~' (<u>131</u>) = (13 x 1) = (`-<u>13</u>) = "**THEY** were to have `-<u>MURDERED</u> (`-<u>13</u>) `-**PEOPLE**" = "**A VERY PIVOTAL # `-NUMBER**"!!!~' (`-**234**) = **PROPHETIC-LINEAR-PROGRESSION-PLP**!!!~' SHE `-<u>DIED</u> on a (`-<u>23</u>rd) at the `-<u>AGE</u> of (`-<u>23</u>)!!!~'

BLANCHE BARROW'S `-**BIRTHDAY # `-NUMBER** = (<u>1</u>/<u>1</u>/1911) = (<u>1</u> + 1 + 19 + 11) = (`-<u>32</u>) = -a **PROPHETIC # `-NUMBER**!!!~' HER `-**DEATH/DAY** # `-**NUMBER** = (12/24/1988) = (12 + 24 + 19 + 88) = (`-<u>143</u>) = (43 x 1) = (`-<u>43</u>) = RECIPROCAL = (`-<u>34</u>)!!!~' (143 (-) 32) = (`-<u>111</u>) = "`-BIRTHDAY (*ALL-IN-ONE-#-NUMBER*)"!!!~' (88 (-) 19 (-) 24 (-) 12) = (`-<u>33</u>)!!!~' **WAS** `-**MARRIED** to `-**BUCK BARROW** from (`-19<u>31</u> to `-19<u>33</u>)!!!~' (31 + 33) = (`-<u>64</u>) = (2 x 32)**!!!~'**

189

BUCK BARROW (CLYDE BARROW'S BROTHER) `-BIRTHDAY # `-NUMBER = (3/14/1903) = (3 + 14 + 19 + 03) = (`-39)!!!~' SAME `-BIRTHDAY # `-NUMBER (`-39) as JOHN DILLINGER'S EX-WIFE BERYL HOVIOUS!!!~' HIS `-DEATH/DAY # `-NUMBER = (7/29/1933) = (7 + 29 + 19 + 33) = (`-88) = "THE `-YEAR `-HIS `-EX-WIFE BLANCHE BARROW had `-DIED (`-88)"!!!~' (7 x 29) = (`-203) = (23 + 0) = (`-23) = -a PROPHETIC # `-NUMBER!!!~' (88 (-) 39) = (`-49)!!!~' (49 (BUCK BARROWS) (-) 26 (CLYDE BARROWS) = (`-23) = -a PROPHETIC # `-NUMBER!!!~'

AMERICAN ACTOR DANNY AIELLO "THE `-GODFATHER PART II" (`-86) (BIRTH: JUNE 20, 1933) (DEATH: DECEMBER 12, 2019)!!!~'

`-MARRIED to SANDY COHEN since (`-1955) = (`-64) YEARS!!!~'

BIRTHDAY # `-NUMBER = (6 + 20 + 19 + 33) = **78**

DEATH/DAY # `-NUMBER = (12 + 12 + 20 + 19) = **63**

(78 (-) 63) = (`-15)!!!~'

(78 + 63) = (`-141) = (14 + 1) = (`-15) = RECIPROCAL = (`-51)!!!~'

HE DIED (`-190) DAYS BEFORE HIS NEXT BIRTHDAY!!!~'

(365 (-) 190) = (`-175) = (17 x 5) = (`-85) = RECIPROCAL = (`-58)!!!~'

RECIPROCAL `-HERE `-OF = "AMERICAN ACTOR of "BENSON" AND "STAR TREK" (RENE AUBERJONOIS) (175/190)"!!!~'

HE DIED AT THE `-AGE of (`-**86**) = RECIPROCAL = (`-**68**) = "THE `-**MARK**"!!!~' (8 x 6) = (`-**48**)!!!~'

JUNE 20 = (6 x 20) = (`-**120**)!!!~'

DECEMBER 12 = (12 x 12) = (`-**144**)!!!~'

(144 (-) 120) = (`-**24**) = "JUNE 20, 1933"!!!~'

JUNE 20, 1933 = (6 + 2 + 0 + 1 + 9 + 3 + 3) = (`-**24**) = RECIPROCAL = (`-**42**)!!!~'

DECEMBER 12, 2019 = (1 + 2 + 1 + 2 + 2 + 0 + 1 + 9) = (`-**18**) = RECIPROCAL = (`-**81**)!!!~'

(**24** + **18**) = (`-**42**) = RECIPROCAL = (`-**24**)!!!~'

(`-**1933**) = (33 (-) 19) = (`-**14**)!!!~'

(`-**2019**) = (20 + 19) = (`-**39**)!!!~'

(14 + 39) = (`-**53**)!!!~'

(39 (-) 14) = (`-**25**)!!!~'

(53 (-) 25) = (`-**78**) = `-**AGE** of `-**DEATH** of **AMERICAN SINGER/ SONGWRITER ROBERT HUNTER LYRICIST FOR "THE GRATEFUL DEAD" & AMERICAN ACTOR ROBERT FORSTER (`-78) & HALL OF FAME FOOTBALL PLAYER WILLIE BROWN (`-78)!!!~'**

$(1212 + \underline{620})$ = (`-$\underline{1832}$) = $(18 + 32)$ = (`-$\underline{50}$)!!!~'

$(1212 (-) \underline{620})$ = (`-$\underline{592}$) = $(59 \times 2)$ = (`-$\underline{118}$)!!!~'

$(118 (-) 50)$ = (`-$\underline{68}$) = RECIPROCAL = (`-$\underline{86}$) = "$\underline{AGE}$ of `-$\underline{DEATH}$ for AMERICAN ACTOR DANNY AIELLO (`-$\underline{86}$)"!!!~'

JUNE 20 (**BIRTH**) + DECEMBER 12 (**DEATH**) = $(6 + 20 + 12 + 12)$ = (`-$\underline{50}$)!!!~'

`-DIED in (`-$\underline{12}$) & was `-BORN in (`-$\underline{6}$) = (`-$\underline{12/6}$) = $(12 \times 6)$ = (`-$\underline{72}$)!!!~'

$(50 + 72)$ = (`-$\underline{122}$) = $(22 + 1)$ = (`-$\underline{23}$) = -a PROPHETIC # `-NUMBER!!!~'

THOMAS ALVA EDISON - AN AMERICAN INVENTOR & BUSINESSMAN -

`-AGE of `-DEATH = (`-$\underline{84}$)!!!~' $(8 \times 4)$ = (`-$\underline{32}$) = -a PROPHETIC # `-NUMBER!!!~'

`-BIRTHDAY # `-NUMBER = FEBRUARY 11, 18$\underline{47}$ = (2/11/18$\underline{47}$) = $(2 + 11 + 18 + \underline{47})$ = (`-$\underline{78}$)!!!~'

$(18 + 47)$ = (`-$\underline{65}$)!!!~'

`-DEATH/DAY # `-NUMBER = OCTOBER 18, 19$\underline{31}$ = (10/18/19$\underline{31}$) = $(10 + 18 + 19 + \underline{31})$ = (`-$\underline{78}$)!!!~'

$(78 + 78)$ = (`-$\underline{156}$) = $(56 \times 1)$ = (`-$\underline{56}$) = "YEAR NIKOLA TESLA was `-BORN in (`-$\underline{56}$)"!!!~'

(`-**56**) = RECIPROCAL = (`-**65**) = **"YEAR MALCOLM X was `-ASSASSINATED (`-65)"!!!~'**

NIKOLA TESLA - A SERBIAN/AMERICAN INVENTOR, ELECTRICAL/MECHANICAL ENGINEER -

`-**AGE of `-DEATH** = (`-**86**)!!!~' (`-**86**) = RECIPROCAL = (`-**68**) = **"THE `-MARK"!!!~'**

`-**BIRTHDAY # `-NUMBER** = JULY 10, 18**56** = (7/10/18**56**) = (7 + 10 + 18 + **56**) = (`-**91**)!!!~'

`-**DEATH/DAY # `-NUMBER** = JANUARY 7, 19**43** = (1/7/19**43**) = (1 + 7 + 19 + **43**) = (`-**70**)!!!~'

(91 + 70) = (`-**161**) = (16 x 1) = (`-**16**) = (4 x 4) = `-**DEATH/DAY of `-MARTIN LUTHER KING, JR. (4/4)!!!~'**

`-**AGE of `-DEATH** = (`-**39**)!!!~' (39 + 39) = (`-**78**)!!!~'

MALCOLM X `-BIRTH** = MAY 19, 1925 = (5 + 19 + 19 + 25) = (`-68**) = **"YEAR that MARTIN LUTHER KING, JR. & ROBERT FRANCIS KENNEDY were `-ASSASSINATED (`-68)"!!!~'**

(5 + 19 + 19) = (`-**43**) = **"YEAR of `-DEATH for NIKOLA TESLA (`-43)"!!!~'**

MALCOLM X `-DEATH** = FEBRUARY 21, 19**65** = (2 + 21 + 19 + **65**) = (`-107**)!!!~'

(2 x 21) = (`-**42**) = **"AGE of `-DEATH of ROBERT FRANCIS KENNEDY (`-42)!!!~'**

(107 (-) 68) = (`-**39**) = **"AGE of `-DEATH for `-HIMSELF (`-MALCOLM X) & MARTIN LUTHER KING, JR. (`-39)"!!!~'**

193

(65 (-) 19 (-) 21 (-) 2) = (`-**23**) = -a PROPHETIC # `-NUMBER!!!~'

(107 + 68) = (`-**175**) = (75 x 1) = (`-**75**) = "BIRTHDAY # `-NUMBER for ROBERT FRANCIS KENNEDY (`-**75**)"!!!~'

`-AGE of `-DEATH = (`-**39**)!!!~' (39 + 39) = (`-**78**)!!!~'

MARTIN LUTHER KING, JR. `-**BIRTH** = JANUARY 15, 1929 = (1 + 15 + 19 + 29) = (`-**64**)!!!~'

(19 + 29) = (`-**48**) = RECIPROCAL = (`-**84**) = "AGE of `-DEATH of THOMAS ALVA EDISON (`-**84**)"!!!~'

(19 + 29) = (`-**48**) /|\ (48 (-) 15 (-) 1) = (`-**32**) = -a PROPHETIC # `-NUMBER!!!~'

MARTIN LUTHER KING, JR. `-**DEATH** = APRIL 4, 19**68** = (**4** + **4** + 19 + **68**) = (`-**95**)!!!~'

(95 (-) 64) = (`-**31**) = "**YEAR** that THOMAS ALVA EDISON `-**DIED** (`-**31**)"!!!~'

(95 (-) 64) = (`-**31**) = RECIPROCAL = (`-**13**) = "A VERY PIVOTAL # `-NUMBER"!!!~'

(68 (-) 19 (-) 4 (-) 4) = (`-**41**)

(41 + 23 (MALCOLM)) = (`-**64**) = RECIPROCAL = (`-**46**) = "AGE of `-DEATH of #35/PRESIDENT JOHN F. KENNEDY (`-**46**)"!!!~'

(41 + 23 (MALCOLM)) = (`-**64**) = "MARTIN LUTHER KING, JR. `-BIRTHDAY # `-NUMBER (`-**64**) & `-AGE of `-DEATH of JACQUELINE KENNEDY ONASSIS (`-**64**)"!!!~'

`-AGE of `-DEATH = (`-42)!!!~'

ROBERT FRANCIS KENNEDY `-BIRTH = NOVEMBER 20, 1925 = (11 + 20 + 19 + 25) = (`-75)!!!~'

ROBERT FRANCIS KENNEDY `-DEATH = JUNE 6, 1968 = (6 + 6 + 19 + 68) = (`-99)!!!~'

(99 (-) 75) = (`-24) = "AGE of `-ASSASSIN SIRHAN SIRHAN (`-24)"!!!~'

(`-24) = RECIPROCAL = (`-42) = "AGE of `-DEATH of ROBERT FRANCIS KENNEDY (`-42)"!!!~'

(24 + 42) = (`-66) = (6/6) = JUNE 6th = "ROBERT F. KENNEDY'S `-DATE of `-DEATH (`-66)"!!!~'

(99 + 75) = (`-174) = (74 x 1) = (`-74) = RECIPROCAL = (`-47) = THOMAS ALVA EDISON was `-BORN in (`-47)!!!~'

(44 (MARTIN) /|\ 66 (ROBERT) = (44/66) = (`-46) = "AGE of `-DEATH of #35/PRESIDENT JOHN F. KENNEDY (`-46)"!!!~'

(44 x 66) = (2904) = (29 x 04) = (`-116) = "SWIPE 1" = "NIKOLA TESLA (`-161)"!!!~'

`-MARK of the `-BEAST = MARTIN LUTHER KING, JR. / BIRTH = (1/15/1929) & DEATH = (4/4/1968)!!!~' MALCOLM X / BIRTH = (5/19/1925) & DEATH = (2/21/1965)!!!~' FROM BIRTHDAY to BIRTHDAY there are (`-124) DAYS & FROM DEATH/DAY to DEATH/DAY there are (`-42) DAYS!!!~' (`-24) = RECIPROCAL = (`-42)!!!~'

`-MARK = MARTIN LUTHER KING, JR. `-DIED at the `-AGE of (`-39)!!!~' MALCOLM X `-DIED at the `-AGE of (`-39)!!!~'

(39 + 39) = (`-**78**`) = (7 x 8) = (`-**56**`) = RECIPROCAL = (`-**65**`)!!!~'
MARTIN was `-**BORN** in (`-**1929**`) = (19 + 29) = (**48**)!!!~' (`-**48**`) =
RECIPROCAL = (`-**84**`)!!!~' **MALCOLM** was `-**ASSASSINATED**
in (`-**1965**`) = (19 + 65) = (`-**84**`)!!!~'

A DANISH-FRENCH ACTRESS ANNA KARINA (`-**79**`)
(BIRTH: SEPTEMBER 22, 1940) (DEATH: DECEMBER 14,
2019)!!!~'

BIRTHDAY # `-NUMBER = (9 + 22 + 19 + 40) = **90**

DEATH/DAY # `-NUMBER = (12 + 14 + 20 + 19) = **65**

(90 (-) 65) = (`-**25**`) = RECIPROCAL = (`-**52**`)!!!~'

(90 + 65) = (`-**155**`) = (55 + 1) = (`-**56**`) = RECIPROCAL = (`-**65**`) =
"DEATH/DAY # `-NUMBER (`-65`)"!!!~'

SHE DIED (`-**83**`) DAYS AFTER HER LAST BIRTHDAY!!!~'

(365 (-) 83) = (`-**282**`) = (28 x 2) = (`-**56**`) = RECIPROCAL = (`-**65**`)
= **"DEATH/DAY # `-NUMBER (`-65`)"**!!!~'

SHE DIED AT THE `-AGE of (`-**79**`)!!!~' (**7** x **9**) = (`-**63**`)!!!~'

SEPTEMBER 22 = (9 x 22) = (`-**198**`) = (98 x 1) = (`-**98**`) =
RECIPROCAL = (`-**89**`) = **"AGE of `-FORMER `-HUSBAND
JEAN-LUC GODARD (`-89`) at the `-TIME of `-HER
`-DEATH"**!!!~'

DECEMBER 14 = (12 x 14) = (`-**168**`)!!!~'

(198 + 168) = (`-**366**`)!!!~'

SEPTEMBER 22, 1940 = (9 + 2 + 2 + 1 + 9 + 4 + 0) = (`-**27**) = RECIPROCAL = (`-**72**)!!!~'

DECEMBER 14, 2019 = (1 + 2 + 1 + 4 + 2 + 0 + 1 + 9) = (`-**20**) = RECIPROCAL = (`-**02**)!!!~'

(**27** + **20**) = (`-**47**) = RECIPROCAL = (`-**74**)!!!~'

(`-1940) = (40 (-) 19) = (`-**21**)!!!~'

(`-2019) = (20 + 19) = (`-**39**)!!!~'

(21 + 39) = (`-**60**)!!!~'

(39 (-) 21) = (`-**18**)!!!~'

(60 + 18) = (`-**78**) = `-**AGE** of `-**DEATH** of **AMERICAN SINGER/ SONGWRITER ROBERT HUNTER LYRICIST FOR "THE GRATEFUL DEAD" & AMERICAN ACTOR ROBERT FORSTER (`-78) & HALL OF FAME FOOTBALL PLAYER WILLIE BROWN (`-78)!!!~'**

(**1214** + **922**) = (`-**2136**) = (21 + 36) = (`-**57**) = **"DANISH-FRENCH ACTRESS ANNA KARINA was (5' 7") in `-HEIGHT"!!!~'**

(**1214** (-) **922**) = (`-**292**) = **"SWIPE 1"** (`-**922**) = **RECIPROCAL-SEQUENCING-NUMEROLOGY-RSN!!!~'**

SEPTEMBER 22 (**BIRTH**) + DECEMBER 14 (**DEATH**) = (9 + 22 + 12 + 14) = (`-**57**) = **"DANISH-FRENCH ACTRESS ANNA KARINA was (5' 7") in `-HEIGHT"!!!~'**

`-**DIED** in (`-**12**) & was `-**BORN** in (`-**9**) = (`-**12/9**) = (12 x 9) = (`-**108**) = RECIPROCAL = (`-**810**) = **"AUGUST 10ᵗʰ"!!!~'** FORMER `-**HUSBAND DENNIS BERRY** was `-**BORN** on AUGUST 11

(`-**811**) and (`-**75**) at the `-**TIME of** `-**HER** `-**DEATH** = (`-**75**) = RECIPROCAL = (`-**57**)!!!~' **BIRTH = (AUGUST 11, 1944) = (8 + 11 + 19 + 44) = (`-82)** = "THE `-**YEAR** `-**THEY** were `-**MARRIED** (`-19**82**)"!!!~'

`-**SHE** `-**DIED** (`-**65**) **DAYS** AFTER FORMER `-HUSBAND DANIEL DUVAL `-**WHO** `-**DIED in** (`-**2013**)!!!~' FORMER `-HUSBAND PIERRE FABRE `-**DIED on** (`-**323**)!!!~' FORMER `-HUSBAND JEAN-LUC GODARD **was** `-**BORN on (12/3)**!!!~' SHE `-**DIED** (`-**266**) **DAYS AWAY** from FORMER `-HUSBAND PIERRE FABRE **who** `-**DIED in** (`-**2006**) and `-**THEY** were `-**MARRIED for** (`-**6**) `-**YEARS**!!!~'

STAR TREK ENCOUNTER same `-**AGE** of `-**DEATH** (`-**79**) as for AMERICAN ACTOR of "BENSON" AND "STAR TREK" RENE AUBERJONOIS (`-**79**)!!!~'

MEXICAN/AMERICAN ACTOR & ENTERTAINER CHUY BRAVO "CHELSEA HANDLER'S LATE-NIGHT SIDEKICK" (`-**63**) (BIRTH: DECEMBER 7, 1956) (DEATH: DECEMBER 14, 2019)!!!~'

`-DEATH/DAY # `-NUMBER = (`-**65**)!!!~' (`-**65**) = RECIPROCAL = (`-**56**) = "**CHUY BRAVO was `-BORN in (`-56)**"!!!~' **CHELSEA HANDLER was (5' 6")**!!!~'

BIRTHDAY # `-NUMBER = (12 + 7 + 19 + 56) = **94**

(9 x 4) = (`-**36**) = RECIPROCAL = (`-**63**) = "**AGE of `-DEATH of CHUY BRAVO (`-63)**"!!!~'

DEATH/DAY # `-NUMBER = (12 + 14 + 20 + 19) = **65**

(94 (-) 65) = (`-**29**)!!!~'

CHELSEA HANDLER `-**BIRTH** = FEBRUARY 25, 1975 = (75 (-) 19 (-) 25 (-) 2) = (`-**29**)!!!~'

(94 + 65) = (`-**159**) = (59 (-) 1) = (`-**58**) = (29 + 29)!!!~'

HE DIED (`-**7**) DAYS AFTER HIS LAST BIRTHDAY!!!~'

(365 (-) 7) = (`-**358**) = (58 x 3) = (`-**174**)!!!~'

HE DIED AT THE `-AGE of (`-**63**) = (6 x 3) = (`-**18**)!!!~'

DECEMBER 7 = (12 x 7) = (`-**84**)!!!~'

DECEMBER 14 = (12 x 14) = (`-**168**)!!!~'

(168 (-) 84) = (`-**84**)!!!~'

DECEMBER 7, 1956 = (1 + 2 + 7 + 1 + 9 + 5 + 6) = (`-**31**) = RECIPROCAL = (`-**13**)!!!~'

DECEMBER 14, 2019 = (1 + 2 + 1 + 4 + 2 + 0 + 1 + 9) = (`-**20**) = RECIPROCAL = (`-**02**)!!!~'

(**31** + **20**) = (`-**51**) = RECIPROCAL = (`-**15**)!!!~'

(51 + 15) = (`-**66**) = (6 x 6) = (`-**36**) = RECIPROCAL = (`-**63**) = **"AGE of `-DEATH of CHUY BRAVO (`-63)"**!!!~'

(`-1956) = (56 (-) 19) = (`-**37**)!!!~'

(`-2019) = (20 + 19) = (`-**39**)!!!~'

(37 + 39) = (`-**76**)!!!~'

(39 (-) 37) = (`-**2**)!!!~'

(76 + 2) = (`-**78**) = `-**AGE** of `-**DEATH** of **AMERICAN SINGER/ SONGWRITER ROBERT HUNTER LYRICIST FOR "THE GRATEFUL DEAD" & AMERICAN ACTOR ROBERT FORSTER (`-78) & HALL OF FAME FOOTBALL PLAYER WILLIE BROWN (`-78)!!!~'**

(**1214** + **127**) = (`-**1341**) = (13 + 41) = (`-**54**)!!!~'

(**1214** (-) **127**) = (`-**1087**) = (10 + 87) = (`-**97**)!!!~'

(97 (-) 54) = (`-**43**) = "CHUY BRAVO was (**4' 3"**) in `-HEIGHT (`-**43**)"!!!~' (43 + 43) = (`-**86**) = RECIPROCAL = (`-**68**) = "THE `-**MARK**"!!!~'

DECEMBER 7 (**BIRTH**) + DECEMBER 14 (**DEATH**) = (12 + 7 + 12 + 14) = (`-**45**)!!!~' HE DIED AT THE `-AGE of (`-**63**) = (6 x 3) = (`-**18**)!!!~' (45 + 18) = (`-**63**) = "**AGE** of `-**DEATH** of CHUY BRAVO (`-**63**)"!!!~'

(63 + 63) = (`-**126**) = DECEMBER 6[th] = "The `-**DAY** before `-**HIS** `-**BIRTH** (**12/6**)"!!!~'

`-**DIED** in (`-**12**) & was `-**BORN** in (`-**12**) = (`-**12/12**) = (12 x 12) = (`-**144**) = (44 x 1) = (`-**44**) = "**AGE** of CHELSEA HANDLER at the `-**TIME** of CHUY BRAVO'S `-**DEATH**"!!!~'

`-**BACK** (**COVER**) of `-**BOOK**!!!~'

The BIBLE says that there will be an IMMORTALITY for CHRIST'S BROTHERS!~' HOW can INDIVIDUALS who have only LIVED a 100 YEARS or LESS have IMMORTALITY due to

TRIBULATIONS when the ANGELS never became DEMONS and have been FAITHFUL unto `-GOD `-for BILLIONS of YEARS and ARE not `-BLESSED with IMMORTALITY!

The BIBLE says that the LIONS will EAT GRASS; and, that the CHILD will play upon the COBRA'S DEN!~' PEACE would be RESTORED to what was PRIOR to ADAM & EVE'S SIN!~ THE DINOSAURS were there before ADAM & EVE!~' Was LIFE then; that PEACEFUL & PERFECT for DINOSAURS, for THOSE MILLIONS of YEARS!

Hmm, `-LION; a `-CYCLE of `-LIFE!~' THE `-BIBLE SAYS that SATAN is a ROARING LION SEEKING to DEVOUR SOMEONE!~' THAT'S `-FOOD for `-THOUGHT!~' "THE LION KING"!~' IF A REAL PROPHET were HERE right now; here on EARTH; WOULD you BE ABLE to IDENTIFY HIM!~' ONE that TALKS with `-GOD!~'

WITH ADAM & EVE BEING CREATED PERFECT IN A PARADISE WOULD GOD HAVE SECLUDED THEIR RECOGNITION, MINDS AND BEHAVIORS TO NEVER SEE BAD FOR IF THEY HADN'T EATEN OF THE TREE OF THE KNOWLEDGE OF GOOD AND BAD!~' BAD NATURALLY EXISTS IN `-ALL OTHER CREATIONS ALL AROUND US!~' HOW WOULD GOD HAVE HIDDEN THIS FROM THEM!

WOULD A WISE GOD HONESTLY ALLOW ANOTHER CREATION OF HIS TO EXIST (SATAN the DEVIL) AND WREAK HAVOC ON HIS OTHER CREATION (MANKIND) PERPETUALLY JUST BECAUSE ONE SPECIFIC CREATION (MAN) ATE A FORBIDDEN FRUIT HAVING THE KNOWLEDGE OF GOOD & BAD THAT ALREADY HAD EXISTED AROUND THEM BY GOD'S HAND!~ SATAN TO LIVE FOR EONS of `-TIME to `-TEST & TORMENT GOD'S

OTHER CREATION (DAILY) that `-ATE GOD'S FORBIDDEN FRUIT that `-HE DIDN'T WANT THEM `-EAT so that `-THEY could `-LIVE (TO STAY ALIVE) in a `-WAY; to `-PROVE that `-HIS `-LAWS, were to be `-RESPECTED!!!~'

HOW MANY THAT HAVE CHILDREN WOULD DISCIPLINE THEM SO SEVERELY FOR MAKING `-ONE `-MISTAKE AND GIVE THEM `-DEATH!~' THAT ALL OF THEIR FUTURE CHILDREN SHOULD HAVE TO PAY THE PRICE FOR THEIR `-ONE `-MISTAKE WITH `-DEATH!~' HOW MANY INVENTORS WOULD DESTROY THEIR CREATIONS BECAUSE YOU WANTED TO TEACH THEM (YOUR CREATIONS) A LESSON OF YOUR SELF IMPORTANCE!!!~'

IT `-WAS `-ALL in this `-BOOK!!!~' `"-/||\ **REAL MESSAGES of `-GOD I, II; & III**-!!!~ /||\'

AMERICAN HIGH SCHOOL FOOTBALL COACH HERMAN BOONE, COACH MADE FAMOUS BY THE MOVIE "REMEMBER THE TITANS" (`-**84**) (BIRTH: OCTOBER 28, 1935) (DEATH: DECEMBER 18, 2019)!!!~'

BIRTHDAY # `-NUMBER = (10 + 28 + 19 + 35) = **92**

DEATH/DAY # `-NUMBER = (12 + 18 + 20 + 19) = **69** = (**3** x **23**)!!!~'

(92 (-) 69) = (`-**23**) = RECIPROCAL = (`-**32**) = -a PROPHETIC # `-NUMBER!!!~'

(92 + 69) = (`-**161**) = (61 + 1) = (`-**62**) = RECIPROCAL = (`-**26**)!!!~'

HE DIED (`-**51**) DAYS AFTER HIS LAST BIRTHDAY!!!~'

(365 (-) 51) = (`-**314**) = (34 x 1) = (`-**34**) = RECIPROCAL = (`-**43**)!!!~'

`-LOOK `-TO: AMERICAN FILM/TELEVISION PRODUCER LEONARD GOLDBERG (`-51) from the `-OTHER `-SIDE!!!~'

HE DIED AT THE `-AGE of (`-**84**) = (8 x 4) = (`-**32**) = RECIPROCAL = (`-**23**) = **-a PROPHETIC # `-NUMBER!!!~'**

OCTOBER 28 = (10 x 28) = (`-**280**)!!!~'

DECEMBER 18 = (12 x 18) = (`-**216**)!!!~'

(280 (-) 216) = (`-**64**) = (**2** x **32**)!!!~'

OCTOBER 28, 1935 = (1 + 0 + 2 + 8 + 1 + 9 + 3 + 5) = (`-**29**) = RECIPROCAL = (`-**92**) = **`-BIRTHDAY # `-NUMBER!!!~'**

DECEMBER 18, 2019 = (1 + 2 + 1 + 8 + 2 + 0 + 1 + 9) = (`-**24**) = RECIPROCAL = (`-**42**)!!!~'

(**29** + **24**) = (`-**53**) = RECIPROCAL = (`-**35**) = **"YEAR of `-BIRTH (`-35)"!!!~'**

(`-1935) = (35 (-) 19) = (`-**16**)!!!~'

(`-2019) = (20 + 19) = (`-**39**)!!!~'

(16 + 39) = (`-**55**) = (23 + 32)!!!~'

(39 (-) 16) = (`-**23**)!!!~'

(55 + 23) = (`-**78**) = **`-AGE of `-DEATH of AMERICAN SINGER/ SONGWRITER ROBERT HUNTER LYRICIST FOR "THE**

GRATEFUL DEAD" & AMERICAN ACTOR ROBERT FORSTER (`-78) & HALL OF FAME FOOTBALL PLAYER WILLIE BROWN (`-78)!!!~'

(1218 + 1028) = (`-2246) = (22 + 46) = (`-68) = "THE `-MARK"!!!~'

(1218 (-) 1028) = (`-190)!!!~'

(190 (-) 68) = (`-122) = (22 + 1) = (`-23) = -a PROPHETIC # `-NUMBER!!!~'

OCTOBER 28 (**BIRTH**) + DECEMBER 18 (**DEATH**) = (10 + 28 + 12 + 18) = (`-68) = "THE `-MARK"!!!~'

`-BIRTHDAY = (28 (-) 10) = (`-18) = "DAY of `-DEATH (`-18)"!!!~'

`-DIED in (`-12) & was `-BORN in (`-10) = (`-12/10) = (12 x 10) = (`-120)!!!~'

(`-84) = RECIPROCAL = (`-48) = "AT `-AGE (`-48) COACHED in (`-1971) the T. C. WILLIAMS HIGH SCHOOL FOOTBALL TEAM to a (13-0) SEASON & with a STATE CHAMPIONSHIP!!!~' MOVIE "REMEMBER the TITANS" HAD a RUNNING TIME of (`-113) MINUTES; WHICH, had a `-RELEASE `-DATE of (9/29/2000) = "BIRTHDAY # `-NUMBER (`-92)"!!!~' (92 + 92) = (`-184) = (84 x 1) = (`-84) = "AGE of `-DEATH for AMERICAN HIGH SCHOOL FOOTBALL COACH HERMAN BOONE (`-84)"!!!~'

A FRENCH ACTRESS CLAUDINE AUGER (JAMES BOND GIRL) (`-78) (BIRTH: APRIL 26, 1941) (DEATH: DECEMBER 18, 2019)!!!~'

CLAUDINE AUGER'S FORMER HUSBAND PIERRE GASPARD-HUIT was (`-**23**) **YEARS OLDER THAN HER**; and, in (`-19**63**) `-**DIRECTED** ANNA KARINA **WHO HAS THE SAME** `-BIRTHDAY # `-NUMBER (`-**90**) AS FRENCH ACTRESS CLAUDINE AUGER (`-**90**)!!!~' FRENCH ACTRESS CLAUDINE AUGER `-**ACTED** in `-**SEVERAL** of PIERRE GASPARD-HUIT'S `-**FILMS** JUST AS WELL!!!~' THEY were `-**MARRIED** in (`-19**59**)!!!~' ANNA KARINA `-**DIED** on a (`-**14**th) & CLAUDINE AUGER `-**DIED** on an (`-**18**th) = (1**4** + 1**8**) = (`-**32**) = -a PROPHETIC # NUMBER!!!~'

BIRTHDAY # `-NUMBER = (4 + 26 + 19 + 41) = **90**

DEATH/DAY # `-NUMBER = (12 + 18 + 20 + 19) = **69** = (**3** x **23**)!!!~'

(90 (-) 69) = (`-**21**)!!!~' FORMER `-HUSBAND PIERRE GASPARD-HUIT (`-**99**) `-LIVED (`-**21**) YEARS LONGER in `-LIFE than FRENCH ACTRESS CLAUDINE AUGER (JAMES BOND GIRL) (`-**78**)!!!~'

(90 (-) 69) = (`-**21**) = RECIPROCAL = (`-**12**)!!!~' FORMER `-HUSBAND PIERRE GASPARD-HUIT was (`-**212**) (ALL-IN-ONE-#-NUMBER) DAYS AWAY in `-DEATH from `-TURNING (`-**100**) YEARS of `-AGE!!!~'

(90 + 69) = (`-**159**) = (59 x 1) = (`-**59**) = RECIPROCAL ~ (`-**95**) = "CLAUDINE AUGER WAS `-**MARRIED** to PIERRE GASPARD-HUIT in (`-**59**)"!!!~'

SHE DIED (`-**129**) DAYS BEFORE HER NEXT BIRTHDAY!!!~'

(365 (-) 129) = (`-**236**) = (23 x 6) = (`-**138**) = (38 x 1) = (`-**38**) = "**PART** of the `-**DEATH** # `-**NUMBERS** (`-**38**)"!!!~'

(365 (-) 129) = (`-**236**) = (23 + 6) = (`-**29**)!!!~'

SHE DIED AT THE `-AGE of (`-**78**)!!!~' (**7** x **8**) = (`-**56**) = RECIPROCAL = (`-**65**) = "**THUNDERBALL was `-RELEASED in (`-65)**"!!!~'

APRIL 26 = (4 x 26) = (`-**104**)!!!~'

DECEMBER 18 = (12 x 18) = (`-**216**)!!!~'

(216 + 104) = (`-**320**) = (32 + 0) = (`-**32**) = -a **PROPHETIC # `-NUMBER!!!~'**

APRIL 26, 1941 = (4 + 2 + 6 + 1 + 9 + 4 + 1) = (`-**27**) = RECIPROCAL = (`-**72**)!!!~' **EQUALS the `-SAME as `-DANISH/FRENCH `-ACTRESS ANNA KARINA (27/72)!!!~'**

DECEMBER 18, 2019 = (1 + 2 + 1 + 8 + 2 + 0 + 1 + 9) = (`-**24**) = RECIPROCAL = (`-**42**)!!!~'

(**27** + **24**) = (`-**51**) = RECIPROCAL = (`-**15**)!!!~'

(`-1941) = (41 (-) 19) = (`-**22**)!!!~'

(`-2019) = (20 + 19) = (`-**39**)!!!~'

(22 + 39) = (`-**61**)!!!~'

(39 (-) 22) = (`-**17**)!!!~'

(61 + 17) = (`-**78**) = `-**AGE** of `-**DEATH** of **AMERICAN SINGER/ SONGWRITER ROBERT HUNTER LYRICIST FOR "THE GRATEFUL DEAD" & AMERICAN ACTOR ROBERT FORSTER (`-78) & HALL OF FAME FOOTBALL PLAYER**

WILLIE BROWN (`-78) & FRENCH ACTRESS CLAUDINE AUGER (JAMES BOND GIRL) (`-78)!!!~'

(1218 + 426) = (`-1644) = (16 + 44) = (`-60) = (19 + 41) = "BORN in (`-1941)"!!!~'

(1218 (-) 426) = (`-792) = (79 x 2) = (`-158) = (58 x 1) = (`-58) = 5' 8" = "FRENCH ACTRESS CLAUDINE AUGER (JAMES BOND GIRL) was 5' 8" IN `-HEIGHT (`-58)"!!!~'

APRIL 26 (**BIRTH**) + DECEMBER 18 (**DEATH**) = (4 + 26 + 12 + 18) = (`-60) = (19 + 41) = "BORN in (`-1941)"!!!~'

`-DIED in (`-12) & was `-BORN in (`-4) = (`-12/4) = (12 x 4) = (`-48) = ANNA KARINA `-BIRTHDAY (`-22) & CLAUDINE AUGER'S BIRTHDAY (`-26) = (22 + 26) = (`-48)!!!~'

`-DIED in (`-12) & was `-BORN in (`-4) = (`-12/4) = (12 x 4) = (`-48) = RECIPROCAL = (`-84) = "JAMES BOND'S "THUNDERBALL" was `-RELEASED in (`-1965) = (19 + 65) = (`-84)!!!~'

THUNDERBALL **RELEASE** `-YEAR = (`-1965)!!!~' (`-65) = RECIPROCAL = (`-56) = **BUDGET: $5.6 MILLION USD!!!~'**

THUNDERBALL **RELEASE** `-DAY = (12/22) = (12 + 22) = (`-34) = RECIPROCAL = (`-43)!!!~'

CLAUDINE AUGER'S & PIERRE GASPARD-HUIT'S `-DEATH `-DATES are (`-134); OR, (`-231) DAYS AWAY from `-EACH `-OTHER!!!~'

The # `-NUMBER (`-168)!!!~'

#**1**/PRESIDENT GEORGE WASHINGTON'S `-**PRODUCT of** `-**DEATH** from `-**DAY of** `-**DEATH** = (`-**168**)!!!~'

#**2**/PRESIDENT JOHN ADAMS `-**PRODUCT of** `-**DEATH** from `-**DAY of** `-**DEATH** = (`-**28**)!!!~' #**3**/PRESIDENT THOMAS JEFFERSON `-**PRODUCT of** `-**DEATH** from `-**DAY of** `-**DEATH** = (`-**28**)!!!~'

#**4**/PRESIDENT JAMES MADISON `-**PRODUCT of** `-**DEATH** from `-**DAY of** `-**DEATH** = (`-**168**)!!!~'

#**5**/PRESIDENT JAMES MONROE `-**PRODUCT of** `-**DEATH** from `-**DAY of** `-**DEATH** = (`-**28**)!!!~' (28 + 28 + 28) = (`-**84**)!!!~' (`-84) x 2) = (`-**168**)!!!~'

#**6**/PRESIDENT JOHN QUINCY ADAMS `-**DAY of** `-**DEATH** (2/**23**) = (22 x **3**) = (`-**66**)!!!~' (`-**66**) for the (`-**6TH**) PRESIDENT = (`-**666**)!!!~' **DEATH/DAY #** `-**NUMBER** = (`-**91**)!!!~'

`-BORN JULY 11th, 1**767** = (7 + 11 + 17 + 67) = (`-**102**) /|\ `-DIED FEBRUARY **23**rd, 1**848** = (2 + 23 + 18 + 48) = (`-**91**)

(67 (-) 17 (-) 11 (-) 7) = (`-**32**) = -**a PROPHETIC #** `-**NUMBER!!!~'** (102 + 32) = (`-**134**)!!!~' (34 x 2) = (`-**68**)!!!~'

`-**1767** = (17 + 67) = `-**84** = **RECIPROCAL** = `-**48** = **DIED** in the **YEAR** of (`-**48**)!!!~'

#**7**/PRESIDENT ANDREW JACKSON `-**DAY of** `-**DEATH** = **JUNE(6) 8** = (`-**6/8**) = (6 x 8) = `-**48** = RECIPROCAL = `-**84**!~'

`-**AND;** `-**HE** `-**DIED** on the `-**DAY** of (6/8)!!!~' **DEATH/DAY #** `-**NUMBER** = (`-**77**)!!!~'

`-BORN MARCH 15<sup>th</sup>, 17**67** = (3 + 15 + 17 + 67) = (`-**102**) (**SAME as #6/PRESIDENT**) /|\ `-DIED **JUNE 8<sup>th</sup>**, 1845 = (6 + 8 + 18 + 45) = (`-**77**)

(67 (-) 17 (-) 15 (-) 3) = (`-**32**) = -a **PROPHETIC #** `-**NUMBER!!!~'** (102 + 32) = (`-**134**)!!!~' (34 x 2) = (`-**68**)!!!~'

`-**ADD UP** `-**DEATH/DAY** **#** `-**NUMBERS** for **#6** & **#7** = (**91** (**ADAMS**) + **77** (**JACKSON**)) = (`-**168**)!!!~'/|\ **FROM** `-**BIRTH** to `-**BIRTH** IT `-**EQUALS** (`-**168**) for **PRESIDENTS #6 & #7,** `-**Too!!!~'** From `-**BIRTH** to `-**BIRTH**; and, from `-**DEATH** to `-**DEATH** = `-**EQUALS** = (`-**168**)!!!~'

THERE ARE (`-**247**) **DAYS** `-**IN-BETWEEN** from `-**BIRTH** to `-**BIRTH** with **#6**/PRESIDENT JOHN QUINCY ADAMS & **#7**/PRESIDENT ANDREW JACKSON!!!~' (`-**247**) = (24 x 7) = (`-**168**)!!!~'

#8/PRESIDENT MARTIN VAN BUREN `-**PRODUCT of** `-**DEATH** from `-**DAY of** `-**DEATH** = (`-**168**)!!!~' **#8**/MARTIN VAN BUREN `-**DAY of** `-**DEATH** = **JULY 24<sup>th</sup>** = (**7**/**24**) = (7 x 24) = `-**168!**~' `-**RECIPROCAL** (**7**/**24**) of **6**/PRESIDENT JOHN QUINCY ADAMS & **#7**/PRESIDENT ANDREW JACKSON!!!~' (`-**247**) = (**24** x **7**) = (`-**168**)!!!~' **#6, #7,** & **#8** `-**PRESIDENTS** (`-**ALL**) `-**ADD** `-**UP** `-**TOGETHER** (**6**-to-**8**)!!!~' AGAIN, the `-**TIME** `-**BETWEEN** `-**BIRTHS** (**#6, #7**) PRESIDENTS (`-**24** x **7**) = `-**EQUALS** = the `-**RECIPROCAL** = "To the `-**DAY** of `-**DEATH** /|\ of the `-**VERY** `-**NEXT** `-**PRESIDENT** **#8**/ PRESIDENT MARTIN VAN BUREN (**7** x **24**)"!!!~'

#9/PRESIDENT WILLIAM HENRY HARRISON `-**DIED** at the `-**AGE** of (`-**68**)!~'

`-BORN FEBRUARY 9ᵗʰ, 17**73** /|\ `-DIED APRIL **4**ᵗʰ, 18**41** /|\ (41 (-) 18) = (`-**23**) = -a PROPHETIC # `-NUMBER!!!~'

`-**BIRTH** = (2 + 9 + 17 + **73**) = `-**101** /|\ `-**DEATH** = (4 + 4 + 18 + 41) = `-**67**

(101 + 67) = (`-**168**)!!!~'

#**12**-PRESIDENT = ZACHARY TAYLOR `-**BORN** NOVEMBER 24ᵗʰ, 17**84** /|\ `-**DIED** JULY 9ᵗʰ, **1850**!!!~'

(11 + 24 + 17 + 84) = (`-**136**)!!!~' /|\ (7 + 9 + 18 + 50) = (`-**84**) = **DEATH/DAY** # `-**NUMBER** = `-**EQUALS** = "**YEAR** of `-**BIRTH** (`-**84**)!!!~' (84 + 84) = (`-**168**)!!!~'

(84 (-) 17 (-) 24 (-) 11) = (`-**32**) = -a PROPHETIC # `-NUMBER!!!~' (136 + 32) = (`-**168**)!!!~'

`-17**84** = (84 (-) 17) = `-**67**!!!~' (6 x 7) = (`-**42**)!!!~' (`-42 x 2) = (`-**84**)!!!~'

(50 (-) 18) = (`-**32**) = -a PROPHETIC # `-NUMBER!!!~'

`-**1850** = (18 + 50) = (`-**68**)!!!~' (6 x 8) = (`-**48**) = RECIPROCAL = (`-**84**)!!!~' (84 + 84) = (`-**168**)!!!~'

`-**DOPAMINE**; and, the `-**POWER** `-**OF**!!!~'

DOPAMINE, SEROTONIN, OXYTOCIN; and, ENDORPHINS are `-RESPONSIBLE for `-OUR `-HAPPINESS & CONTENTMENT!!!~' WHETHER IT'S `-MARRIAGE, `-SEX, `-DRUG `-USE, `-GOOD `-FOOD, `-A GREAT `-BOOK, being a `-TERRORIST, `-LOVING `-WAR, `-EXERCISING,

`-MEDITATING, `-FAMILY `-FIRST; the `-LIST GOES `-ON & `-ON.... IT `-PUTS `-US in a `-QUEST to SATISFY these so `-NECESSARY `-URGES!!!~' WE `-MUST get in `-FRONT of `-THEM; and, `-CONTROL `-ALL of `-THESE `-CRAVINGS, no `-MATTER what `-THEY `-ARE!!!~' AND; IF `-THEY `-VIOLATE the `-SATISFACTION & CONTENTMENT of `-SOMEONE `-ELSE, `-THEY MUST be `-BROUGHT to an `-ABRUPT `-HALT!!!~' SELF-CONTROL is a `-NECESSARY `-TOOL in this `-ENDEAVOR to `-OUR `-COMPLETE `-SATISFACTION OF `-LIFE!!!~' EVEN to the `-FIGHTING of `-ADDICTIONS!!!~' AT `-TIMES doing `-WITHOUT some of `-THESE is the `-BEST `-PLAN of `-ACTION!!!~' KNOWING the `-TIME & `-PLACE for `-EACH; and, `-EVERY `-SITUATION is a `-MUST!!!~' HARNESSING a `-BALANCE of these `-ENDEAVORS brings `-PEACE to the `-WORLD!!!~' PEACE & HARMONY: To `-EVERY `-HUMAN, `-INSECT, `-ATOM & the `-ENVIRONMENT; and, EVEN `-NECESSARILY to the `-COSMOS as `-WELL!!!~' NOW; FIND `-YOUR `-BALANCE; and, `-FIND `-YOUR `-PEACE!!!~' The `-**PROPHET!!!~'**

NASCAR HALL OF FAME DRIVER JUNIOR JOHNSON (`-**88**) (BIRTH: JUNE 28, 1931) (DEATH: DECEMBER 20, 2019)!!!~'

BIRTHDAY # `-NUMBER = (6 + 28 + 19 + 31) = **84**

DEATH/DAY # `-NUMBER = (12 + 20 + 20 + 19) = **71**

DEATH/DAY = (12 + 20) = (`-**32**) = **-a PROPHETIC # `-NUMBER!!!~'**

(84 (-) 71) = (`-**13**) = **"A VERY PIVOTAL # `-NUMBER"!!!~'**

(84 (-) 71) = (`-**13**) = **WAS** `-**MARRIED** in (`-**1994**) **TO** `-**HIS** `-**WIFE LISA JOHNSON** = (19 + 94) = (`-**113**)!!!~'

(84 + 71) = (`-**155**) = (55 x 1) = (`-**55**) = (**23** + **32**)!!!~'

HE DIED (`-**190**) DAYS BEFORE HIS NEXT BIRTHDAY!!!~'

(365 (-) 190) = (`-**175**) = (17 x 5) = (`-**85**) = RECIPROCAL = (`-**58**)!!!~'

`-**RECIPROCAL** of **AMERICAN ACTOR** of **"BENSON"** AND **"STAR TREK" RENE AUBERJONOIS** (**175**/**190**)!!!~'

HE DIED AT THE `-**AGE** of (`-**88**) = (8 x 8) = (`-**64**) = RECIPROCAL = (`-**46**) = (**23** x **2**)!!!~'

JUNE 28 = (6 x 28) = (`-**168**) = `-**BIRTHDAY** of **NASCAR HALL OF FAME DRIVER JUNIOR JOHNSON** (`-**68**) = **"The** `-**MARK"**!!!~'

DECEMBER 20 = (12 x 20) = (`-**240**)!!!~'

(240 (-) 168) = (`-**72**) = RECIPROCAL = (`-**27**)!!!~'

JUNE 28, 1931 = (6 + 2 + 8 + 1 + 9 + 3 + 1) = (`-**30**) = RECIPROCAL = (`-**03**)!!!~'

DECEMBER 20, 2019 = (1 + 2 + 2 + 0 + 2 + 0 + 1 + 9) = (`-**17**) = RECIPROCAL = (`-**71**) = `-**DEATH/DAY** # `-**NUMBER** (`-**71**)!!!~'

(**30** + **17**) = (`-**47**) = RECIPROCAL = (`-**74**) = (7 x 4) = (`-**28**) = `-**DAY** of `-**BIRTH** (`-**28**)!!!~'

(`-**1931**) = (31 (-) 19) = (`-**12**)!!!~'

(`-**2019**) = (20 + 19) = (`-**39**)!!!~'

212

(12 + 39) = (`-**51**)!!!~'

(39 (-) 12) = (`-**27**)!!!~'

(51 + 27) = (`-**78**) = `-**AGE** of `-**DEATH** of **AMERICAN SINGER/ SONGWRITER ROBERT HUNTER LYRICIST FOR "THE GRATEFUL DEAD" & AMERICAN ACTOR ROBERT FORSTER** (`-**78**) **& HALL OF FAME FOOTBALL PLAYER WILLIE BROWN** (`-**78**) **& FRENCH ACTRESS CLAUDINE AUGER (JAMES BOND GIRL)** (`-**78**)!!!~'

(**1220** + **628**) = (`-**1848**) = (18 + 48) = (`-**66**) = **DIED** at the `-**AGE** of (`-**88**) = (66/88) = (`-**68**) = "The **MARK**!!!~'

(`-**1848**) = (`-**48**) = RECIPROCAL = (`-**84**) = `-**BIRTHDAY #** `-**NUMBER** (`-**84**)!!!~'

(**1220** (-) **628**) = (`-**592**) = (59 x 2) = (`-**118**)!!!~'

(118 + 66) = (`-**184**) = (**84 x 1**) = (`-**84**) = (8 x 4) = (`-**32**) = -a **PROPHETIC #** `-**NUMBER**!!!~'

(118 + 66) = (`-**184**) = (**84 x 1**) = (`-**84**) = `-**BIRTHDAY #** `-**NUMBER** (`-**84**)!!!~'

JUNE 28 (**BIRTH**) + DECEMBER 20 (**DEATH**) = (6 + 28 + 12 + 20) = (`-**66**) = **DIED** at the `-**AGE** of (`-**88**) = (66/88) = (`-**68**) = "The **MARK**!!!~'

`-**DIED** in (`-**12**) & was `-**BORN** in (`-**6**) – (` **12/6**) = (12 x 6) = (`-**72**)!!!~'

(66 + 66) = (`-**132**) = (32 x 1) = (`-**32**) = -a **PROPHETIC #** `-**NUMBER**!!!~'

JOSEPH SEGEL, QVC AND FRANKLIN MINT FOUNDER, DEAD AT (`-**88**) (BIRTH: **JANUARY 9**, 1931) (DEATH: **DECEMBER 21**, 2019)!!!~'

`-**BORN** on (**1/9**); and, `-**DIED** in (**19**)!!!~' /|\ (`-**1931**) = (31 (-) 19) = (`-**12**); and, `-**DIED** in the `-**MONTH** of (`-**12**) on the `-**DAY** of (`-**21**)!!!~'

BIRTHDAY # `-NUMBER = (1 + 9 + 19 + 31) = **60**

DEATH/DAY # `-NUMBER = (**12** + **21** + 20 + 19) = **72**

(72 (-) 60) = (`-**12**) = RECIPROCAL = (`-**21**) = **"DAY of `-DEATH"**!!!~'

(72 + 60) = (`-**132**) = (32 x 1) = (`-**32**) = **-a PROPHETIC # `-NUMBER!!!~'**

HE DIED (`-**19**) DAYS BEFORE HIS NEXT BIRTHDAY!!!~' (`-**19**0) DAYS for NASCAR HALL OF FAME DRIVER JUNIOR JOHNSON (`-**19**0) `-**DIED** at (`-**88**) as **WELL!!!~'**

(365 (-) 19) = (`-**346**) = (46 x 3) = (`-**138**) = (38 x 1) = (`-**38**) = **"PART of the `-DEATH # `-NUMBERS (`-38)"**!!!~' `-3(8's) = (`-**888**)!!!~'

HE DIED AT THE `-AGE of (`-**88**) = (8 x 8) = (`-**64**) = RECIPROCAL = (`-**46**) = (**23** x **2**)!!!~'

JANUARY 9 = (1 x 9) = (`-**9**)!!!~'

DECEMBER 21 = (12 x 21) = (`-**252**) = **RECIPROCAL-SEQUENCING-NUMEROLOGY-RSN!!!~'**

(252 (-) 9) = (`-**243**) = (24 x 3) = (`-**72**) = `-**DEATH/DAY # `-NUMBER!!!~'**

(252 (-) 9) = (`-**243**) = (43 x 2) = (`-**86**) = RECIPROCAL = (`-**68**) = "The `-**MARK**"!!!~'

JANUARY 9, 1931 = (1 + 9 + 1 + 9 + 3 + 1) = (`-**24**) = RECIPROCAL = (`-**42**) = "The `-**MARK**"!!!~'

DECEMBER 21, 2019 = (1 + 2 + 2 + 1 + 2 + 0 + **1** + **9**) = (`-**18**) = RECIPROCAL = (`-**81**)!!!~'

(**24** + **18**) = (`-**42**) = RECIPROCAL = (`-**24**)!!!~'

(`-1931) = (31 (-) 19) = (`-**12**)!!!~'

(`-2019) = (20 + 19) = (`-**39**)!!!~'

(12 + 39) = (`-**51**)!!!~'

(39 (-) 12) = (`-**27**)!!!~'

(51 + 27) = (`-**78**) = `-**AGE** of `-**DEATH** of **AMERICAN SINGER/ SONGWRITER ROBERT HUNTER LYRICIST FOR "THE GRATEFUL DEAD" & AMERICAN ACTOR ROBERT FORSTER** (`-**78**) **& HALL OF FAME FOOTBALL PLAYER WILLIE BROWN** (`-**78**) **& FRENCH ACTRESS CLAUDINE AUGER (JAMES BOND GIRL)** (`-**78**)!!!~'

(**1221** + **19**) = (`-**1240**) = (12 + 40) = (`-**52**)!!!~'

(**1221** (-) **19**) = (`-**1202**) = (12 + 02) = (`-**14**)!!!~'

(52 + 14) = (`-**66**) = (66/88) = (`-**68**) = "The `-**MARK**"!!!~'

(52 (-) 14) = (`-**38**) = "**PART of the `-DEATH # `-NUMBERS** (`-**38**)"!!!~' `-3(8's) = (`-**888**)!!!~'

JANUARY 9 (**BIRTH**) + DECEMBER 21 (**DEATH**) = (1 + 9 + 12 + 21) = (`-**43**) = (43 x 2) = (`-**86**) = RECIPROCAL = (`-**68**) = "The **MARK**!!!~'

`-**DIED** in (`-**12**) & was `-**BORN** in (`-**1**) = (`-**12/1**) = (12 x 1) = (**ALL-IN-ONE-#-NUMBER**) for (**12/21**) = `-**DEATH/DAY** for **JOSEPH SEGEL / QVC AND FRANKLIN MINT FOUNDER**!!!~'

(**88 + 88**) = (`-**176**) = (**76 x 1**) = (`-**76**) = (7 x 6) = (`-**42**) = "The `-**MARK**"!!!~'

NASCAR HALL OF FAME DRIVER JUNIOR JOHNSON (`-**88**) /|\ JOSEPH SEGEL, QVC AND FRANKLIN MINT FOUNDER, DEAD AT (`-**88**) /|\ `-**BACK-to-BACK-**' (`-**88**) "**ONE** `-**AFTER** the `-**NEXT**"!!!~'

"**ENTER THE DRAGON**" /|\ "THE **BROTHERHOOD** of **SATAN**" /|\

FILM ACTRESS **AHNA CAPRI** (ANNA MARIE NANASI) `-**DIED** at the `-**AGE** of (`-**66**) after (`-**11**) DAYS in a **COMA** and on **LIFE SUPPORT**!!!~'

(66 + 66) = (`-**132**) = (32 x 1) = (`-**32**) = -a **PROPHETIC #** `-**NUMBER**!!!~'

BIRTH: **JULY 6, 1944** = (7/6/1944) = (7 + 6 + 19 + 44) = (`-**76**)!!!~'

HER `-**BIRTHDAY # **`-**NUMBER** (`-**76**) = `-**EQUALS** = "HER `-**BIRTHDAY** (**7/6**)"!!!~'

SHE was `-**BORN** in (`-**44**); and, `-**DIED** (`-**44**) DAYS after `-**HER** `-**LAST** `-**BIRTHDAY**!!!~'

(365 (-) 44) = (`-**321**) = **PROPHETIC-LINEAR-PROGRESSION-PLP!!!~'**

(44 + 44) = (`-**88**)!!!~'

(66/88) = (`-**68**) = "The `-**MARK** of the `-**BEAST**"!!!~'

DEATH: AUGUST 19, 2010 = (8/19/2010) = (8 + 19 + 20 + 10) = (`-**57**) = RECIPROCAL = (`-**75**)!!!~' SIBLING'S `-**BIRTH/YEAR** = (`-**1956**) = (19 + 56) = (`-**75**)!!!~'

AUGUST 19 = 8 (9(-)1) = (`-**88**)!!!~'

(88 + 88) = (`-**176**) = (76 x 1) = (`-**76**) = "**BIRTHDAY** (**7/6**) & **BIRTHDAY** # `-**NUMBER** (`-**76**)"!!!~'

(57 + 75) = (`-**132**) = (32 x 1) = (`-**32**) = **-a PROPHETIC #** `-**NUMBER!!!~'**

DEATH: AUGUST 19, 2010 = (8/19/2010) = (8 + 19 + 20 + 10) = (`-**57**) = "**WAS `-SHE 5' 7" in `-HEIGHT**"???~'

(93 (-) 57) = (`-**36**) = RECIPROCAL = (`-**63**)!!!~'

(8/19) = (8 + 19) = (`-**27**) + (`-**66**) = (`-**93**)!!!~'

(8/19) = (19 (-) 8) = "**ELEVEN `-DAYS in a `-COMA**"!!!~'

(8/19) = (19 (-) 8) = (8/11) = "**SIBLING was `-BORN on (8/10)**"!!!~'

SIBLING ACTOR PETER ROBBINS `-**BIRTH** = (8/10/1956) = (8 + 10 + 19 + 56) = (`-**93**)!!!~' **CURRENTLY `-HE is (`-63) YEARS of `-AGE!!!~'**

`-**BORN** in (`-**56**); AND, HIS `-**SIBLING'S `-HEIGHT** was (**5' 6"**) for **AHNA CAPRI-!!!~'**

(93 + 63) = (`-**156**) = (56 x 1) = (`-**56**)!!!~'

`-**YEARS** of `-**HIS** `-**SIBLINGS** (AHNA CAPRI'S) `-**LIFE** (`-**1944**) & `-**DEATH** (`-**2010**) = (19 + 44 + 20 + 10) = (`-**93**) = `-**SIBLING'S** PETER ROBBINS' `-**BIRTHDAY** # `-**NUMBER** (`-**93**)!!!~' (93 + 93) = (`-**186**) = (86 x 1) = (`-**86**) = RECIPROCAL = (`-**68**) = "The `-**MARK** of the `-**BEAST**"!!!~' WE'RE `-**ALL** `-**INTERTWINED** in `-**TIME**!!!~'

`-**WHO IS** `-**EVERYWHERE**!!!~' (JAH)!!!~'

`-**AMAZING** how `-**EVERY** `-**CREATION** /|\ from `-**MAN** to `-

INSECT, from `-**STAR** to `-**MOON**; and, `-**COSMIC** to `-

ATOMIC /|\ are `-**UNDER** the `-**HINGED** `-**CONTROL** /|\ via `-

TIME /|\ of `-**OUR** `-**ENDEARING** & `-**LOVING** `-**EXPANDING** /\

`-**JEHOVAH** `-**GOD-**'!!!~'

`-**A** `-**PATTERN** in the `-**DAY** of `-**BIRTHS** for the `-**PRESIDENTS**!!!~'

#**1**-PRESIDENT = GEORGE WASHINGTON `-**DAY** of `-**BIRTH** = FEBRUARY 22nd, 17**32** = (2/22) = (2 x 22) = `-**44**!' `-DAYS in a `-SINGLE `-YEAR TILL `-NEXT `-PRESIDENT'S `-BIRTHDAY = (`-**115**); or, (`-**250**)!!!~'

#2-PRESIDENT = JOHN ADAMS `-DAY of `-BIRTH = OCTOBER 30th, 1735 = (10/30) = (10 x 30) = `-**300**!' `-DAYS in a `-SINGLE `-YEAR TILL `-NEXT `-PRESIDENT'S `-BIRTHDAY = (`-**165**); or, (`-**200**)!!!-'

#3-PRESIDENT = THOMAS JEFFERSON `-DAY of `-BIRTH = APRIL(**4**) 13th, 17**43** = (4/13) = (4 x 13) = `-**52**!-' (43 + 43) = (`-**86**) = RECIPROCAL = (`-**68**) = "The `-**MARK**"!!!-' `-DAYS in a `-SINGLE `-YEAR TILL `-NEXT `-PRESIDENT'S `-BIRTHDAY = (`-**28**); or, (`-**337**)!!!-'

#4-PRESIDENT = JAMES MADISON `-DAY of `-BIRTH = MARCH 16th, 1751 = (3 x 16) = `-**48**!' (`-**1751**) = (17 + 51) = (`-**68**) = "The **MARK**"!!!-' `-DAYS in a `-SINGLE `-YEAR TILL `-NEXT `-PRESIDENT'S `-BIRTHDAY = (`-**43**); or, (`-**322**)!!!-'

#5-PRESIDENT = JAMES MONROE `-DAY of `-BIRTH = APRIL 28th, 1758 = (4/28) = (4 x 28) = `-**112**!-' `-DAYS in a `-SINGLE `-YEAR TILL `-NEXT `-PRESIDENT'S `-BIRTHDAY = (`-**74**); or, (`-**291**)!!!-'

#6-PRESIDENT = JOHN QUINCY ADAMS `-DAY of `-BIRTH = JULY 11th, 1767 = (7/11) = (7 x 11) = `-**77**!' `-DAYS in a `-SINGLE `-YEAR TILL `-NEXT `-PRESIDENT'S `-BIRTHDAY = (`-**118**); or, (`-**247**)!!!-'

#7-PRESIDENT = ANDREW JACKSON `-DAY of `-BIRTH = MARCH 15th, 1767 = (3/15) = (3 x 15) = `-**45**!-' `-DAYS in a `-SINGLE `-YEAR TILL `-NEXT `-PRESIDENT'S `-BIRTHDAY = (`-**100**); or, (`-**265**)!!!-'

#8-PRESIDENT = MARTIN VAN BUREN `-DAY of `-BIRTH = DECEMBER 5th, 1782 = (12/5) = (12 x 5) = `-**60**!-' `-DAYS in a

`-SINGLE `-YEAR TILL `-NEXT `-PRESIDENT'S `-BIRTHDAY = (`-**66**); or, (`-**299**)**!!!~'**

#9-PRESIDENT = WILLIAM HENRY HARRISON `-**DAY of `-BIRTH** = FEBRUARY(2) 9ᵗʰ, 1773 = (**2/9**) = (2 x 9) = `-**18**!~' `-DIED (4/4) = (4 x 4) = (`-**16**)**!!!~'** (18/16) = (86 x 1 x 1) = (`-**86**) = RECIPROCAL = (`-**68**) = **"The `-MARK"!!!~'** `-**DIED** at the `-**AGE** of (`-**68**)!~' `-DAYS in a `-SINGLE `-YEAR TILL `-NEXT `-PRESIDENT'S `-BIRTHDAY = (`-**48**); or, (`-**317**)**!!!~'**

#10-PRESIDENT = JOHN TYLER `-**DAY of `-BIRTH** = MARCH **29**ᵗʰ, 1790 = (3/29) = (3 x 29) = `-**87**!~' `-DAYS in a `-SINGLE `-YEAR TILL `-NEXT `-PRESIDENT'S `-BIRTHDAY = (`-**147**); or, (`-**218**)**!!!~'** **#9 & #10 are `-CLOSE to being `-RECIPROCALS-' of `-EACH `-OTHER!!!~'**

#11-PRESIDENT = JAMES K. POLK `-**DAY of `-BIRTH** = NOVEMBER 2ⁿᵈ, 1795 = (11/2) = (11 x 2) = `-**22**!~' `-DAYS in a `-SINGLE `-YEAR TILL `-NEXT `-PRESIDENT'S `-BIRTHDAY = (`-**22**); or, (`-**343**)**!!!~'**

#12-PRESIDENT = ZACHARY TAYLOR `-**DAY of `-BIRTH** = **NOVEMBER 24**ᵗʰ, 17**84** = (11/24) = (11 x 24) = `-**264**!~' `-DAYS in a `-SINGLE `-YEAR TILL `-NEXT `-PRESIDENT'S `-BIRTHDAY = (`-**44**); or, (`-**321**)**!!!~'** (64 / 2) = (`-**32**) = -a **PROPHETIC #** `-**NUMBER!!!~'**

#13-PRESIDENT = MILLARD FILLMORE `-**DAY of `-BIRTH** = JANUARY 7ᵗʰ, 1800 = (1/7) = (1 x 7) = `-**7**!~' `-**DIED** at the `-**AGE** of (`-**74**) = (**JULY 4**ᵗʰ)**!!!~'** `-DAYS in a `-SINGLE `-YEAR TILL `-NEXT `-PRESIDENT'S `-BIRTHDAY = (`-**45**); or, (`-**320**)**!!!~'** **#12 & #13 are `-CLOSE to being `-EXACT!!!~'**

#14-PRESIDENT = FRANKLIN PIERCE `-DAY of `-BIRTH = NOVEMBER 23rd, 1804 = (11/23) = (11 x 23) = `-253!!!~' `-DAYS in a `-SINGLE `-YEAR TILL `-NEXT `-PRESIDENT'S `-BIRTHDAY = (`-151); or, (`-214)!!!~' NOTICE #12 (`-1784) & #14 (`-1804)!!!~' `-BIRTHS = (23/24) = (23 + 24) = (`-47) = RECIPROCAL = (`-74) = "AGE of `-DEATH of the `-PRESIDENT #13 IN-BETWEEN `-THEM"!!!~' `-RECIPROCALS-`!!!~'

#15-PRESIDENT = JAMES BUCHANAN `-DAY of `-BIRTH = APRIL(4) 23rd, 1791 = (4/23) = (4 x 23) = `-92!~' `-DAYS in a `-SINGLE `-YEAR TILL `-NEXT `-PRESIDENT'S `-BIRTHDAY = (`-70); or, (`-295)!!!~'

#16-PRESIDENT = ABRAHAM LINCOLN `-DAY of `-BIRTH = FEBRUARY 12th, 1809 = (2/12) = (2 x 12) = `-24!~' `-DIED in (`-1865 at the `-AGE of (`-56)!!!~' `-DAYS in a `-SINGLE `-YEAR TILL `-NEXT `-PRESIDENT'S `-BIRTHDAY = (`-45); or, (`-320)!!!~' NOTICE the `-# `-NUMBERS for #13/#16 PRESIDENTS (45/320)!!!~'

#17-PRESIDENT = ANDREW JOHNSON `-DAY of `-BIRTH = DECEMBER 29th, 1808 = (12/29) = (12 x 29) = `-348!~' `-DAYS in a `-SINGLE `-YEAR TILL `-NEXT `-PRESIDENT'S `-BIRTHDAY = (`-119); or, (`-246)!!!~' NOTICE the `-# `-NUMBERS `-BETWEEN #17/#18 PRESIDENTS (119/246)!!!~' NOTICE the `-# `-NUMBERS `-BETWEEN #6/#7 PRESIDENTS (118/247)!!!~'

#18-PRESIDENT = ULYSSES S. GRANT `-DAY of `-BIRTH = APRIL 27th, 1822 = (4/27) = (4 x 27) = `-108!~' `-DAYS in a `-SINGLE `-YEAR TILL `-NEXT `-PRESIDENT'S `-BIRTHDAY = (`-205); or, (`-160)!!!~'

#**19**-PRESIDENT = RUTHERFORD B. HAYES `-**DAY of** `-**BIRTH** = **OCTOBER 4**th, 1822 = (10/4) = (10 x 4) = `-**40!**~' `-DAYS in a `-SINGLE `-YEAR TILL `-NEXT `-PRESIDENT'S `-BIRTHDAY = (`-**46**); or, (`-**319**)!!!~'

#**20**-PRESIDENT = JAMES A. GARFIELD `-**DAY of** `-**BIRTH** = NOVEMBER 19th, 1831 = (11/19) = (11 x 19) = `-**209!**~' `-DAYS in a `-SINGLE `-YEAR TILL `-NEXT `-PRESIDENT'S `-BIRTHDAY = (`-**45**); or, (`-**320**)!!!~' **NOTICE the** `-**#** `-**NUMBERS for #13/#16/#20 PRESIDENTS (45/320)!!!**~' **NOTICE the** `-**#** `-**NUMBERS for #19 PRESIDENT (46/319) & #20 PRESIDENT (45/320) = **`-**RECIPROCALS**-` **(10/11/10)!!!**~' **#19 & #20 are** `-**CLOSE to being** `-**EXACT!!!**~'

#**21**-PRESIDENT = CHESTER A. ARTHUR `-**DAY of** `-**BIRTH** = **OCTOBER 5**th, 18**29** = (10/5) = (10 x 5) = `-**50!**~' `-DAYS in a `-SINGLE `-YEAR TILL `-NEXT `-PRESIDENT'S `-BIRTHDAY = (`-**164**); or, (`-**201**)!!!~'

#**22/#24**-PRESIDENT = GROVER CLEVELAND `-**DAY of** `-**BIRTH** = MARCH 18th, 1837 = (3/18) = (3 x 18) = `-**54!**~' BORN (`-**318**) in `-YEAR (**183**) = "SWIPE 1"!!!~' **#22-to-#23!**~' `-DAYS in a `-SINGLE `-YEAR TILL `-NEXT `-PRESIDENT'S `-BIRTHDAY = (`-**155**); or, (`-**210**)!!!~' **#24-to-#25!**~' `-DAYS in a `-SINGLE `-YEAR TILL `-NEXT `-PRESIDENT'S `-BIRTHDAY = (`-**48**); or, (`-**317**)!!!~' **NOTICE the** `-**#** `-**NUMBERS for #9 PRESIDENT (48/317) & #24 PRESIDENT (48/317) = **`-**RECIPROCAL**-` **to** `-**HIMSELF!!!**~'

#**23**-PRESIDENT = BENJAMIN HARRISON `-**DAY of** `-**BIRTH** = AUGUST 20th, 1833 = (8/20) = (8 x 20) = `-**160!!!**~' **#23-to-#24!**~' `-DAYS in a `-SINGLE `-YEAR TILL `-NEXT `-PRESIDENT'S `-BIRTHDAY = (`-**155**); or, (`-**210**)!!!~'

#25-PRESIDENT = WILLIAM MCKINLEY `-**DAY of** `-**BIRTH** = JANUARY **29**th, 18**43** = (1/29) = (1 x 29) = `-**29!!!~'** `-DAYS in a `-SINGLE `-YEAR TILL `-NEXT `-PRESIDENT'S `-BIRTHDAY = (`-**94**); or, (`-**271**)**!!!~'**

#26-PRESIDENT = THEODORE ROOSEVELT `-**DAY of** `-**BIRTH** = OCTOBER **27**th, 1858 = (10/27) = (10 x 27) = `-**270!!!~'** `-DAYS in a `-SINGLE `-YEAR TILL `-NEXT `-PRESIDENT'S `-BIRTHDAY = (`-**42**); or, (`-**323**)**!!!~'** `-**NOTE** (**#23**) & (**#32**) within `-**HIS** `-**FAMILY** & `-**PRESIDENCY!!!~'**

#27-PRESIDENT = WILLIAM HOWARD TAFT `-**DAY of** `-**BIRTH** = SEPTEMBER 15th, 1857 = (9/15) = (9 x 15) = `-**135!~'** `-DAYS in a `-SINGLE `-YEAR TILL `-NEXT `-PRESIDENT'S `-BIRTHDAY = (`-**104**); or, (`-**261**)**!!!~'**

#28-PRESIDENT = WOODROW WILSON `-**DAY of** `-**BIRTH** = DECEMBER 28th, 1856 = (12/28) = (12 x 28) = `-**336!!!~'** `-DAYS in a `-SINGLE `-YEAR TILL `-NEXT `-PRESIDENT'S `-BIRTHDAY = (`-**56**); or, (`-**309**)**!!!~'**

#29-PRESIDENT = WARREN G. HARDING `-**DAY of** `-**BIRTH** = NOVEMBER 2nd, 1865 = (11/2) = (11 x 2) = `-**22!!!~'** WAS `-**BORN** on a (`-**2**nd) & `-**DIED** on a (`-**2**nd)**!!!~'** `-DAYS in a `-SINGLE `-YEAR TILL `-NEXT `-PRESIDENT'S `-BIRTHDAY = (`-**121**); or, (`-**244**)**!!!~'**

#30-PRESIDENT = CALVIN COOLIDGE `-**DAY of** `-**BIRTH** = **JULY 4**th, 1872 = (7/4) = (**7** x **4**) = `-**28!!!~'** `-DAYS in a `-SINGLE `-YEAR TILL `-NEXT `-PRESIDENT'S `-BIRTHDAY = (`-**37**); or, (`-**328**)**!!!~'** **NOTE #3** PRESIDENT (`-**28**); or, (`-**337**)**!!!~'** **SWAP the #3** `-**RECIPROCALS-'!!!~'**

#31-PRESIDENT = HERBERT HOOVER `-**DAY of** `-**BIRTH** = AUGUST 10ᵗʰ, 18**74** = (8/10) = (8 x 10) = `-**80**!-` `-DAYS in a `-SINGLE `-YEAR TILL `-NEXT `-PRESIDENT'S `-BIRTHDAY = (`-**173**); or, (`-**192**)!!!-`

#32-PRESIDENT = FRANKLIN D. ROOSEVELT `-**DAY of** `-**BIRTH** = JANUARY 30ᵗʰ, 1882 = (1/30) = (1 x 30) = `-**30**!-` `-DAYS in a `-SINGLE `-YEAR TILL `-NEXT `-PRESIDENT'S `-BIRTHDAY = (`-**98**); or, (`-**267**)!!!-`

#33-PRESIDENT = HARRY S. TRUMAN `-**DAY of** `-**BIRTH** = MAY 8ᵗʰ, 1884= (5/8) = (5 x 8) = `-**40**!-` `-DAYS in a `-SINGLE `-YEAR TILL `-NEXT `-PRESIDENT'S `-BIRTHDAY = (`-**206**); or, (`-**159**)!!!-`

#34-PRESIDENT = DWIGHT D. EISENHOWER `-**DAY of** `-**BIRTH** = OCTOBER 14ᵗʰ, 1890 = (10/14) = (10 x 14) = `-**140**!-` `-DAYS in a `-SINGLE `-YEAR TILL `-NEXT `-PRESIDENT'S `-BIRTHDAY = (`-**227**); or, (`-**138**)!!!-` **#33** & **#35** **PRESIDENTS are** `-**RECIPROCALS**-` via **#34** **PRESIDENT**!!!-` (33 + 35) = (`-**68**) = "The `-**MARK**"!!!-`

#35-PRESIDENT = JOHN F. KENNEDY `-**DAY of** `-**BIRTH** = MAY **29**ᵗʰ, 1917 = (5/29) = (5 x 29) = `-**145**!-` `-DAYS in a `-SINGLE `-YEAR TILL `-NEXT `-PRESIDENT'S `-BIRTHDAY = (`-**90**); or, (`-**275**)!!!-`

#36-PRESIDENT = LYNDON B. JOHNSON `-**DAY of** `-**BIRTH** = AUGUST 27ᵗʰ, 1908 = (8/27) = (8 x 27) = `-**216**!-` `-DAYS in a `-SINGLE `-YEAR TILL `-NEXT `-PRESIDENT'S `-BIRTHDAY = (`-**135**); or, (`-**230**)!!!-` (`-**23**) = **RECIPROCAL** = (`-**32**)!!!-` (`-**216**) = (2 x 16) = (`-**32**)!!!-`

#37-PRESIDENT = RICHARD NIXON `-DAY of `-BIRTH = JANUARY 9th, **1913** = (1/9) = (1 x 9) = `-**9!~**' `-DAYS in a `-SINGLE `-YEAR TILL `-NEXT `-PRESIDENT'S `-BIRTHDAY = (`-**186**); or, (`-**179**)!!!~' (`-**1913**) = (19 + 13) = (`-**32**) = -a PROPHETIC # `-**NUMBER!!!~'**

#38-PRESIDENT = GERALD FORD `-DAY of `-BIRTH = **JULY** 14th, **1913** = (**7**/1**4**) = (7 x 14) = `-**98!~**' `-DAYS in a `-SINGLE `-YEAR TILL `-NEXT `-PRESIDENT'S `-BIRTHDAY = (`-**79**); or, (`-**286**)!!!~' `-NOTE (#**37**) & (#**38**) PRESIDENTS are `-**RECIPROCALS**-' of `-EACH `-OTHER (**79**/**86**)!!!~' (`-**1913**) = (19 + 13) = (`-**32**) = -a PROPHETIC # `-**NUMBER!!!~'**

#39-PRESIDENT = JIMMY CARTER `-DAY of `-BIRTH = OCTOBER 1st, 1924 = (10/1) = (10 x 1) = `-**10!~**' `-DAYS in a `-SINGLE `-YEAR TILL `-NEXT `-PRESIDENT'S `-BIRTHDAY = (`-**128**); or, (`-**237**)!!!~'

#40-PRESIDENT = RONALD REAGAN `-DAY of `-BIRTH = **FEBRUARY(2) 6**th, 1911 = (2/6) = (2 x 6) = `-**12!~**' `-DAYS in a `-SINGLE `-YEAR TILL `-NEXT `-PRESIDENT'S `-BIRTHDAY = (`-**126**); or, (`-**239**)!!!~' #**39** & #**40** are `-**CLOSE** to being `-**EXACT!!!~'**

#41-PRESIDENT = GEORGE H. W. BUSH `-DAY of `-BIRTH = JUNE 12th, 1924 = (6/12) = (6 x 12) = `-**72!~**' `-DAYS in a `-SINGLE `-YEAR TILL `-NEXT `-PRESIDENT'S `-BIRTHDAY = (`-**68**); or, (`-**297**)!!!~'

#42-PRESIDENT = BILL CLINTON `-DAY of `-BIRTH = AUGUST 19th, 1946 = (8/19) = (8 x 19) = `-**152!~**' `-DAYS in a `-SINGLE `-YEAR TILL `-NEXT `-PRESIDENT'S `-BIRTHDAY = (`-**44**); or, (`-**321**)!!!~' #**12** PRESIDENT being (`-**44**/`-**321**) just as WELL!!!~'

#**43**-PRESIDENT = GEORGE W. BUSH `-**DAY of** `-**BIRTH** = **JULY 6**ᵗʰ, 1946 = (**7**/**6**) = (7 x 6) = `-**42**!~` `-DAYS in a `-SINGLE `-YEAR TILL `-NEXT `-PRESIDENT'S `-BIRTHDAY = (`-**29**); or, (`-**336**)!!!~`

#**44**-PRESIDENT = BARACK OBAMA `-**DAY of** `-**BIRTH** = **AUGUST 4**ᵗʰ, 1961 = (**8**/**4**) = (8 x 4) = `-**32**!~` (`-**1961**) = (61 (-) 19) = (`-**42**) = "**The** `-**MARK**"!!!~` `-DAYS in a `-SINGLE `-YEAR TILL `-NEXT `-PRESIDENT'S `-BIRTHDAY = (`-**51**); or, (`-**314**)!!!~` #**14** **PRESIDENT** = (`-**151**); or, (`-**214**)!!!~` `-**CHANGE** the (**1**,**2**,**3**) = **PROPHETIC-LINEAR-PROGRESSION-PLP**!!!~`

#**45**-PRESIDENT = DONALD TRUMP `-**DAY of** `-**BIRTH** = JUNE 14ᵗʰ, 1946 = (6/14) = (6 x 14) = `-**84**!~` `-DAYS in a `-SINGLE `-YEAR TILL `-NEXT `-PRESIDENT'S `-BIRTHDAY = (`-**PENDING**); or, (`-**PENDING**)!!!~`

NOTICE #**41** & #**42** (**JUNE(6)/AUGUST(8)**) = (**6**/**8**) = "The `-**MARK**"!!!~`

(41 + 42) = (`-**83**)!!!~`

NOTICE #**45** & #**44** (**JUNE(6)/AUGUST(8)**) = (**6**/**8**) = "The `-**MARK**"!!!~`

(45 + 44) = (`-**89**)!!!~` (89 + 83) = (`-**172**) / 2 = (`-**86**) = RECIPROCAL = (`-**68**) = "The `-**MARK**"!!!~` (17 x 2) = (`-**34**) = RECIPROCAL = (`-**43**)!!!~`

WITH #**43** **RIGHT** in the `-**MIDDLE** = (43 + 43) = (`-**86**) = RECIPROCAL = (`-**68**) = "The `-**MARK**"!!!~` **WITH** #**43** **BEING A** (**7**/**6**) = **JULY 6**ᵗʰ `-**BIRTH** = (7 x 6) = (`-**42**) = "The `-**MARK**"!!!~`

226

NOTICE #41 & #42 (JUNE(6)/AUGUST(8)) (`-68) = RECIPROCAL = #44 & #45 (AUGUST(8)/JUNE(6)) = (8/6)!!!~'

The `-MARK IS `-INEVITABLE (`-68) THROUGHOUT `-TIME!!!~'

The `-**LIST** goes `-**ON**; and, `-**ON!!!~'** JUST `-**WATCH** the `-**NEWS** `-**STATIONS**; and, `-**USE** & `-**CALCULATE** these `-**DEATHS** with `-**ALL** of the `-**FORMULAS** `-**PRESENTED** within; and, by `-**ALL**; of the `-**PENNED** `-**BOOKS** of the `-**PROPHET!!!~'**

BY: THE `-PROPHET - DWAYNE W. ANDERSON!!!~'

Printed in the United States
By Bookmasters